THE
SECRET
REVEALED

THE
SECRET
REVEALED

Exposing the Truth
About the Law of Attraction

JAMES L. GARLOW *and*
RICK MARSCHALL

New York   Boston   Nashville

FaithWords
Hachette Book Group USA
237 Park Avenue
New York, NY 10017

Visit our Web site at www.faithwords.com.

Printed in the United States of America

First Edition: August 2007
10 9 8 7 6 5 4 3 2 1

FaithWords is a division of Hachette Book Group USA, Inc.
The FaithWords name and logo is a trademark of Hachette Book Group USA, Inc.

Library of Congress Cataloging-in-Publication Data

Garlow, James L.
  The secret revealed : exposing the truth about the law of attraction / by James L. Garlow and Rick Marschall.—1st ed.
    p. cm.
  ISBN-13: 978-0-446-19796-0
  ISBN-10: 0-446-19796-3
  1. Success—Religious aspects—Christianity.   2. Byrne, Rhonda. Secret.   I. Title.
  BV4598.3.G37 2007
  131—dc22
                                                                2007018772

DEDICATION

From Jim:

I have, over the years, dedicated books to my wife, my parents, my children, my son-in-law, my daughter-in-law and my grandchildren, my sisters, my brothers, and to some former teachers.

And now…

This book is lovingly dedicated to my parents-in-law, Richard and Vivian Luckert; my sister-in-law and brother-in-law, Larry and Kathy Goad, and to their family; my brother-in-law and sister-in-law, John and Mary Luckert, and to their family.

Thank you for welcoming me into the family.

From Rick:

I dedicate this book to Nancy Wilson Marschall, my wife of thirty-two years, best mother to the best children Christian parents could pray for.

In the face of unbelievable health problems and so many other pressures, you have never doubted, never broken down, never shaken your fist at the universe or your Father in heaven.

Your example, your strength, your knowledge, and your faith are no secrets.

I thank God our "Attraction" came when it did.

ACKNOWLEDGMENTS

Every book has "enablers" who, by direct assistance or silent encouragement, help authors in mighty and essential ways. We were blessed to have a circle of such people lift us up at the right moments, with the right things, in our work. With only a fear that we might leave someone out, we are grateful to acknowledge their assistance.

Jeff Dunn is a literary agent, writer, and editor, and dreamer of the first rank: *The Secret Revealed* was his conception. This amazing man convinced us to write it on the basis of his confidence and has handled the inevitable business end of matters with aplomb. He catches visions and shares his passion like nobody else in the field. He even can catch aplomb in his teeth in the field—amazing. Seriously, this is his book, too, and it never would have happened without his inspiration and nurture. Thank you, Jeff. You drew us into *The Secret Revealed,* and you were the one who insisted I (Jim) coauthor *Cracking Da Vinci's Code.* You have a wonderful and gentle way of "throwing me to the wolves." (Keep doing it.)

Thank you to Craig Bubeck: we brought him on to the team early, and his role morphed from General Editor and Traffic Cop of the research crew, to Father Confessor, Sounding Board, and Facts Checker. His personality and his superb editing talents are between the lines of every page of this book.

From Jim:

Thank you, Skyline Church family, for being a superbly supportive church. You prayed for us, encouraging us to press forward. Thank you for your prayers for me—both as pastor-teacher and as "cultural responder."

Thank you to: fellow pastors on staff, Church Board members, Pastor's Prayer Partners, the Intercession & Healing Team, and the specially formed TSR Intercession Team. All of you were incredible. You were spectacular "cheerleaders" for this project.

Thank you, Winifred Garlow, not only for being Mom, but for transcribing—even as you approach your eighty-sixth birthday—tape after tape of my occasionally garbled comments into the late hours of the night. Thank you, Pam Dahl and Elaine Snelson, for keeping the writing team supplied so we could work day and (much of the) night.

And so many others! Bob Siegel, your intellect was so brilliant. John Debus, your research was exceptional. Christine Demery, your insights were helpful. April Williams, your discoveries were insightful. Melissa Hatt, your graphics were professional. Special thanks to other members of the "rapid response" Research Team: Rick Augustine, Ross Chenault, Samuel Ferrer, Silvia Flores, Sally Jadlow, Jennifer Kuyper, Barry Neely, Gerard Reed, Gail Romaine, Roxanne Swails, and Wendy Ware. And to so many not mentioned here—to the entire team of persons who were there, thank you for lifting, helping, and encouraging.

And especially, thank you to my family, for allowing me intently to focus on this project, and for gently asking "How is the book coming?" each time I thought I could not do more.

From Rick:

My wife, Nancy, and her family have been supportive during the hectic process of writing this book—a traumatic time of health and household moving concerns. I was allowed to concentrate on the goal of this book, and for that I am grateful. My son Ted has been of assistance, with advice and research help. Jerry and Marit Vincent generously opened their Granite Hills home outside San Diego to, variously, one, two, and three of us as we wrote, researched, Googled, and (occasionally) slept. By making their home an unlikely literary factory for a time, they helped more than they can know. And Matthew kept things loose at the right moments. Marlene Bagnull of the Christian Writers' Conferences in Estes Park, Colorado, and Philadelphia, Pennsylvania, is one of God's prayer warriors who interceded, and without her, this team might not even know each other. Greg Johnson—agent, friend, counselor—is also due thanks. Jo Lauter is my prayer partner and accountability partner on books we each write: she is a friend who cannot possibly know how much she is appreciated.

Workers, friends, partners who went above and beyond: Larry Hoagland of PPS San Diego: I "shutter" to think what I'd look like without your snap decisions; Skip Elmore, early encourager; Tim Ewing of *Rare Jewel Magazine*; James Grifiths; John and Roberta Province; Georgene and John Kruzel; Patrick Russo; Aubrey Grable; Beth Davies; Sally and Three-Chord Charlie Basbas; James Clarence Cusser for hours spent discussing Plato and Aristotle, setting me on the right course; Ed Norton; and Tom Heintjes.

The leadership and members of my home church, Deliverance

Tabernacle, Pentecostal Church of God, Burton, Michigan, have been of splendid support. I have been prayed over, encouraged, and cared for. Particularly I want to thank Pastor Ernest and Sister Ellen Davis, Pastor Don and Sister Louise Werden, Brother Butch and Sister Peggy Martin, Brother Wade and Sister Julia Mainer, Brother Jack and Sister Linda Arrand, and Brother Autrey McIlroy.

CONTENTS

PART III   WHAT NOW?

STATEMENT OF PURPOSE

ZAPENATH-PANEAH

"Christ . . . was chosen before the creation of the world, but was revealed in these last times for your sake."
—1 PETER 1:20

IN THE BEGINNING, GOD

PART I

FOUNDATIONS

"You will know the truth, and the truth will set you free."
—JOHN 8:32

Chapter 1

BRAIN-DEAD

Belief: Keep Your Mind Engaged

S tan Lee of Marvel Comics has a wonderful phrase he uses about the art and craft of writing superhero comics, and of being a fan of them. He says we have to "suspend disbelief." Actually, with many forms of fiction, the watchword is to "suspend belief"—it's those times we are asked to go a step further, mentally, emotionally, rationally.[1] True to form, *The Secret* requires that we suspend disbelief. Its ideas are abstract, its evidence is vague, its promises are grand, and it arouses suspicion in the most casual reader's mind.

In its first months, *The Secret*'s DVD and book versions sold millions of copies—of course, the word spread, even though its propositions sounded too good to be true. Once *The Secret* got out, many news programs, comedy shows, and pop commentators—the type of people in today's culture who normally fall over each other to endorse the latest feel-good or self-help fad—instead criticized or ridiculed the book. Yet it continued on its whirlwind course, with reports of bookstores unable to stock copies, of additional DVDs in production, even of a high-ticket marketing scheme based on *The Secret*, and more. So it finds an audience of fans.

Up-front, we must acknowledge we are not among them. You might ask then, if we think *The Secret*'s ideas far-fetched and implausible, why do we bother countering them? Why should we consider them worth discussing? More so, some fellow skeptics will protest that any effort to deal with this philosophy will backfire, giving further publicity for *The Secret*.

Our first answer to questions about whether *The Secret* is even worth answering is this: there are many claims by author Rhonda Byrne and her team, from unsupported varieties of dream therapy to "history" built on paranoid fantasies, and it's important for some of these matters that the record be set straight.

THE FLAW OF ATTRACTION

The Law of Attraction is a recently coined phrase, but its ideas are hardly new. Easily it can be seen in the Bible's account of the Garden, where the serpent issued the temptation "You will be like God" (Gen 3:5). That is the clear (and stated) thesis of The Secret. *This book will review history's other philosophies, heresies, and doctrines similar to the Law of Attraction. Gnosticism is a belief that has persisted for centuries. We will review others in succeeding chapters, but here are comments on gnosticism.*

Gnostics believed that God is good and the world is evil. Since God is good, He could not have created the world. There was an emphasis on knowledge (*gnosis* is Greek for "knowledge"). This knowledge, which led to salvation, was secret, reserved for the elite.

"The Gnostic movement posed as the bearer of a secret tradition stemming from Christ, or from the apostles." J. Guitton, *Great Heresies and Church Councils* (New York: Harper & Row, 1965).

"Gnostics claimed to have a secret knowledge which was the key to salvation." David Christie-Murray, *A History of Heresy* (London and New York: Oxford University Press, 1976).

"The Gnostic position asserts that over and above the simple Gospel…there is a secret, higher knowledge reserved for an elite." Harold O. J. Brown, *Heresies: The Image of Christ in the Mirror of Heresy and Orthodoxy from the Apostles to the Present* (New York: Doubleday & Company, 1984).

We might grant that if the threat amounted to no more than a group of people being invited to a presentation or seminar where they are offered this collection of "facts," it would perhaps amount to no more than an unfortunate waste of an evening. But in fact *The Secret* has become a craze that has swept the nation, affected peoples' behavior, and taken their money. Such a phenomenon demands further examination.

But second, we believe *The Secret* represents something unfortunate, even dangerous, in contemporary life. Because it is packaged in the language of happiness, wealth, and feeling good, it masquerades as a harmless prescription for…well, everything unfortunate, even harmful, in contemporary life.

What's ironic is that there is a materialistic aspect to *The Secret*: a me-oriented, wealth-obsessed selfishness that flies in the face of most religions, philosophies, and value-systems through all history, all over the world.

Even the more contemporary schools of thought tending toward materialism pay at least minimal lip service to charity and service. Yet *The Secret* actually ridicules the concept of sacrifice. Even if *The Secret*'s popularity is due to the fact that such ideas strike a chord in present-day America, we consider that alone a reason to raise an alarm, and not passively accept some sort of planetary convergence of new morals.

Our third reason for "answering" *The Secret* is no less important: hurting people are seeking answers from Rhonda Byrne to life's toughest questions.

Many readers of our book are already familiar with *The Secret*. Some will merely know of the controversy Rhonda Byrne's book has stirred; some have a curiosity engendered by a magazine cover or a *Nightline* report on television; some might have even reacted to a word-of-mouth recommendation of our book.[2] Maybe some have bought the book itself, maybe the video, maybe some attended seminars or bought into *The Secret*'s new multilevel marketing scheme. Others have been persuaded by its presentation; indeed many are enthusiastic recruits. To a large extent, we address these readers.

We firmly believe others will benefit from the reading of our book: in fact, we have designed *The Secret Revealed* to inform anyone, even those (if there are any such left in the world) who have not heard of *The Secret*.

But it's especially to those who have reached out for the answers *The Secret* offers—it's with these audiences we need to identify. And we do empathize. There are billions of people in the world, all different in countless ways, yet among the few common characteristics of everyone on earth are the need to be loved, a desire for security, and a feeling of self-worth. We see that. We all share these fundamental human characteristics. It is clear why *The Secret* can appeal to people on its surface.

But the desire for security shouldn't have to lead to a value system that excludes caring. A feeling of self-worth should not morph into an ethic of selfishness. Did *The Secret* intrigue you because of what it promised? That's not to say your needs are inappropriate, but we will unpack together some more lucid ways to confront whatever hurts or fears, confusion or desires you might have.

THE LAW OF ATTRACTION IS IN THE CLASSROOM

Have you ever wondered why:

- teachers in your local government-run public school cannot speak of God or Jesus, our Lord, and Savior, and even having a Bible on school grounds could be cause for disciplinary action, but the same prohibition on "religion" does not exist for Islam, Hinduism, or Buddhism?
- children study the spirituality of the Native American Indians; their spiritual wheels and animal spirits, shamans, dream catchers, and the like, are [acceptable] topics and art projects for the classroom, but speaking of God or coloring a picture of Christ is taboo?
- children cannot wear clothing proclaiming their belief in God to school, but clothing depicting Satan, the peace symbol, or the yin/yang symbol do not receive the same censorship?
- children cannot pray to God in the classroom, but they can go on guided fantasies and guided visualizations to meet spirit guides (demons) in the classroom?

Do you get the impression the only discrimination going on, in the realm of religion in the government-run public schools, is against Christianity? If you do, you are absolutely correct.

Why is that? Very simple: "systems theory"—that which provides the foundation upon which the transformation of America from a constitutional republic to a participatory democracy is built—cannot tolerate the individual; and true Christianity teaches we are all individuals.

Enter the New Age movement, one of the precepts of which is that we are one with one another, one with God, in communion with God 24/7: "as above, so below."

(Lynn Stuter's commentary on the Law of Attraction's infection of America's classrooms is from: http://www.newswithviews.com/Stuter/stuter96.htm.)   ∞∞

Along the way we will also expose some of the more outlandish arguments we have seen in *The Secret*. We will hear real wisdom from genuine sages from throughout history. We will offer the authentic, not the theoretical.

Up-front, we'll tell you: we hold no secrets, we allege no secrets, we reveal no secrets. But we *will* tell you the truth, and we will speak of the great Mystery. If you've read *The Secret* or seen its DVD, you know it walks a tightrope of apparent inconsistencies. We're asked to believe that mighty men possessed the Secret and kept it secret for millennia, yet today here it is for all to see. It was guarded, yet at the same time it was published in a number of books a century ago. The Christian church even is supposed to have hidden the Secret, but likewise the church passed it along.

Prominent people are likewise supposed to have held the Secret. Beethoven, although we are not told what he did with it, evidently failed to realize he should have been able to wish away his cruel deafness in the manner outlined in the Secret. Andrew

Carnegie blessed mankind with millions of dollars given in charity and was a great benefactor of peace to societies and the arts. Yet we are to believe it simply didn't occur to him to share the Secret with any of his fellow souls.

We will invent no nonsense nor pass along fabricated history. *Real* history is more interesting. To those who might say, "Look where history has got us," we reply with George Santayana that those who do not learn from history are doomed to repeat it. We will share some ancient truths, not secrets, and try to present them in a new way, just as every generation has had to discover them anew.

We harbor no secrets...promise.

But we do know of mysteries, beautiful mysteries. Mysteries that flood our souls. Mysteries we will visit by the end of this book, that are more fulfilling to behold than the Secret. We will even point you to all the claims of *The Secret*'s road map for life. Like certain life forms, we believe the claims cannot stand the exposure of the light. In short, we have a better way to show you.

Chapter 2

THE FLAW OF ATTRACTION

Conspiracy: Stop Imagining

When Theodore Roosevelt ran for president on the Progressive Party platform in 1912, he delivered one of his many observations on the American culture that stated facts precisely and colorfully; unforgettable phrases fell like crumbs from his plate but are still wise a century later: "We shall have done nothing in this country if all we do is replace the greed of arrogance with the greed of envy."[1]

TR saw something in the American makeup that swung like a pendulum—resentment of the rich, oppression of the poor; governmental actions to protect the upper class or to "soak the rich"; and governmental programs to keep the lower class at bay through massive handout programs. So on and so forth it goes...to this day.

Through it all, there has been a dark underside to the American experience. The blessings of an open continent, fertile land, and freedoms established by faithful patriots have been responsible for optimism prevailing over cynicism. We became a nation of shared values, not just a country with a growing population. Over the bumpy roads of slavery and other evils, a unified nation generally shared values that encouraged a broad prosperity and civic justice.

But increasingly, despite the advances in general wealth and justice, there has been a movement steeped in paranoia. The envy and greed TR warned of is being preached, not just as something to observe, but something to practice.

THE STYLE OF PARANOIA

In 1964 Professor Richard Hofstadter wrote a famous essay called "The Paranoid Style in American Politics," looking left and right at hate groups, at the twisted lenses through which movements saw events. In 1999, Professor Daniel Pipes wrote a book called *Conspiracy: How the Paranoid Style Flourishes and Where It Comes From,* which broadens the analysis and sees this civic cancer as spreading.[2]

For some reason, this us-*versus*-them view of the world resonates today in America. It is safe to say a lot of the interest in *The Da Vinci Code* was not its persuasive history—in fact, it wasn't always airtight fiction, much less history—but the secretive, paranoiac atmosphere it attained.

The Secret must be seen in that same growing tradition. Its very name, of course, tempts the uninitiated: "We know something you don't know!" "Pssst! Hey, you wouldn't believe what the powerful have been keeping from you!" "Step right up! See what all the power brokers have been keeping from you and me!"

And who doesn't love a detective story? Our popular-culture media bombard us with so many stories, what's one more? We live in such a saturation of sensations that what is merely plausible *becomes* real to many people. Oliver Stone's movies rewrite history, but many viewers are not just intrigued by his premises but believe they have actually witnessed documentary truth. Conspiracy theorists abound in politics, and, in the words of the old song, millions of people still say, "Lie to me!"

Enter *The Secret*, and Rhonda Byrne's personal story is now famous: an Australian television producer (the Down-Under Freddie de Cordova[3]), she made a video of *The Secret* that met with scant appreciation in Australia; she took it to America where, fine-tuned and with a book version, it met with astonishing success.

As the world knows, and as we will trace here, the primary elements of *The Secret* are not eternal secrets of any sort—certainly not of any deep or profound sort—but a collection of antiquated heresies and more contemporary nostrums, suggestions, and promises. For approximately a century, Rhonda's ideas and those of her team have bounced around and been variously practiced under the banners of New Thought, Science of the Mind, Laws of Attraction, and various New Age manifestations sprinkled with ancient occultism.

In truth, there is nothing "new" about "New Age"; it arguably might be called "Old Age" (or even by its mirror-image, "age old"). For the "New Age" movement is based on age-old ideas, none of them new, nor uplifting...nor proven successful. The New Age movement's foundations are so old as to be found in the most ancient of human stories, the account of Adam and Eve in the Garden. As that Bible story goes, these were the first recorded instances of promoting self over others, all springing from the fundamental temptation for humans to think they were equal to God.

But if the prescriptions in *The Secret* are not really new, neither are they secrets. If they seem obscure to you, it is more likely because the majority of people regard the practitioners of the Law of Attraction as marginal cultists, not liberators of alleged secrets closely guarded throughout history by some conspiracy of the powerful.

FATAL ATTRACTION

One has to admit there is a strange attraction to the theories. Maybe it is that very style of paranoia itself. But you have to wonder, with all of *The Secret*'s prescriptions, suggestions, and promises, why does Rhonda Byrne feel the need to push a story of us-*versus*-them? Because with all of her sure system of success and untold wealth that has been denied the masses, there are no footprints—there is no documentation.

Indeed, there are numerous quotations in *The Secret*, salted through the pages of its book version, by some of the most eminent names in history. And yet none of them are preceded nor followed by documented connections to any sort of Secret to which they were privy.

WAS PLATO WOO-WOO?

Woo-Woo. adj., concerned with emotions, mysticism, or spiritualism; other than rational or scientific; mysterious; new agey. Also n., a person who has mystical or new age beliefs. The term refers to ideas considered irrational or based on extremely flimsy evidence or that appeal to mysterious occult forces or powers. When used by skeptics, woo-woo is a derogatory and dismissive term used to refer to beliefs one considers nonsense or to a person who holds such beliefs. Sometimes woo-woo is used by skeptics as a synonym for *pseudoscience, true-believer,* or *quackery* ("Woo Woo" definition and discussion from The Skeptic's Dictionary, http://skeptic.com/woowoo.html).

To those readers who have the impression that Rhonda Byrne and her Secret santas either made up the list of history's great names (as possessors and profiteers of the Law of Attraction) or put words in their mouths (see our research on Churchill, Emerson, et al.), there is the question of Plato.

More careful research on Byrne's part might have prompted her to retroactively anoint Aristotle instead of his friend and rival, Plato. Plato (of ancient Athens, before Christianity) believed in absolute truth and abstract right and wrong. His philosophy was congenial to the early Christian church. Many of its leaders and thinkers were neo-Platonists, including St. Augustine and Martin Luther, to name a couple. Aristotle's views that there was no knowable right and wrong, that every generation had to decide its own standards and morals, gave birth to relativism; his descendents in this admittedly broad-brush characterization included Thomas Aquinas, Spinoza (called the first modern Pantheist), Hegel, Marx.

Add these unmistakable legacies and published beliefs to the fact that—typically—Rhonda Byrne offers no documentation about famous figures' involvement with a Law of Attraction, and you have proof that truth is all Greek to her.   ∞

For that matter, lest there be any confusion, there actually is no documented evidence for an original Secret attributable to anything resembling an original author. And there certainly is no timeline for any of its owners or its supposed protectors, and no information about *how* it might have been used by a vast array of conspirators.

The absence of any evidence should be troubling enough. But, as viewers of the DVD are aware, the portion of the movie dealing with history's supposed suppression of the Secret is accompanied by quick-cut stock footage of dark dungeons, galley slaves in manacles, and workers from the days of crowded factory rooms, grainy film effects, and the twelve-hour work-day. Some pictures may be worth a thousand words, but we need to ask ourselves, are these films of actual citizens actually being denied wealth and material progress by actual misers of the Secret?

Defying Description

Not only is one hard-pressed to define *The Secret*'s sources, but its category (and therein its purpose) is tough to call as well. Many bookstores are placing it in their self-help sections for now. Of course, when it recedes from the bestseller tables and displays, it will have to go somewhere. Because it makes extravagant prom-ises about achieving personal fortunes, *The Secret* could be placed on financial shelves. On the other hand, its claim that people might both wish diseases upon themselves and easily wish them away, *The Secret* might just find a home on health shelves. Place-ment among philosophy books would be a little presumptuous, considering its lightweight and popular treatment of some pretty heady issues. And there is always the broadly spanning and generally welcoming occult shelf.

"Self-help" is actually something of an interesting desig-nation when one realizes *The Secret*'s major characteristic is religion. Self-help is such a nonconfrontational term. Yet *The Secret* aggressively asserts a value system, a cosmology (explanation of the universe and its origins), a theology (presentation and explanation of God—or denial of Him), ethics, and morals, all in the manner of a major religion.

So perhaps the religion section is best suited to this little book, though probably not the Christian subsection of religion. *The Secret* misinterprets the Old and New Testaments, and it mentions Jesus less frequently than Buddha and avatars, which suggests at least an indifference to Christianity, if not a hostility to biblical truth.

Actually, even the current designation of self-help is arguably a misleading label, considering the roots of the Secret's philosophy. As we explore more in depth later, many of the movements from which it derived proudly touted their identities as occult and Eastern mystical philosophies.

FRYING THEIR BACON

"Knowledge is power," said Sir Francis Bacon, the "father of inductive reasoning." *The Secret* names the seventeenth-century philosopher as possessor of the Secret but quotes nothing of his work nor cites how he used or profitted from the Secret. Many of the quotations of the book's great names are difficult to trace. How do you prove a negative, so to speak, especially when—as we show here—quotations are sometimes taken out of context or misapplied?

Shakespeare wrote many plays. They all provided brilliant insights on human nature. Is it plausible that never once, in soliloquy or dialog, Shakespeare was tempted to share mankind's greatest Secret (supposedly) with his audience? *Et tu*, Rhonda? And she accuses Lincoln of knowing the Secret and not sharing it. Couldn't he have wished the Rebellion away...or told the slaves to wish their shackles fall off? *The Secret* cannot long endure half lies and half nonsense, can it?

Bacon said, "Knowledge is power." Fast-forward a couple of centuries, and now it's *The Secret* that explains science, truth, and reality to us. And it becomes a bestselling book and DVD. Today, ignorance is power!

(By the way, we should not confine our searches to nonexistent words from historical figures. We endeavored to discover the credentials of *The Secret*'s expert panel, too, since their backgrounds are suspiciously obscured. "Dr. Joe" Vitale reportedly is a graduate of the IMM University, a mail-order diploma mill (of quantum physics) that currently offers study-at-home degrees. It invites applicants to leapfrog directly to a doctorate without those messy bachelors and masters programs, for "80 percent discounts" of $90 down and $25 a month. To repeat: ignorance is power! (The diploma mill can be found at www.metaphysics.com.)   ∞∞

Return to Oz

Like the Wizard of Oz, Rhonda Byrne has constructed an Emerald City of smoke machines and sound effects and great spectacle. And what she *really* says is, "Pay no attention to what's behind that curtain."

What's behind the curtain is an impressive array of smoke and mirrors—"facts" that don't exist and a Hall of Fame list of historical names that are propped up like mannequins in a department-store window but are wearing costumes for a masquerade ball. They are not wearing anything genuine.

Take just a moment to visit with some of *The Secret*'s phantom endorsers: Churchill, Plato, Shakespeare, Bacon, Beethoven, Emerson, Henry Ford, Einstein. Frankly, readers could be forgiven for imagining Rhonda Byrne, having finished her project, thumbing through a copy of *Bartlett's Familiar Quotations*. She's skimming through the pages, stopping at familiar names; or perhaps her finger runs down the big index, searching for key words like secret, attraction, and perhaps even gullible.

In fact, most of her quotations themselves, allegedly from history's pantheon of distinguished thinkers, are suspect. But since *none* of the quotations are attributed, readers are given no courtesy if they desire to dig deeper or learn more. And those quotations that are attributable are taken out of context. But for several quotations, one is left to wonder if they have ever been previously written or spoken at all.

Ralph Waldo Emerson allegedly originated the very last line in *The Secret*: "The secret is the answer to all that has been, all that is, and all that will ever be." Because of its placement, we realize Rhonda Byrne intends this as a motto, a brand, an emblem to be sealed with wax on her entire dissertation. Except...*where's Waldo?* As far as one is able to discern (again, lacking any citation), the quotation doesn't exist.[4]

ANOTHER LONDON BLITZ: *THE SECRET* MISQUOTES CHURCHILL

On page 36 of The Secret, *there is a statement attributed to Winston Churchill, rather remarkable because it supports Rhonda Byrne's thesis and appears at the proper spot to maximize the* ex post facto *endorse-*

ment by the British statesman of the Law of Attraction. The words
are Churchill's. But the full story is an embarrassing disclosure for The
Secret*: "You create your own universe as you go along" is taken out of*
context. More, it is from a passage in Churchill's autobiography when
he actually rejected and ridiculed the notion. He was paraphrasing
his cousins' odd views, and he even warns his young readers to treat
such arguments "as a game," calling the ideas "absurd." The Secret*'s*
reliance on this outright distortion is sloppy at best and fraudulent at
worst. If she has to twist the words of Churchill and others, how confi-
dent is she of her views? Here is the passage from Churchill's book:

"Some of my cousins who had the great advantage of University education used to tease me with arguments to prove that nothing has any existence except what we think of it. The whole creation is but a dream; all phenomena are imaginary. You create your own universe as you go along. The stronger your imagination, the more variegated your universe. When you leave off dreaming, the universe ceases to exist. These amusing mental acrobatics are all right to play with. They are perfectly harmless and perfectly useless. I warn my younger readers only to treat them as a game. The metaphysicians will have the last word and defy you to disprove their absurd propositions. I always rested upon the following argument which I devised for myself many years ago. We look up in the sky and see the sun. Our eyes are dazzled and our senses record the fact. So here is this great sun standing apparently on no better foundation than our physical senses. But happily there is a method, apart altogether from our physical senses, of testing the reality of the sun. It is by mathematics. By means of prolonged processes of mathematics, entirely separate from the senses, astronomers are able to calculate when an eclipse will occur. They predict by pure reason that a black spot will pass across the sun on a certain day. You go and look, and your sense of sight immediately tells you that their calculations are vindicated. So here you have the evidence of the senses reinforced by the entirely separate evidence of a vast independent process of mathematical reasoning. We have taken what is called in military map-making "a cross bearing." We have got independent testimony to the reality of the sun. When my metaphysical friends tell me that the data on which the astronomers made their calculations, were necessarily obtained originally through the evidence of the senses, I say, "No." They might, in theory at any rate be obtained by automatic calculating-machines set in motion by the light falling upon them without admixture of the human senses at any stage. When it is persisted that we should have to be told about the calculations and use our ears for that purpose, I reply that the mathematical process has a reality and virtue in itself, and that once discovered it constitutes a new and independent fact. And I am also at this point accustomed to reaffirm with emphasis my conviction that the sun is real, and also that it is hot—in fact as hot as Hell, and that if the metaphysicians doubt it they should go there and see."

(Winston Churchill's quotation—from his early autobiography, written when he was nearly indigent and thought his career ended—was cited in Salon. com's blog, Tuesday, March 06, 2007 www.Salon.com, also *ScienceWeek*, http://scienceweek.com/2000/sw000310.htm, and *The Language of Mathematics*, http://www.chemistrycoach. com/language.htm. Churchill's book is *My Early Life*, Fontana, London, 1972 reprint, pp. 123–124.)

This is not merely trivia—the equivalent importance of shouting out a *Jeopardy!* answer to your TV. Emerson is one of the privileged men of history who was a keeper of the Secret, according to Rhonda Byrne. As Blair Warren said on the *Twisted Wisdom* site, "Surely, if Emerson was speaking of 'the great secret' when he supposedly said this, it would be prominently featured in his writings and referenced in other places than just the film" and book. But of course it's not. And yet *The Secret* offers no *hint* of the quotation's source of special revelation.

Our suspicions should also be aroused when Einstein—one of *The Secret*'s most important props, because he was not just famous but a scientist whose jargon *The Secret* can appropriate or approximate in its mystical libretto—is falsely represented. "From [Einstein's] poor background and poor beginnings, you would have thought it impossible for him to achieve all that he did. Einstein knew a great deal of the Secret...and eventually [became] one of the greatest scientists who ever lived" (pp. 79, 80), says our historical guide Rhonda Byrne.

In fact, Einstein was born into a comfortable bourgeois family; his father was a salesman who progressed to co-ownership of an engineering company. Once again, these are not like cards in a game of Trivial Pursuit: Rhonda Byrne asserts that Albert Einstein's rise from poverty was due to the existence of a "secret" and Einstein's possession of it.[5]

DISTORTING THE WORDS AND BELIEFS OF DR. MARTIN LUTHER KING

On page 57 of *The Secret*, there is a quotation from Dr. Martin Luther King, a respected American icon of the highest standing: "Take the first step in faith. You don't have to see the whole staircase. Just take the first step." This appears in the chapter "How to Use the Secret," immediately after a quotation by Jack Canfield about plowing forward in life, and text by Rhonda Byrne asserting her successful use of *The Secret*'s principles. In other words, Dr. King was one of history's possessors of the Secret.

For this book we interviewed Dr. King's niece, Dr. Alveda C. King, founder of King for America. She was asked if Dr. King possessed the "secrets" described by Rhonda Byrne, or whether she thought Dr. King would endorse *The Secret* today. She said:

Dr. Martin Luther King Jr. was not self-empowered; Dr. King was Christ-empowered. God's love is not a secret, and neither was Dr. King's faith. The weakness of Ms. Byrne's book The Secret *is that it lacks the greatest gift of all, the power of Christ.*

He also said that one night at midnight, while praying, he heard the voice of Jesus say, "Stand up for truth, stand up for justice, and lo I will never leave you."

Dr. M. L. King also wrote, touching on metaphysics, " I have always believe[d] in the personality of God. But in the past the idea of a personal God was little more than a metaphysical category that I found theologically and philosophically satisfying. Now it is a living reality that has been validated in the experience of everyday life. God has been profoundly real to me in recent years."

(The information about Dr. Martin Luther King Jr. was from an exclusive interview conducted for this book with Dr. Alveta King, niece of Dr. Martin Luther King Jr., April 12, 2007.)

(The quotation of Dr. Martin Luther King Jr. is from "Martin Luther King, Jr., and the African-American Social Gospel" in *African-American Christianity*, Paul E. Johnson, editor, University of California Press, 1994.)

This is a shocking and revealing manifestation of the dubious validity and reliability of *The Secret*. The book and DVD base much of their case on the existence of a sacred secret and personal possession by these figures. The absurdity of that proposition is underscored by the baseless claims, faulty research, and cavalier presentations.

So we have seen that two of the major foundations of *The Secret* are specious, the nutritional equivalent of balloon soup. The "fact" essential to its premise—that there has been this Secret, that it has been kept secret, that the most successful and powerful people in history have known it—is ridiculous, and neither Rhonda Byrne nor any of her team members even attempt to document the "fact." Another foundation stone crumbles when we visit the historical vault-keepers, respectable historical figures who supposedly passed the Secret to each other through the years: quotation after quotation of theirs has been taken out of context.

You have to hand it to the author, editors, publishers, and others of the world who implicitly endorse this mass deception: their gall is amazing, since these things can so easily be checked.

PART II

A BETTER WAY TO LIVE

"And now I will show you the most excellent way."
—1 CORINTHIANS 12:31

Chapter 3

IT'S ALL ABOUT ME

Self: Check Your Ego

We now move (or rather are pushed by *The Secret* agenda) from paranoia, which we identified and discussed in the previous chapter as central to that book's validity, to Pragmatism.

Pragmatism is a philosophical movement that regards beliefs and values according to their utility or usefulness. Consistent with that, the Pragmatists were concerned with a rough scientific empiricism; that is, "what works" in questions between self and the world. Therefore it came to be known as a practical (everyday) variety of philosophy, instead of theoretical.

On the other hand, it generally led to social movements and political/economic theories that infected America with things like Progressive Education, egalitarianism, Reform Democracy, pluralism, codes of "tolerance" (political correctness), and other pestilential panaceas. The founders of Pragmatism were children of Kant, so to speak, and therefore clad themselves in costumes of "virtue," seeking to ameliorate itchy consciences or impress the audience in the pit, instead of measuring their acts against either abstract truth or objective reality.

Thus the Pragmatists clearly served as the crazy uncles to the Law of Attraction: they rejected a standard of right and wrong, and (although they were too "stuffy" to say it this way) anointed the Feel-Good gospel.

Pragmatism, which started oozing to the surface of American intellectual life in the late nineteenth century, was long viewed as America's lone contribution to the canon of world philosophies. Four New Englanders (Oliver Wendell Holmes Jr., Charles S. Peirce, William James, and John Dewey) share the credit, or blame. Author Lewis Menard distilled their positions thus: "They all believed that ideas were not 'out there' waiting to be discovered, but are tools—like forks and knives and microchips—that people devise to cope with the world in which they find themselves," a view existentialism up-ended with no measurable consequences in the world.[1]

However, the Pragmatists *did* have an influence on their times and on almost all areas of American life. Just as few architects deviated from the ugly and impractical precepts of the Bauhaus for decades, so did Pragmatism rule the socio-industrial complex. Ironically, a philosophy dedicated to empirical "success" never recanted, much less reKanted, when, after a century, the American welfare state, educational establishment, and intellectual landscape were decimated in large part to their theories... an early day Law of Attraction as social policy.

William James, evidently with a clear conscience and straight face, said: "Ideas (which themselves are but parts of our experience) become true just in so far as they help us to get into satisfactory relation with other parts of our experience."[2]

Pragmatism seems an especially good fit to the American personality. This worldview does seem to illustrate a law of attraction as well, but perhaps not quite as Rhonda Byrne defines it. To the thinking of many people, Pragmatism is a codification of the more selfish aspects of human nature: "What works for me," "If it makes me prosper, that makes it good for me," "How can it be wrong when it feels so right?" and, ultimately, "If it feels good, do it."

Pragmatism as a philosophy or epistomolgy (explanation of a system of knowledge) is in the tradition of Aristotle, not Plato; that is, the school of thought that tends to regard values as right or wrong for each new generation, according to personal conditions, instead of as eternal truths or absolutes despite our own ignorance, knowledge, reason, or experience.

The years preceding the formation of Pragmatism saw the application of similar tendencies in economics (socialism and communism) and sociology (determinism and Social Darwinism). Indeed, the theory of evolution itself fed the rise of Pragmatism— allowing people to be comfortable with the concept that whatever worked must be meant to work. Or, what prevails is meant to prevail.

In the nascent discipline of sociology in the 1880s, it was called "survival of the fittest" and Social Darwinism. William Graham Sumner wrote a book called *Folkways*, an otherwise fascinating and remarkable (for its time, when worldwide travel was inconvenient at best) book about habits and mores around the world. Its subtext, which Sumner didn't have to go near to tell his story, was Darwinian evolution, still a hot fad. Among schoolyard bullies and aggressive countries alike, these practices are called "Might makes right." Ironically, it's also the same ethic that is the root problem in the story about Robert, the gay comedian profiled in the book and DVD.

In Tune with Robert

In that story, Robert wrote to Bill Harris, one of *The Secret*'s stars, about the "grim reality" of teasing and ridicule he endured. So "Robert's circumstances changed because he changed his thoughts. He emitted a different frequency out into the universe. The universe *must* deliver the pictures of the new frequency, no matter how impossible the situation might seem. Robert's new thoughts became his new frequency, and the pictures of his entire life changed" (page 19 of *The Secret*).

In the DVD where once we saw (actors' portrayals of) paper cups being thrown at Robert onstage, the final scene has him at the same microphone, his audience laughing uproariously. "Good night, everybody!"

The story does not lead to pronouncements on the right-makes-right bullies, or how a survival-of-the-fittest ethic might end tragically in Robert's case. Tellingly, *The Secret* never discussed Robert's case in terms of right or wrong—not Robert's own choices, nor the rude people at his office, the bullies on the sidewalk, or even the rude patrons at the Comedy Club.

No, when Robert "changed" his "thoughts," "emitting" a different "frequency" out into the "Universe," and when the "Universe" obediently "delivered" the "pictures" of the new "frequency" (in spite of the apparent impossibility of the situation), Robert's "new thoughts" became his "new frequency," and the "pictures" of his "entire" life changed.

Cutting through the nonsense (and all those quotation marks), here is what Robert's story adds up to: the worst situations we can experience, in *The Secret*'s value system, are not sin, brutality, or cruelty, but inconvenience, embarrassment, and annoyance. Robert is not counseled to consider his own situation, nor are the bullies held to account for their unloving offenses. No—it is all tuned away, like changing stations on a radio dial.

There is no right or wrong in the world of *The Secret*. If something makes you whine, wish it away. In the name of happiness, joy is sublimated...and neither is achieved.

SERENITY NOW!

The books and renegade theorists from which *The Secret* borrowed cooked up their stews from equal parts Pragmatic philosophy, materialism, and the American "can-do" ethic, perhaps with a healthy dash of greed. Rhonda Byrne altered the recipe slightly, adding envy and selfishness. The agenda is not so secret at all, and rather brazen about its value system. In fact, *The Secret* seems quite pleased to state that if everybody operated according to its program of "Me First," we'd all have serenity now.

THE LAW OF ATTRACTION AT YOUR FRIENDLY NEIGHBORHOOD BOOKSTORE

It wasn't my target on this research trip, but there, on the road near the airport, was a huge store in a strip mall, The Psychic Eye Book Shop. The next day I returned to take its pulse. This is actually a chain of stores—the new landscape of American culture might include such Cults-R-Us hither and yon—and it was almost a caricature: smoky incense, sitar music, amulets. On the bookshelves I noted *The Coming of the Cosmic Christ*, *The Drag Queen of Elfland*, and, next to a whole shelf of "goddess studies," a book titled *Practical*

Candle-Burning Rituals. A wall of jars and bowls was labeled "Aids in Manifesting Wishes/Desires," and I noted a pile of "Mojo Wish Beans." I hurriedly took notes because the incense was overtaking me, but as I left I noticed a whole table of new books, many titles, stacked neatly and offered for sale—all from the *Chicken Soup for the Soul* series. The connection of the series' founder, Jack Canfield, and the Law of Attraction (through *The Secret*) was not noted—but it didn't have to be, not by a sign, anyway. The books were "at home."   ∞∞

But there is another fatal flaw in *The Secret*'s program: It's the everyday, nonclassroom use of the word *pragmatism*, similar in meaning but not as formal: "Does it work?"; "Does this make sense?"; "When all is said and done, is this practical?" On that level, also, we must deal with *The Secret*, especially because all of its claims and promises are presented as definitive answers to life's problems. It sets the bar high ... and then runs under it.

On a pragmatic level—a basic, nuts-and-bolts "Does it work?" context—*The Secret* fails its followers. Not only does it not work, but the book and DVD present very few examples of its succeeding for others (besides the team of professional motivational speakers and self-help seminar executives). Little effort is expended to assert its effectiveness.

The closest thing to *The Secret*'s offering any empirical test is the application of what's called the "pragmatic fallacy"—basically, that something is valid because "it works." What "works" is not clearly defined; control factors and variables are not tracked. The basic criteria is just, "Wow, it works." As the psychological phenomenon of "autosuggestion" tends to suggest, making up your mind to be "positive" is sure to make you feel ... well, positive. But beyond that, the effectiveness of the pragmatic fallacy amounts to little more than what politicians call "putting a positive spin on things."

A check of the biographies reveals that the majority of *The Secret* team, when boasting of their wealth, lists the operation of get-wealthy Web sites and seminar programs as the sources of their fortunes. Getting rich by having other people pay you to tell them how to get rich is a nifty business model (until people catch on), but hardly a universal prescription for prosperity. Likewise there are few examples of physical healing, and none about personal appearance, even among the gallery of Attractionists at the back of the book (or in front of the hidden treasure map backdrop in the DVD).

A RECENT REFERENCE TO THE LAW OF ATTRACTION ... BY WITCHES

Law of Attraction: Following on from the Law of Polarity, such opposites are attracted to each other. Hence, male and female may find magical attraction within a circle (something that should not be misunderstood as sexual attraction). There is also another aspect of this law (sometimes known as the Law of Opulence or Law of Synthesis) which states that if you wish to attract something, give away that which you already have of it. Quite simply, by bringing two forces together you create a third. This is summed up in the old Oriental saying, "If you have two loaves, sell one and buy a lily."

Farrar, Janet, and Gavin Bone, *Progressive Witchcraft: Spirituality, Mysteries, and Training in Modern Wicca* (The Career Press, 2004).

BUT DOES IT WORK?

Such questions, standing alone, might be considered potshots. But when the fundamental proof of a philosophy's validity hinges on the argument "its bottom line works," the question begs to be answered.

There are deeper concerns, more serious questions, to be asked of *The Secret* and its rostrums like the Law of Attraction. There are dangers in a lifestyle dedicated to self-absorption. As we have pointed out, it might be the logical extension of a pragmatic philosophy...but is it pragmatic in your life? Does it work for individuals? Can it work in the world? *Should* it work in a world of friends and family, in communities of interdependency?

If It Works for Me, It's Right

For instance, most of us know deep in our hearts there is a difference between our *wants* and our *needs*, and we're not always the best judges! Yet on page xii of *The Secret*, we find the promise: "You can have, or be, anything you want."

Apart from the effects of such limitless power on other people, most of us sense there is danger in an unbridled appetite for anything on your radar screen. Yet to *The Secret*'s way of thinking, self-indulgence, going overboard, and being out of control are either minor points or major pluses in the New Self-ism religion. Yet the closing words to *The Secret*'s readers affirm its bias for regarding ego-driven desire as a positive virtue: "Whatever you choose is right" (p. 184).

From the Bible down to our grandmothers, we have been taught that a positive principle of life is to think of others, to serve our fellow men and women, and of course, to not cut in line. This is not just a matter of saying please and thank you, but a practical means of interacting with others. Some might affectionately refer to it as good old-fashioned love and humility.

But *The Secret* rejects this universal impulse: "Many of us were taught to put ourselves last, and as a consequence we attracted feelings of being unworthy and undeserving... You must change that thinking" (p. 119). At least for some of us, it seems a bit of a stretch to imagine Jesus saying, "Excuse me, I misspoke about that principle 'the last shall be first'." Apparently Jesus should have demanded that the disciples wash *His* feet instead of His washing theirs in humility. Or maybe a more contemporary application: Mother Teresa might have done better to demand the poor of Calcutta gather up food and cook *her* meals?

THE LAW OF ATTRACTION ON OTHER FREQUENCIES

Theron Q. Dumont (believed to be one of the assumed names of William Walker Atkinson), wrote *The Power of Concentration* in 1915 (Advanced Thought Publishing Co). Whether it was researched or otherwise used by Rhonda Byrne, its similarities to *The Secret*'s Law of Attraction are striking:

- "When you once learn the laws of thought and think of nothing but Good, Truth, Success, you will make more progress with less effort than you ever made before" (p. 49).
- "By concentrated thought you can make yourself what you please.... How many attract poverty instead of riches?" (cover).
- "Concentrate on what you want and get it...By the law of concentration you can achieve your heart's desire. This law is

so powerful that that which at first seems impossible becomes attainable" (p. 146).

- "This is the law. Make yourself a concentrated dynamo from which your thoughts vibrate to others. Then you are a power in the world" (p. 71).

- "In a half an hour I showed that man why poverty had always been his companions. He had dressed poorly. He held his lectures in poor surroundings. By his actions and beliefs he attracted poverty. He did not realize that his thoughts and his surroundings exercised an unfavorable influence. I said, 'Thoughts are moving forces; great powers. Thoughts attract wealth. Therefore, if you desire wealth you must attract the forces that will help you secure it'" (passim). ·

- "It is within your power to gratify your every wish. Success is the result of the way you think.… The power to rule and attract success is within yourself" (p. 45).　　　　　∞∞

Don't Need Your Love

On page 45 of *The Secret*, Aladdin makes his first appearance. Role-modeling, wish fulfillment, and positive references surround Aladdin's repeat performances. Followers of the Law of Attraction are told to hold up the vision of rubbing a lamp and expecting miracles. Byrne and her team aggressively assert as a foundational principle a new and superior ethic of wish fulfillment.

It not only rejects but almost mocks the type of better impulses with which everyone's conscience resonates. In principle, this concept of wish fulfillment must repulse the proverbs, wisdom, and literature of wise men from every time, every movement. And most significantly, it must stand opposed to the words and whole purpose of Jesus' ministry. Though *The Secret* never says so directly, in so many words it cannot accept love as the higher good, that sacrifice is love in action, and that we find self-worth in sacrificing for others.

The Secret takes great pains to clarify, "There is a big difference between giving and sacrificing. Giving from a heart that is overflowing feels so good. Sacrificing does not feel good. Don't confuse the two—they are diametrically opposed.... One feels good and one does not feel good. Sacrifice will eventually lead to resentment" (p. 108).

One can't help but wonder what must be the response from so many readers who have served or sacrificed for loved ones, who have gone out of their way to help strangers in need or with hurts. Hopefully they can at least feel profound pity for the leaders of *The Secret's* directorate whose naïve words bear such bitterly cold ramifications. Many find the biblical ideals a much warmer comfort.

Service, or Serve Us?

In light of this new ethic of self-serving over service—or the foundations of this new religion—browsing through *The Secret* reveals the following numbers of references and terms within 184 pages of text:

- *Feel good* (feeling good, feels good): 58 occurrences
- *Believe* (belief, believing, believable, believed): 91 occurrences
- *Happy* (happiness, happier, happily): 36 occurrences
- *Joy* (joyous, joyful): 55 occurrences

This brings us to the question many tentative followers of *The Secret* might ask: what harm can there be in reinforcing positive views of yourself? Especially to the emotionally wounded, that is a question that might resonate. Even to the pragmatic thinker, it might seem plausible we cannot be any good to others until we are whole ourselves.

There is a logic to that rationale that appeals to self-preservation in order to rescue another, except even that is not *The Secret*'s logic. None of its manifestations—book, DVD, and certainly not any marketing plan—pretend to point to nobler motives even over the horizon. The payoff is to *self*, not society. The promises are for *me*, not any other member of humanity.

The tragic truth is, the injury will be to the "I" in *The Secret*—to whoever transforms his or her value system to the so-called Law of Attraction. This gossamer drapery of choice covering the new religion of New Selfism is adorned by two prominent terms: "feeling good" and "belief." They appear over and over in *The Secret*, yet they lie below the surface meaning. Despite appearances, the book's usage of these terms makes a beeline for the most selfish, me-oriented, exclusionary of meanings.

Spread the Love

Of course, no one wants to discourage feeling good. In and of itself, the feeling is not what is so self-destructively hedonistic. It is a positive human impulse; something parents want for their children. It's also something a loving God desires for His children in the Bible—that we be fulfilled, have life, and have it more abundantly.

Yet in *The Secret* it is not coupled with spreading the feeling or encouraging it in others, except to urge others to adopt the very same inward-directed priority. Because we wouldn't want to share them. A world of independent feel-good islands, each self-absorbed, is the heaven on earth of the New Selfist.

In the same way, *The Secret* touts "belief"; it does repeatedly encourage us "to believe." But, at the risk of being picky, Rhonda Byrne has some additional serious problems...with her grammar. Please indulge a writer a moment of editorializing.

Some verbs are transitive; some are intransitive. To illustrate the point, the word "believe" (indeed, the *concept* of belief) only makes sense when followed in the sentence by *in something.* So the natural question is, believe in what? In the same way, *The Secret* also talks about "being grateful," but doesn't specify *about what* or *to whom.* Predictably, the same goes for Byrne's suggestion to "give thanks"; the subject line is there, but never a recipient (to God, for instance).

Bad grammar. Worse philosophy. Horrible neighbor, actually.

Ya Gotta Believe

Perhaps an illustration from the world of sports will bring this a little closer to home. In 1973 the New York Mets were woefully underachieving—for all practical purposes, out of contention by mid-season. On July 9 the team's chairman of the board, M. Donald Grant, visited the clubhouse and delivered a pep talk to the players.

The Mets' irrepressible relief pitcher Tug McGraw, after he thought Grant had left and was of out earshot, bellowed, "Ya gotta believe!"

He wondered why his teammates didn't respond, then

realized Grant was still in the vicinity and heard the yell. For a moment everyone wondered whether McGraw was mocking the pep talk. He repeated it with animation, everyone joined in, and eventually the fans did too.

The rallying cry became one of the most famous of all baseball chants.

McGraw had a grammar problem too—he never stipulated *what* ya gotta believe in. Winning the World Series, perhaps? But after a surprising rallying winning streak, the Mets lost the World Series.

Turning the season around, perhaps? But the 1973 team was less than Hall of Fame caliber, finishing an anemic 82–79. (The worst of all play-off contenders, actually.) Byrne, McGraw, and the '73 Mets' fans are not alone in their grammatical shortcoming. Our culture has come to treat the word "believe" as if the commitment doesn't need completion. "It doesn't matter what you believe," people say, "just as long as you believe in something." "Just believe." In the same way people refer to rather ordinary circumstances as "unbelievable" when in fact the circumstances routinely are quite believable.

Tug McGraw was often asked whether his shouting "Ya gotta believe!" was indeed a mock of his boss. His several answers through the years were always delivered with a smile. It's hard to tell whether *The Secret* is similarly smiling when it tells its followers to *believe* but not that *believing in something or someone* is what makes all the difference.[3]

Happy Happy, Joy Joy

One final point of grammar—that is, how Rhonda Byrne plays fast and loose with the terms "happiness" and "joy." We have already discussed why feeling good cannot be a bad thing but is a better thing when it represents more than mere self-indulgence; and how "belief" is a positive thing but is meaningless unless it means *believing in something* or *someone*. In the same way, a distinction should be made between *happiness* and *joy*.

The culture tends to join Byrne in fuzzing the distinctions (the "denotations," as the grammarians like to call it), but that doesn't mean there are no distinctions.

There was an editor who wanted to call something in a book "penultimate" (with lots of exclamation points, no less), emphasizing his meaning: "the best." It was pointed out to him that "penultimate" literally means "next to last," about as close to the bottom as you can get. No matter: he *thought* "penultimate" sounded like "the best!!!"...and he ensured that it was published in that context.

If you *think* something is right, it's right? In that same manner, a lot of people think "happiness" and "joy" are interchangeable.

THE BIBLE'S TAKE ON LOVE

If I speak in the tongues of men and of angels, but have not love, I am only a resounding gong or a clanging cymbal. If I have the gift of prophecy and can fathom all mysteries and all knowledge, and if I have a faith that can move mountains, but have not love, I am nothing. If I give all I possess to the poor and surrender my body to the flames, but have not love, I gain nothing.

Love is patient, love is kind. It does not envy, it does not boast, it is not proud. It is not rude, it is not self-seeking, it is not easily angered, it keeps no record of wrongs. Love does not delight in evil but rejoices with the truth. It always protects, always trusts, always hopes, always perseveres.

Love never fails. But where there are prophecies, they will cease; where there are tongues, they will be stilled; where there is knowledge, it will pass away. For we know in part and we prophesy in part, but when perfection comes, the imperfect disappears. When I was a child, I talked like a child, I thought like a child, I reasoned like a child. When I became a man, I put childish ways behind me. Now we see but a poor reflection as in a mirror; then we shall see face to face. Now I know in part; then I shall know fully, even as I am fully known.

And now these three remain: faith, hope and love. But the greatest of these is love.

—*The apostle Paul, 1 Corinthians 13*　　　∞

You can rejoice when you feel happy, or be happy when joy comes into your life, but here's the distinction: *Happiness* is a sense or feeling based on circumstances. *Joy* is a deeper perspective based on knowledge of more than circumstances—for instance, Christians know it by its biblical meaning: security, trust in God, love.

One can experience joy even when there is little happiness about circumstances, but not vice versa.

REALITY CHECK

Perhaps these faults can seem a bit on the abstract or theoretical side, and some might question what can seem to be petty nit-picking. But ours are actually very much practical concerns that are utterly relevant to how we all live and respond to reality. In fact, the harmful effect of *The Secret*'s essential misunderstanding of these concepts can be illustrated by a story—a true story.

A young girl, Elise, recently engaged and deliriously in love, was a church worker who did some missions work overseas and yearned to do one more service project with the people she loved serving. Her fiancé, Art, urged her to take the trip before their wedding and held out the possibility that he, also a church worker, might even make a career shift and join her in that type of work.

Beneath this storybook picture was a hidden secret. Art engaged in homosexual practices. Art sank deeper into denial as the truth became known—to Elise, and at his job—until he lost both. Elise is still overseas, serving in missions work, and finds it hard to trust relationships after her feelings of betrayal. But she is working on it.

This is a story, however, of even deeper wrongs, deeper hurts, and deeper parallels to *The Secret*. Elise and Art had a deeper disagreement even before her departure and the subsequent betrayal. The arguments revolved around "happiness." Art was doing and was urging his friends to do things, all with "happiness" as the justification. Elise was astonished that her fiancé would sublimate judgment, prudence, his lifetime of beliefs—not to mention jeopardize his friendships and job—over what he defended as "bringing happiness."

Elise had no conception of all he was actually doing in the name of "happiness," yet the very same menu of the Law of Attraction and *The Secret*'s worldview was being played out.

She wrote this letter when she learned, overseas, that Art

encouraged his friend to cheat on *his* girlfriend in a similar way (yet before she knew the extent of his own unfaithfulness to her):

> You do all this in the name of "finding happiness"? You led him places, lied to his girlfriend, hid him from his group at a convention? You told his parents you didn't know where he was when they were frantic…but you knew? So, you think he is "happy" now, and that's your excuse, but since when is happiness the most important principle in life? Happiness is junk; it comes and goes. Who promises happiness? God promises joy and that is drastically different than happiness. And in the name of so-called "happiness" you think you made for your friend, there are so many people hurt and scarred and wounded.

And here is the actual end to that story—or to a chapter of that story. The "friend" of Art contracted HIV-AIDS. Actions have consequences. In the real world—where the Laws of Attraction have no force of law—you cannot wish things away so glibly. One love, a possible marriage, several friendships, and a man's health and life…all sacrificed on the altar of "happiness."

(Though based on a true story, names have been altered to protect privacy.)

The Secret never explains—and in fact it is impossible to reconcile—what happens when the "Universe" doesn't listen to the same radio of your "frequency," when different peoples' conceptions of "happiness" clash, when the logical extensions of a philosophy of New Selfism clash.

Instead, it more or less smiles blithely back at us and repeats its maxim: "Don't worry, be happy."

Chapter 4

FOR EVERYTHING ELSE, THERE'S MASTERCARD

Wealth: Find True Prosperity

A man was walking in the park and saw another guy on a bench. He looked so sad, as if he were about to cry. The walker was moved to reach out and asked, "Are you okay? Excuse me for bothering you, but you look so troubled! Is there anything wrong? Is there anything I can do for you?"

The guy looked up and said, "Hey, thanks for asking. But, no ... I just got a call from my mom. My uncle, my favorite uncle, who lives on the other side of the country, is real sick, it seems. He's, like, on death's door. They said he's given up all hope."

The man who had been strolling through the park was a disciple of the Secret, a believer in the Law of Attraction. So he got very earnest and animated: "Listen to me! This is all about negative thoughts! I'll bet your uncle has been attracting negative forces to him—it's all in his mind! He can turn this around. He's got to send positive frequencies to the Universe. They'll return! You meet me here tomorrow and tell me how your uncle has changed! Listen to me—he only thinks he's sick!"

45

Next morning, same spot in the park, they meet. "How's your uncle?"

"He thinks he's dead."

SPREADING THE LOVE OF MONEY

Wealth is the thematic preoccupation of *The Secret*, as well of many of its progenitors among fringe movements and obscure merchandisers of the past century. Health is mentioned almost as often in the book, and then few other ideals. The chapter on relationships veers toward love but typically discusses it in terms of "self-love," along with a sure-to-be-famous line about "wanting to kiss myself" (p. 121). Abstract goals like justice and affirmation are scarcely mentioned. Happiness is—in *The Secret*'s cosmology—creature comforts, which are more or less an application of self-love. By way of illustration, in the DVD we are treated to a boy who dreams of a bicycle, clips photos of bicycles, dreams some more of a bicycle...and awakens one morning to find a bicycle on his family's doorstep.

Both book and movie then go on to boast a kind of materialistic exhibitionism that seems especially vulgar coming from Jack Canfield, considering it is he who originated the nominally altruistic *Chicken Soup for the Soul* series. He had the opportunity in *The Secret* and DVD to share any satisfaction he had in, say, touching people's lives in some way, maybe sharing some soulful letters of appreciation and gratitude he received through the years. In true *Secret* form, however, he rushed straight to gaudy self-adulation: "I live in a four-and-a-half-million-dollar mansion" (p. 40).

The Secret evidently assumes its followers are similarly obsessed with cash over all other aspects of life, by evidence of its arguments, recommendations, and incantations. In Byrne's land of Oz, there is an emphasis on wealth *behind* the curtain, too, and we do need to pay attention to it.

THE LAW OF ATTRACTING MONEY

"Critics of *The Secret,* and even some fans, are bothered by its obsession with using ancient wisdom to acquire material goods. In one segment, a kid who wants a red BMX bicycle cuts out a picture in a catalog, concentrates real hard, and is rewarded with the spiffy two-wheeler. *The Secret* 'is like having the universe as your catalog,' says Joe Vitale, who is called a 'metaphysician' in the film but whose website bills him as 'Mr. Fire'—a marketing consultant with the power to sway consumers with a 'hypno-buying trance.' 'The get-rich-quick parts really bothered me,' says [metaphysical bookshop] Bodhi Tree buyer Harmony Allor. 'It's my hope that people won't use creative visualization to obtain wealth for themselves, but in more positive, altruistic ways.'

"The film's backers say they deliberately aimed to make 'wealth enhancement' a major element of the project. 'We desired to hit the masses, and money is the number one thing on the masses' minds,' says Bob Rainone, a former IBM salesman and telcom exec who now serves as Byrne's U. S. business partner. Wealth enhancement is also part of the *The Secret*'s business plan. Among the spinoff books expected in 2007 are *The Secret Workbook* and a collection of *The Secret* success stories. Byrne will also begin filming a sequel to *The Secret* in January, for an August release; Rainone says it will explore 'the next step, the next level' in the process of achieving one's life goals. Meanwhile, the original DVD is about to be distributed in

Europe and Asia; German, Spanish and Portuguese translations are nearly completed, with French, Japanese and Chinese to follow."

Jeffrey Ressner, *"The Secret* of Success," *TIME* magazine, Dec. 28, 2006 (http://www.time.com/time/arts/article/0,8599,1573136,00. html).   ∞∞

Conflicting Messengers

Jerry and Esther Hicks run a business called Abraham-Hicks. In books and seminars they claim to speak for—no, actually they claim to "speak the mind" *of*—Abraham. (No, not *that* Abraham of the Bible, but a group of disembodied minds calling themselves Abraham—more relevant perhaps to another group of biblical characters described in Mark 5:10 and referring to itself as "Legion.") The Abraham Jerry and Esther Hicks describe has led them to a set of beliefs similar to the Law of Attraction.

As celebrities of sorts in their particular circles, they were contacted by the Australian TV producer Rhonda Byrne when she dreamed up the idea of doing a documentary. Originally they played a major role in the DVD, but problems, including money, led to their exclusion. In their words:

> We received an e-mail from the producer of *The Secret* lovingly explaining (we never have received correspondence from her that was anything other than extremely loving) that the contract that we had all agreed upon and signed was no longer sufficient for their further distribution of the project…after conferring with our publisher, and then our intellectual property rights attorney, and

finally with Abraham, allowing them to edit us out was the path of least resistance....

Financially speaking, we have been very well paid for our participation with this project...which has amounted to a staggering amount of money. And if money were the most important factor, we assure you, we would have found some way of staying involved.[1]

Receiving comfortable compensation, Esther and Jerry make no public splash over their disagreements with *The Secret*'s corporate activities.

Some of those who remained on the team, however, are overtly distancing themselves now also. James Ray, one of the stars, was interviewed on KKLA's *Frank Pastore Show*. He is more blatant than some of his fellows regarding his focus on "true wealth and prosperity," as his biography states; he developed the "Science of Success and Harmonic Wealth," a program whose title is always accompanied by a trademark symbol. In the interview he said, "I'm not a spokesman for *The Secret*" when pressed on questions of wealth, evil, and creation.

Pastore posed a hypothetical question: if wealth could be attracted by thinking about it, after "attracting it," why didn't Ray give his money to the poor or give ideas away instead of charging exorbitant seminar fees? Ray shot back with another "law," the Law of Compensation. Unlike Emerson's more famous Law of Compensation, which reckons a yin-yang-styled ultimate balance to life, Ray's law is a "Universe Law" that allows people to profit, evidently bypassing the annoying necessity to wish for replacement cash if you give some to charity.[2]

Dissension in the Ranks

There are other signs that Team Secret's unity is unraveling. There is potentially much at stake, with enormous sales, a valuable brand, a DVD sequel in production, and reports of a syndicated television program in the works. There were early suspicions in press and public mind that squabbling over the crowns and scepters, and not the canon and commandments, of *The Secret*, would overtake the movement. Even if cut up, *The Secret* has become a big pie.

In the "front of the class" of *The Secret* team are two men who are not shy about their emphasis on wealth, especially when it comes to their own personal wealth. One we have visited—Jack Canfield—and the other is a silver-haired veteran of the wealth-creation seminar industry, Bob Proctor. Their spin-off of *The Secret* is the logical extension of the movement's materialistic foundations. It remains to be seen whether these and other team members are quibbling over random tenets of a patchwork philosophy or are destined to play tug-of-war over spotlights and profits.

Proctor himself was interviewed on ABC News' *Nightline* by Cynthia McFadden, and seemed to draw away from some parts of *The Secret*: "I guess Rhonda Byrne is very good at what she does." And about *The Secret*'s advice to write a check and expect that amount to show up in your life: "I'm not sure...I don't think it works quite like that." And to McFadden's observation that *Secret* adherents "believe that action has no place," Proctor replied, "If people think they can sit and think and 'it will happen,' they're deluding themselves."[3]

Two of the "quantum physicists" who sat on *The Secret*'s gallery of gurus, Fred Alan Wolf and John Hagelin, recently have distanced themselves from the project as well. According to Wolf, many of his points were edited out, leaving his position murky, or at least not as he would have it. Regarding the so-called Law of Attraction, he says, "I don't think it works that way. It hasn't worked that way in my life." Hagelin, a onetime candidate for president of the United States of America on the "Natural Law" ticket, said, "The coherence and effectiveness of our thinking is crucial to our success in life. But this is not, principally, the result of magic."[4]

The Proctor and Canfield Gamble

But lest one think that an apparent crack in *The Secret*'s foundation of unity will sufficiently reveal the archbishops of Attraction's naked materialism for what it is, they have developed an even more audacious scheme. Proctor and Canfield have devised something they call a "seminar," which amounts to little more than a briefcase. They call it a *new* program, but they take the name and ideas from the old book, *The Science of Getting Rich*. They call it wealth-creation, but the contents of the briefcase cost $1,995.00. In a way, it *is* wealth-creation...that is, their own wealth.

Secret watchers noted that on the program's Web site that the first announcement prominently featured the logo of *The Secret*, the faux sealing-wax impression. It has now been removed from the top of the presentation. The first announcement featured three men: Proctor, Canfield, and Michael Beckwith, the leader of a popular Los Angeles–area center called Agape.

In spite of Sunday services, Easter celebrations, a Revelation study series, and even the name Agape (not exclusively Christian, but frequently used by Christians to refer to God's unconditional love), Beckwith's movement is in no way Christian and recognizes no divinity in Jesus.[5] Beckwith is likely the most prominent celebrity among the *Secret*'s stars after Proctor and Canfield. In the first announcement of the pricey MLM spin-off of *The Secret*, he was featured in photos with his hand on Canfield's shoulder. Suddenly he disappeared from the Web site; it is now a two-ring circus.

The evolution from vague hints of altruism in *The Secret* to an out-and-out get-rich-quick scheme is best illustrated by the language of the solicitation itself. In fine print, there is notice of technical independence from *The Secret*, but Proctor and Canfield are identified as stars of the DVD and book; *The Secret* can be purchased through the site; and the graphics, down to the ancient-looking cursive script, mirror the design elements of *The Secret*.

"Bob Proctor's new program is your next step in learning to apply the Law of Attraction to build the ideal life you desire," the prospectus announces. Cleverly inserting the word "secret" into its ad copy, the solicitation continues:

The Law of Attraction reveals The Secret to everything you've ever wanted.... Ever since the world found out about the Law of Attraction through the phenomenon of the movie, people from every corner of the globe have been asking Bob Proctor for more.... The Law of Attraction as explained in *The Secret*, and even in much greater detail in The Science of Getting Rich Program, will teach you whatever it is that you may want or need in your life.

In true hypermarketing fashion (redolent of late-night info-mercials), the astonishing price tag for this grab bag first occurs precisely 73 percent into the pitch by word count. But then again, it *is* called a "secret."[6]

The Root of Evil

Please don't misunderstand. There is nothing wrong with making money. In spite of the fact *The Secret* derides a tenet of capitalism (arguing that "competition is bad"), Christians should acknowledge that Rhonda Byrne herself deserves to profit from her labors. In America people are free to pursue wealth. And for that matter, in the Bible some of God's choice people enjoyed great wealth: for instance, Abraham (yes, *that* Abraham) and King Solomon. Many people think the Bible says "money is the root of all evil," but in fact it says that "the *love* of money is the root of all evil" (1 Tim. 6:10 KJV, emphasis added).

The Secret's problem is the fact it cannot discern the difference between wealth and prosperity. In a way, the meanings are parallel to the distinctions made between happiness and joy, as discussed earlier. Wealth is a mere accumulation of money and treasure. (Many might dispute the connotation of the word "mere," but such is wealth: the ledger sheet.) Prosperity, however, is when blessings flow. You *prosper* when you have money, or sometimes when money is scarce! You also *prosper* when your life abounds in love, security, family, self-worth, and a peace that passes understanding.

This *sense* of prosperity is absent from *The Secret* and the statements of all its materialistic mullahs. Is *this* the cornerstone of an old, profound Secret, and a new, exciting way to live—accumulating shiny objects, as magpies and pack rats do, but never enjoying real, soul-satisfying prosperity . . . or even seeking it? Frankly, that kind of secret should remain kept!

Yet the drumbeat of references to a skewed view of wealth reverberates throughout *The Secret*. One of the more remarkable assertions has to be a statement whose absurdity money can't buy: "Jesus was a millionaire" (p. 109). As this is *The Secret*'s only mention of Jesus, surely Rhonda Byrne must have simply confused her cartoonish image of the Son of God with C. Montgomery Burns of Simpsons fame.

GREED IS GOOD?

Along with *The Secret*'s different slant on the pursuit of wealth, you are asked to:

- accept that the ancient Babylonians, a great civilization, are praised solely for their wealth (p. 5),
- believe "predominant thoughts of wealth are what brought wealth to [keepers of the Secret]" (p. 6),
- you can have faith enough that "you can have whatever you want in your life, no limits" (p. 32),
- envy Canfield's bragging about his mansion so much that you'll find yourself wishing that you could evict him and move in (p. 40),
- acquire objects by "making believe" or imagining that you are Aladdin with a magic lamp (p. 50),

- make a hundred-thousand-dollar bill and tape it to the ceiling over your bed (p. 96),
- fill out a blank check with any amount you desire—"We have received hundreds of stories of people who have brought huge sums of money to them using the 'Secret check.' It's a fun game that works" (p. 99),
- ask, "How can I get more of the green stuff?" (p. 101),
- believe the "hundreds and hundreds of letters from people who have said that since seeing [*The Secret* DVD] they have received unexpected checks in the mail" (p. 104),
- make it your intention to look at everything you like and say to yourself, 'I can afford that. I can buy that'" (p. 111).

The Work Ethic Factor

A more contemporary millionaire, Pete Peterson, who was President Ronald Reagan's secretary of the treasury, was also interviewed on ABC News' *Nightline* and assessed both the Law of Attraction's obsession with wealth and *The Secret*'s unique manual of acquisition methods (including thinking hard, taping fake checks made out to yourself to the ceiling, and tuning a personal frequency toward the "Universe"). "These are dangerous childhood fantasies. It's psychotic. If this were true, why would anyone work?" observed the former treasury secretary.

Peterson was also affirming the nobility of *work*—of setting goals, sacrificing, achieving, and knowing success in the arena. *The Secret* dismisses the struggle of earning money, even to achieve wealth, and knows nothing of the benefits to one's pride and setting the next goals for the ambitious and industrious.

Abraham Lincoln recognized the same principle of intrinsic value in labor itself when he said, "Labor is prior to, and independent of, capital. Capital is only the fruit of labor, and could never have existed if Labor had not first existed. Labor is superior to capital, and deserves much the higher consideration."[7]

Can *The Secret*'s team be excused for not knowing about the true meanings—the true *value*—of work versus wishing, of wealth and prosperity? Fully twenty-one of the twenty-four "experts" who lecture us on "financial frequencies" list their activities as speakers and "thinkers" in the self-help industry— ironically their livelihood and wealth are generated from seminars, books, CDs, and miscellanea sold to the hurting, hungry, needy people who sincerely seek direction.

Worse yet—continuing the ethos of self-absorption we saw in *The Secret*'s Pragmatism—Rhonda Byrne's economic prescriptions are amoral at best. She asks no questions of right or wrong; offers no treatment of naked greed's effect on a person's soul; makes no mention of caring or sharing (except for a few clichés like "imagine what you could do for the world"); gives no acknowledgment of biblical views, civic responsibilities, or the soul-cleansing joy of service and sacrifice. Just the Hindu-and-hippie mantra of "follow your karma." Conspicuous consumption leads to a cold world of tarnished objects that one soon can barely recall even lusting after. This is *The Secret*'s heaven on earth.

HEAVEN ON EARTH? BONO GIVES AN EXPLICIT CONFESSION OF BEING SAVED BY GRACE, NOT BY KARMA

Is Bono, the lead singer and songwriter for the rock group U2, a Christian? He says he is and writes about Christianity in his lyrics. Yet many people question whether Bono is "really" a Christian, due to his notoriously bad language, liberal politics, and rock-star antics (though he has been faithfully married for twenty-three years). But in a new book of interviews, *Bono in Conversation* by Michka Assayas, Bono, though using some salty language, makes an explicit confession of faith.

The interviewer, Mr. Assayas, begins by asking Bono, Doesn't he think "appalling things" happen when people become religious? Bono counters, "It's a mind-blowing concept that the God who created the Universe might be looking for company, a real relationship with people, but the thing that keeps me on my knees is the difference between Grace and Karma."

The interviewer asks, What's that? "At the center of all religions is the idea of Karma. You know, what you put out comes back to you: an eye for an eye, a tooth for a tooth, or in physics—in physical laws—every action is met by an equal or an opposite one," explains Bono. "And yet, along comes this idea called Grace to upend all that…. Love interrupts, if you like, the consequences of your actions, which in my case is very good news indeed, because I've done a lot of stupid stuff."

The interviewer asks, Like what? "That's between me and God. But I'd be in big trouble if Karma was going to finally be my judge," says Bono. "It doesn't excuse my mistakes, but I'm holding out for Grace. I'm holding out that Jesus took my sins onto the Cross, because I know who I am, and I hope I don't have to depend on my own religiosity."

Then the interviewer marvels, "The Son of God who takes away the sins of the world. I wish I could believe in that."

"The point of the death of Christ is that Christ took on the sins of the world, so that what we put out did not come back to us, and that our sinful nature does not reap the obvious death," replies Bono. "It's not our own good works that get us through the gates of Heaven."

The interviewer marvels some more: "That's a great idea, no denying it. Such great hope is wonderful, even though it's close to lunacy, in my view. Christ has His rank among the world's great thinkers. But Son of God, isn't that farfetched?"

Bono comes back, "Look, the secular response to the Christ story always goes like this: He was a great prophet, obviously a very interesting guy, had a lot to say along the lines of other great prophets, be they Elijah, Muhammad, Buddha, or Confucius. But actually Christ doesn't allow you that. He doesn't let you off that hook. Christ says, No. I'm not saying I'm a teacher, don't call me teacher. I'm not saying I'm a prophet. I'm saying: 'I'm the Messiah.' I'm saying: 'I am God incarnate.'… So what you're left with is either Christ was who He said He was—the Messiah—or a complete nutcase…. The idea that the entire course of civilization for over half of the globe could have its fate changed and turned upside-down by a nutcase, for me that's farfetched."

What is most interesting in this exchange is the reaction of the interviewer, to whom Bono is, in effect, witnessing. This hip rock journalist starts by scorning what he thinks is Christianity. But it is as if he had never heard of grace, the atonement, the deity of Christ, the gospel. And he probably hadn't. But when he hears what Christianity is actually all about, he is amazed.

From "Salty Dogma" by Gene Edward Veith, *WORLD* magazine, August 06, 2005.

Health—Getting Personal

"Healthy, wealthy, and wise"? The old American maxim has been repurposed under the watchful eye of the Law of Attraction, not only in terms of wealth, but your health as well. In the *Nightline* program we have cited, reporter Cynthia McFadden interviewed Dr. Richard Wender, president of the American Cancer Society. He dealt with the advice in *The Secret* and speculated that people could die if they carried its ideas about health too far. He dismissed both of the so-called Law of Attraction's attributes—that we can attract cancer, for instance, by thinking about it; and that we can wish it away. This is not just foolish; it is deadly. We can "think" ourselves into bad situations, but to suggest we can attract or cast out cancer cells, bicycles, or mansions (as in *The Secret*), just by pointing thought-waves to the "Universe" seems a cruel panacea to peddle.

Can healing come without medicine, are cures possible that defy explanation? I believe so, because I have witnessed it. Let me introduce my wife, Nancy, whose heart and kidneys were failing her more than a decade ago. Presumably Rhonda would say she wished diabetes on herself, even when she was too young to spell the word. In her adulthood, Nancy grew too weak to sustain dialysis, and her kidneys could no longer deal with the heart medicines in her system. She was listed for transplantation.

But after that story—after she received a heart transplant on Valentine's Day—she had another medical crisis about a year later. She was diagnosed with thyroid cancer. A biopsy/aspiration revealed two kinds of cancer cells. They identified the type of cancer cells, the pictures showed the affected area, and doctors felt the cancerous spot. Our church prayed over her before the surgery.

Nancy did have the thyroid operation, and the affected lobe was removed. The oncologist tested it, to see whether the cancer had perhaps spread to the other lobe. As we heard it, there was panic at first because the staff thought they had removed the wrong lobe—no cancer. No, there was just...no cancer. It was one of the stories you hear: "The doctors can't explain it."

The relation to *The Secret* is this: Nancy prayed for a miracle to free her from facing a heart and kidney transplant. The miracle came in the form of a transplant, which was "flying colors" successful. And with a cancerous thyroid gland, a miracle came when Nancy wasn't pleading for one.

HEALTHY, WEALTHY... AND WISE

One of the hardest things about the whole transplant process was looking out the hospital's seventh-floor window, overlooking the city of Philadelphia, and knowing that someone out there would die if I were to live. That was very difficult.

We all know there are no guarantees in life, but no matter how young or old, we tend to take some things for granted. However, when hospitalized in a heart-failure unit, never knowing what the next minutes might bring, I developed a deeper sense of what was important to me. I prayed for more time—time to be a mother to my children, for us to be together as a family. I cried out to God, "How much longer?" He answered through the words of 1 Peter 5:6–7: "Humble yourselves under the mighty hand of God, that He may exalt you in due time, casting all your care upon Him; for He cares for you" (NKJV). And I learned to trust Him.

In all ways my long hospital stay, before and after the transplants, was a good experience. I came to know God in a more intimate way, to learn to trust Him and His ways, and to appreciate all He has given me. I began praying for the other patients on the floor; first for those on their way to the operating room, then during weekly Bible studies, then prayer support groups.

I have often told people since then, "I would not choose to go through all that again, but I would not trade the experience for anything." That's a mystery, but it is very, very true. And I learned the similarity between a proper view of total health and a holistic view of prosperity.

God can prosper us in so many ways! I feel sorry for those who chase after mere wealth or operate their lives by what they *want* instead of focusing on what they need. And they never trust in what God can supply according to His will, according to His riches in glory.

Nancy (Mrs. Rick) Marschall   ∞∞

Thoughts? Frequencies? Blank checks? "Visualizing" a fancy car...or a cured disease? I must confess this is where *The Secret*'s misconceptions get very personal for me. But all I can do is let some play with the self-deceiving children's games *The Secret* admits are make-believe. But this I believe: better it is to know— and embrace—the *mysteries* of life, and of God and His ways, through which we struggle. It is so much better to summon faith in the person who is God, and through Him...conquer.

Chapter 5

FAULTY TRANSMISSIONS

Thinking: Reason Soundly

Is it true "everything that's coming into your life you are attracting into your life" (p. 4)?

Is it true "there isn't a single thing that you cannot do with this knowledge" (p. xi)?

Is it true thinking positively "knows no limit" (p. xi)?

Is it true your thoughts can "create the world" (p. 11)?

These are the claims of *The Secret*. Consider this question: Do you really buy the idea that you can create your entire world by your thinking? And what is the true value of a positive mental attitude?

THINK POSITIVELY

First of all, a positive mental attitude is a good thing. How many people would rather be around someone with a positive mental attitude than a negative attitude? The answer: all of us! A healthy outlook on life, being filled with a spirit of gratitude and expecting joy for the delights of life are all part of making life good for you and for those around you.

The problem with *The Secret*, however, is that it deifies reality by denying its existence—outside your own thought constructs. The value of a positive mental attitude is that it assists us in interpreting and handling those realities in our lives we *cannot* change. *The Secret*'s emphasis on a positive mental attitude borders on self mental manipulation—claiming, in effect, that reality does not exist, except as I think something to be reality. This type of an emphasis on positive mental attitude is delusional. It causes people to be in denial. And when it fails to deliver the promised result, it leads to disillusionment.

What is needed? A heavy dose of honesty and realism.

The Power of the Mind

The human mind is truly amazing! *The Secret*'s emphasis upon the power of the mind is a worthwhile reminder to us all. The power of the mind is impressively illustrated in Dr. Denis Waitley's explanation regarding Visual Motor Rehearsal (p. 81). Waitley emphasizes that when you visualize certain events, the power of the mind is such that it begins to fire muscles, causing them to respond as if you were actually doing that event. The capacity of human mental power is immense. According to Marci Shimoff, the mind has more than sixty thousand thoughts a day (p. 29).

Dr. Daniel Amen is one of the strongest advocates on the power of the human brain. A nationally known neuropsychiatrist, he has examined more than thirty thousand brain scans. Most remarkable, though, is the sense of wonder he inspires regarding the human mind. In that regard, *The Secret* succeeds in underscoring what is likely obvious to all of us.[1] Byrne is correct when she writes of "unfathomable power and unlimited potential of the human mind" (p. 137).

The problem, however, is Rhonda Byrne's insistence on over-stating the truth. "You can achieve and do anything you want with this knowledge" (p. 169). Anything? Absolutely anything? Anything you want? Can you jump off the top of a building and fly like a bird? Can you swim across the Pacific Ocean? Can you burrow into the ground like a gopher?

The answer to these three questions, and hundreds like them we can think of, is no. You cannot do everything. Most self-help books put appropriate parameters around their claims. *The Secret* fails to do any such thing and thus will lead many to defeat and disappointment.

The Balance of Powers

The Secret consistently overstates its claims regarding the Law of Attraction. In a simpler form, it is true that like attracts like. This axiom is true in nature. Most creatures tend to be inher-ently homogenous—that is, they are found with entities like themselves. Birds of a feather flock together—geese tend to flock with other geese, not with dogs; ants tend to be with each other, rather than crawling around bees.

Likewise, people tend to want to be with people like them-selves.[2] That's why people often cluster together in similar social, economic, ethnic, and gender categories. Ironically, even those who pride themselves in valuing diversity above all will often prefer the company of like-minded people. They're actually rather homogenous, gathering together because of a common value: their belief in diversity. Like tends to attract like. As much as some might wish otherwise, no one can dispute that.

The Secret, in a statement on the Law of Attraction, sheds any attempt at accuracy, suggesting that you can have what you want. Not satisfied to simply state the Law of Attraction, the claim shifts into overdrive: "Are there any limits to this? Absolutely not!" (p. 17). What could have been a helpful book affirming the phenomenal power of the human mind disintegrates into a hedonistic "Grab all you can, as quickly as you can."

A "LAW" OR A PRINCIPLE?

My good friend John Maxwell, a leadership expert, wrote a book several years ago titled *The 21 Irrefutable Laws of Leadership*. The book became a classic in the field, selling over a million copies globally. With his blessing, I wrote a historical follow-up titled *The 21 Laws of Leadership Tested by Time*. My book provided historical examples of people over a two-thousand-year span who followed (or who violated) the leadership principles of John's earlier book.

When I (Jim) used the word *law* in the book, I used it as being interchangeable with the word *principle*. My emphasis was on decisions, a way of conduct, which have consequences.

Law, according to *Merriam Webster*, can be understood several ways, including the following:

- "formally recognized as binding or enforced by a controlling authority," that "implies imposition by a sovereign authority" or
- a "rule of behavior or procedure commonly accepted as a valid guide." (http://www.m-w.com/dictionary/law)

Rhonda Byrne's *The Secret* uses the term *law* in a profoundly emphatic way—stating that it is established in the universe and cannot be violated; it *always* works. She seems to view the *Law* of Attraction as truly imposed, as binding. She appears to use the first dictionary definition, seeing the *Law* of Attraction as absolute.

In contrast, I used the term *law* based upon the second *Merriam Webster* definition, i.e., a "rule of behavior."

My use of the term *law* in my book was an appeal for decisions to be made that promoted the ideal of leadership. Ms. Byrne's use of *law* implies a concept—fixed by an authority beyond us.

Frankly, her "attraction" concept is invalid even if she has used it as a principle, rather than as a law. It becomes ludicrous when she portrays it as a type of *sovereign* Law of Attraction.　　∞

Bordering on abuse of its more naïve readers, Byrne included David Schirmer's simplistic quotation: "It is amazing; today I just get checks in the mail. I get a few bills, but I get more checks than bills" (p. 104). He used to get bills, he claims. But then he changed his focus. In fact, he actually whited out the actual totals on his bank statement—writing in what he wanted them to be. Any person with compassion can anticipate the economic disasters awaiting those who accept this in the manner in which it is stated. If his "whiting out" had been accompanied by such classic concepts as diligence, wise investing, patience, endurance, and—perish the thought—honest work, one could have applauded his "whiting" abilities. But as presented, it is delusional—with potential catastrophic impact on those who assume its truthfulness.

The Secret does, however, have some helpful and *healthful* components. On a positive note, *The Secret* appropriately warns of the danger of wrong uses of the mind. For example: "A person who set his or her mind on the dark side of life, who lives over and over in the misfortunes and the disappointments of the past, prays for similar misfortunes and disappointments in the future" (p. 166). At this point, *The Secret* provides wise counsel to those who are inclined to live life looking in the rearview mirror, rehearsing the damage done to them by someone or some event in the past.

Every person can think of some time when someone deeply wounded him or her. All persons, if they are to enjoy mental, emotional, and spiritual health, have to walk in a state of forgiveness and refuse to dwell on past misdeeds any longer, and to forgive. Unfortunately, these truly balanced and rational explanations are few and far between in *The Secret*.

Resistance Is Futile

But *The Secret* generally overstates the power of thought in multiple ways. For example, Carl Jung stated "What you resist persists" (p. 142). This "resist-persist" relationship is portrayed in a quote from Mother Teresa: "I will never attend an anti-war rally. If you have a peace rally, invite me" (p. 143). This quotation is likely accurate, though the context from which it was taken is not given.

But the very next statements exemplify *The Secret's* antihistorical embellishments: "[Mother Teresa] knew." "She understood *The Secret*" (p. 143). This might be laughable if it were not such a serious mischaracterization of a greatly admired woman. When did Mother Teresa ever teach that you should feel good, so you can have happy thoughts, so that you can emit them into the Universe, at a particular frequency, so that the Universe will give you anything you want? Such a portrayal of one who held the sick and dying in her arms is irresponsible at best and, at worst, offensive to her memory. Such claims about Mother Teresa (and other historical figures cited in *The Secret*) are historically in error.

The statement that whatever you resist will persist lacks historical merit. A couple of examples will suffice. Let's begin with the antislavery movement. Those who laid down their lives to free the slaves did not say or think: "I can't say I'm opposed to slavery, or it will 'persist.' I must call it 'pro-freedom'." The fact is, they fought slavery hard and it was defeated. A recent movie, *Amazing Grace*, features the life of William Wilberforce, who, encouraged by John Newton and John Wesley, was one of the great—and, at times solitary—voices battling Britain's slave trade. According to *The Secret*'s methodology, the "resistance" of slavery would have been negative thinking and would have caused it to "persist." Such was not the case. Brave leaders called it evil—and they won the day.

In America, in 1847, there was a man who died young, largely due to exhaustion and poor health brought on by his vigorous battle against slavery. Orange Scott is rarely remembered today, except for a dormitory named in his honor at Oklahoma Wesleyan University. But he warred against slavery. He resisted it. And as a result, *it did not persist.*[3]

Another example would be the women's suffrage movement. If you are a female and you vote, you owe a debt of gratitude to the women who met in a small Wesleyan church in Seneca Falls, New York, in 1848. They challenged the injustice of male-only voting—and ultimately won! They did not say, in some politically correct—shall we say "*The Secret* correct"—way, "Invite me to a pro-women's rights rally." They called evil "evil"—and "ran to the roar of the lion,"[4] challenging life's inequities. These injustices did not persist. In fact, they desisted because people were courageously resisting them.

Women eventually won the right to be preachers in many pulpits, just like men. The first woman to be ordained to church leadership in America was Antoinette Brown, whose ordination sermon was preached by a Wesleyan, slave-fighting preacher named Luther Lee.[5]

Why are these stories important? Because they illustrate that sufficient resistance does cause something to cease to persist. The "what is resisted must persist" theory is nothing more than a fiction—along with the many other fictions contained in *The Secret*.

Nothing More Than Feelings

After doing a respectful job of making a case for the power of the human mind, *The Secret* turns its focus to the relationship of thoughts and feelings. *The Secret* is obsessed with "feeling good." Any causal reading reveals the many times the reader is instructed to simply "feel good."

The thesis is essentially this: your feelings are an indicator of your thoughts. If you feel bad, you have bad thoughts. If you feel good, you have good thoughts. If you have any bad thoughts, that means you're transmitting them into the Universe at such a frequency, they will bring back bad things to you. In contrast, if you are emitting good thoughts, like a radio transmitter, to the Universe, the Universe will mirror those good thoughts to you in materialized form. Thus, thinking about driving a BMW emits thoughts to the Universe that obligates the Universe to reward you with a BMW sooner or later.

The error of such thinking is that it denies the reality of human experience. As persons, we were made with the capacity for joy and the capacity for grief. Both are gifts from God. Grief does not qualify as "feeling good." Feeling bad is an equally valid part of the human experience. Admittedly, it's not as much fun to feel bad as to feel good. In fact, given the opportunity, all of us would rather feel good than feel bad any day. But there are circumstances within the scope of life that merit feeling bad, whether it is something we have done ourselves, something we have done to others, something done to us, or something done by others. Being aware of a universe that consists of both good and evil mandates we have the capacity for responding with joy, which is authentically good, and responding with sorrow or disappointment to that which is harmful. If one's child is killed by a drunk driver, one should not merely "feel good" in response. Grief is a *bona fide*, legitimate expression of one's humanity.

ACTIONS SPEAK LOUDER

The relationship between thoughts and actions is likely one of the areas in which *The Secret* most misleads its followers. A positive mental attitude, as stated earlier, is a good and wonderful thing. Thinking you can do something Herculean—that is believed to be beyond human capability—is a wonderful drive. We all love being around people who can climb the mountains in their lives, who dream of doing the seemingly impossible. That is the way life should be viewed.

For example, you have to admire the biblical character Caleb, who at age eighty-five finally entered the promised land of Israel. When the leader, Joshua, asked him what portion of the land he'd like to settle in, Caleb said, "Give me the hill country." Why did he want it? Because there were giants to slay, and he wanted the challenge (Josh. 14:6–13). Most accomplishments in life would never have occurred had people not believed they could climb mountains that appeared to be insurmountable.

What is understated (in fact, harmfully so) throughout *The Secret* is the relationship between thoughts *and actions*, and more specifically the impact of actions upon results. Suppose a couple begins to think they want to own a beautiful home. Do they simply *think* about this home hour after hour, day after day, post pictures all over the house, and do nothing about it? Assuredly not! *The Secret* only gives lip service to that tremendous gap between thinking about something and seeing it achieved. That "gap" is called *action*. It could have other labels as well, such as *personal responsibility*.

It's worth noting as well that at no time does *The Secret* allow for a unique and explicable factor in all of life simply called *the favor and blessing of Almighty God....* But back to the role of action.

Let's picture once again the couple thinking about a beautiful home they would like to own. Does thinking about it simply produce it? Honest people know the answer is no. But let's suppose instead of merely thinking about it, the couple begin to take action. Let us suppose they sacrifice in order to accomplish that goal. Sacrifice, according to *The Secret,* is a bad word, a concept that can cause "resentment" (p. 108).

The couple continues to sacrifice diligently. Maybe they avoid eating out at expensive restaurants, avoid buying brandnew cars, avoid purchasing expensive clothing and jewelry. They curb their entertainment expenses. In the meantime, they shop the real estate market carefully, seeking the counsel of wise people. They study and become familiar with real estate. They look at many houses. They continue to think thoughts as *The Secret* insists (picturing their dream house), but they're also taking wise and diligent actions. In time, they will own a home that meets their needs; not because they "thought it into existence" but rather because after their thinking came actions in alignment with that desire.

The Secret may acknowledge "any action we take must be proceeded by a thought" (p. 114), but its mention of *bona fide* action is at best passive. Similarly, while affirming your circumstances do not define who you are, James Ray insists those circumstances are merely the "visual outcome of your thoughts and actions" (p. 72), with actions being relegated to an afterthought.

Even when *The Secret* does acknowledge the relevance of actions in life, it is often in negative terms: "When you want to attract something in your life, make sure your actions don't contradict your desires" (p. 115). Similarly, Ray cautions that would-be believers notoriously "are not doing the things that are going to make them happen" (p. 102).

So it is encouraging when Byrne at least tips her hat by admitting, "When you have an inspired thought you have to trust it and act on it" (p. 96), but even there is a fundamental flaw that again undercuts the truth. What is the *it* in which we are to trust? (In chapter 9, we will examine this single greatest weakness in *The Secret*: its emphasis on trusting an "*it*.")

The phrase "act on it" seems vitally important, but what does it mean? In biblical language, this would be the important combination of faith and works, of trusting *and* acting upon that trust. However, in this case the emphasis is on "think it," and if you think it, it will effortlessly be yours. Many will experience despair and disillusionment after they try following *The Secret*'s guidelines and discover that merely thinking it—without appropriate action—will not bring desired results.

Despite Byrne's admission that "action will sometimes be required," the reality is that action of some sort is crucial. Yet she virtually laments how "action is a word that can imply 'work' to some people, but inspired action will not feel like work at all.... Inspired action is effortless" (p. 55). Sounds nice, but effort isn't all the evil Byrne makes it out to be. And again, this idealized standard, proclaiming that life's blessings should come effortlessly, will also bring much disappointment.

Contrary to the claims of *The Secret*, living life and experiencing its blessings *involves work*. Even Byrne's illustration of the one who received his dream house by thinking good thoughts had to acknowledge he didn't merely attract it, he bought it—which requires effort—and then he renovated it—which, as anyone who has ever remodeled a home knows, requires great effort (p. 90). In other words, he didn't just *think* the house into being, he had to *take action*—with significant initiative—for it to happen.

Sowing and Reaping

Ultimately, the readers of *The Secret* are going to have to decide whether they are going to believe in (1) *The Secret*, and put their confidence in their own mental projections, or (2) a God in whom they can place their confidence.

In the Judeo-Christian tradition there is a concept known simply as *sowing and reaping*. In the physical realm we have no problem understanding that. If you plant apple seeds, you get apple trees. If you plant tomato seeds, you get tomato plants. If you plant corn seeds, you get cornstalks.

It's when we move to the spiritual that we have our greatest difficulties. We believe what is true in the physical world is true in the spiritual world—what you sow you also reap. And so the question for believers of *The Secret* is not that you reap what you sow, but rather *how* you go about sowing. How do you sow something in the unseen world, in the world of the invisible?

According to *The Secret* you sow by simply having good thoughts. Those thoughts are obligated—by virtue of some level of participation with an undefined entity called "the Universe"—to bring you back the good things you were thinking about. However, in the Christian tradition, sowing is seen very differently.

Byrne does affirm the Bible's teaching, "Whatever you sow you reap." But then she goes on to add, "Your thoughts are seeds and the harvest you reap will depend on the seeds you plant" (p. 17).

It's true you reap what you sow. But what is the "ground" for this belief? In other words, what (who?) makes this happen? The underpinnings of the Bible's sowing/reaping reality is a confidence in a God who causes the pattern to occur. In the same way no one can explain why an acorn can produce a gigantic oak tree that pushes up against the law of gravity (how, yes; but not why), so it is in the spiritual realm. No one can explain *why* sowing causes reaping, except that God honors the sowing.

THE TRUE POWER OF BELIEF

Followers of *The Secret* are encouraged to maintain a vision board, "a place where you see it and look at it every day" (p. 91).

At first glance, who can possibly find fault with that? A "vision board" helps one to see the invisible, desiring it to become visible (pp. 57, 168). The visible/invisible connection is perhaps one of the more profound messages of the book.

Christianity also believes the invisible can become visible. The biblical understanding of prayer is, in part, exactly that. In fact, John, the closest friend of Jesus, describes Jesus coming to Earth as the invisible become visible (John 1:14).

Perhaps *The Secret*'s take on the visible/invisible connection is best summarized by Mike Dooley's succinct (if simplistic) statement, "Thoughts become things" (p. 9). But the question *The Secret* readers need to ask themselves is, *Why?* Bob Proctor claims, "Anyone that ever accomplished anything did not know how they were going to do it. They only knew that they were going to do it" (p. 61). Though statements such as these sound noble enough, they fail to address a most pressing issue: it is not how they are going to do it that is the question, but rather through whom.

If Rhonda Byrne and *The Secret* contributors truly believe they can accomplish all they say they can, then why don't they blanket the entire globe with positive thoughts and end hunger, violence, war, and greed this very day?

Are we gods who can speak things into existence? As difficult as it may be to admit, we all know we're not omnipotent—we don't have unlimited power. The one truth humans least like to hear is that we are merely human—we are not God. According to the Bible's account in Genesis 3, it was the very misconception that we can "be like God" that caused all the problems in our world to this day (vv. 4–5). Our power, as all human experience confirms, has limits. If you are going to accomplish something great (and we all should desire to do exactly that), the question is by whose power you are going to accomplish it.

Lisa Nichols does well to call people to "unwavering faith" (p. 52). Likewise, it's exciting to read Rhonda Byrne's joyously enthusiastic "I believed!" (p. 100). One wants to applaud her encouragement to not allow "a thought of doubt to enter your mind" (p. 89). And wise people can do worse than to begin their day with a faith statement akin to "I'm going to have…a pleasant journey" (p. 56).

But what is this faith to be placed in? In you? In your thoughts? Or in something or Someone much greater than you? What is sorely lacking in these noble claims is any recognition of an object to this faith. The fundamental human problem is that we have tried to make life work by having faith in ourselves. But that has resulted in failure (as promised in Genesis 3). The invitation to every seeking human heart is to find the One—to place your faith in the person who is truly God. There is One who has much more power than even your thoughts could dream. One person alone is legitimately called "God."

Vision versus Imagining

Now that takes us back to the "vision board" (p. 91). It is, of course, a good thing to be able to envision the things that you believe, that you are called to do or to receive. But there is an enormous difference between "visioning" and what Byrne characterizes as "imagining." In fact, a better description of her process would be "fantasizing."

A vision is something given to you by God after which you are shown the steps to proceed toward it. For that matter, authentic imagining is likewise a gift from God. But fantasizing is a *make-believe game* in which you try to wish something into being. What is the difference?

For starters: the source. A vision is from God (and imagination is likewise a gift from God for beings created in His image). But fantasizing is from (and for) yourself. A vision is something that spurs you on to do the sacrifice to reach the goal. Fantasizing is merely an excuse to naively attempt to obtain something for which you have not paid the price. It is not childlike, it is childish.

A little advice to the person who wants to achieve some goal in life: don't follow the advice of simply imagining "having all the things you want" (p. 67). No, you are not "blocking your own good from coming to you because you are in a negative frequency" (p. 34).

Do you want something worthwhile? Yes, envision it; then be willing to pay the sacrifice to obtain it.

Ask, Believe, Receive

Interestingly, Rhonda Byrne herself chose to use the Bible as proof for some of her main points. One major component of the alleged Law of Attraction is the three-step procedure: ask, believe, and receive (pp. 54, 60), which directly parallels Jesus' teachings as recorded in Matthew 21:22 and Mark 11:24.

What is this three-step procedure? What does it mean to ask, believe, and receive? Rhonda Byrne correctly references the biblical order of the process: first, ask; second, believe; and third, receive. However, she fails to understand the context in which these very words were stated.

In the Matthew passage, Jesus was answering some of His critics. The story, continuing to verse 27, involved a question of by whose authority Jesus was doing and saying things.

The answer is quite obvious from verse 25. Jesus was operating on the authority of God Himself. Nowhere did Jesus suggest that if you simply emitted transmissions into the Universe that the Universe would have to, somehow, mirror back the request for the desires of your heart. Instead He made the answer contingent upon authority: that is, speaking with the authority of God Himself.

Byrne distorts—knowingly or unknowingly—the biblical texts. She cites Mark 11:24, which reads, "What things so ever ye desire, when ye pray, believe that ye receive them, and ye shall have them" (KJV). Putting that in easier-to-understand language it reads as follows from the New International Version of the Bible: "Therefore I tell you, whatever you ask in prayer, believe that you have received it, and it will be yours."

Byrne uses this verse in an attempt to support the Law of Attraction. After citing the Scripture, she quotes Bob Doyle as saying, "Do whatever you have to, to generate the feelings of having it now" (p. 54).

What she fails to notice, apparently, is that the Mark 11 paragraph begins with the words, "Have faith in God" (v. 22). Nowhere does the biblical text say, "Have faith in your thoughts." It does not suggest emitting thoughts into the Universe like a transmission tower at a particular frequency so you can get things back from the Universe. Faith is founded and rooted in having radical confidence in the personal God who alone is able to answer prayer.

Furthermore, verse 25 says, "When you stand praying, if you

hold anything against anyone, forgive him, so that your Father in heaven may forgive you your sins." In other words, the foundation of this prayer is having a right relationship with other persons, forgiving them harms they've done against you and consequently, having a right relationship with God the Father in heaven, having acknowledged your sins.

Context Is Everything

Rhonda Byrne's *The Secret* has no allowance for even the existence of sin. It never acknowledges the sin, evil, or brokenness of this world. *The Secret* acknowledges no God. *The Secret* does not acknowledge the capacity to have a relationship with God. *The Secret* does not acknowledge going to God and asking for forgiveness for an offense against a friend.

None of these are acknowledged, and yet it's the very foundation of the profound statement. Whatever you *ask* in prayer, *believe* you have *received* it, and it will be yours. In other words, the ask-believe-receive pattern is totally contingent upon an understanding of God, forgiveness of sins, and restoration of proper relationships with those around you. *The Secret* fails to acknowledge any of these conditions.

A similar verse is found in Luke 17:6, when it says, "If you have faith as small as a mustard seed, you can say to this mulberry tree, 'Be uprooted and planted in the sea,' and it will obey you." If you took those few words by themselves, you would think Jesus was trying to teach His followers how to rip trees up and throw them into the sea. That was not the case. If you look at the verses before Luke 17:6, you see that the text specifically talks about how difficult it is to forgive somebody who has wronged you. In dialogue with His closest buddies, Jesus said, if a friend is truly asking forgiveness for having harmed you, then forgive him. If that same friend continues to do harm against you seven times a day but continues to ask forgiveness each of those seven times, then you continue to forgive him (see Luke 17:4).

The followers of Jesus responded the same way any of us would: "Help us to have the faith to be able to do that. That's too hard." It was at that point Jesus explained that if you had a tiny amount of faith—the size of a mustard seed, a very small seed—you'd be able to speak to a mulberry tree and command it to be uprooted and thrown into the sea. In other words, the discussion about the power of your words was based upon uprooting, not trees, but roots of bitterness that can grow in your heart when somebody wrongs you.

You may wonder, what does this have to do with the Mark 11:24 passage Rhonda Byrne quotes in *The Secret*? That verse has the same fundamental teaching: if you are going to *ask, believe, and receive*, then with God's help you will need to forgive all persons who have sinned against you. This "formula" so central to *The Secret*'s strategy to success (ask-believe-receive) has been ripped completely out of its spectacular context, not only by Rhonda Byrne, but by many well-meaning Christians, too.

∞∞∞

OPRAH: CHRISTIAN OR PROMOTER OF NEW AGE?

On Friday, February 16, 2007, two of the promoters of *The Secret* appeared for the second time on the *Oprah* show. For the discerning, what spewed from the mouths of these two men, Michael Beckwith and James Ray, was New Age. One lady, identifying herself as a Christian, spoke about her unease with the seeming focus of *The Secret*. She was quickly shot down by Beckwith and Ray and by Oprah Winfrey, claiming that she too was a Christian....

Let us be reminded that Oprah Winfrey had Marianne Williamson, New Age leader and guru, on her show back in 1992; that it was Winfrey's endorsement of Williamson that skyrocketed Williamson to fame, along with her book expounding the virtues of the New Age "Bible": *A Course in Miracles*. (Source: http://www.reinventingjesuschrist.com) Williamson now appears on *Oprah and Friends XM Satellite Radio* as a "friend and contributor."

(Lynn Stuter, "Christianity or New Age," February 2007, online, www.crossroad.to)   ∞∞

GOOD THINGS COME

Simply stated, ask, believe, and receive is an enthralling biblical formula that has real applications, but only when you are with the plan: that is, God's plan. The choice is yours, whether or not you want to be either in alignment with the "Universe," or in conformity with the plan of a God who loves you.

Consider the contrast between God's will for your life (that is, seeking forgiveness in broken and distorted relationships around you) and that of *The Secret*, which is to "attract" whatever you want.

The Secret even brags of children attracting whatever they want (p. xi). How alarming it would be for young children, who do not know the difference between "want" and "need," to be able to attract whatever they want. That would mean they would want not to go to school but to play all day. It means they would want to stay up until midnight every night watching TV. It would mean they would get their dream of entire days of eating ice cream—without a healthy diet.

Ironically, *The Secret*'s constant pandering to our *wants* reminds one very much of the fundamental difference between being childlike and being childish. *Childlike* is when we have a tender openness before God as a Father to us. *Childishness* is when we want what we want when we want it—a formula for self-destruction.

Yet this reality of childishness and the danger of getting whatever we want is acknowledged by the book in a quotation by Lisa Nichols: "Thank God there is a time delay, that all of your thoughts don't come true instantly. We'd be in trouble if they did. The element of time delay serves you. It allows you to reassess, to think about what you want, and to make a new choice" (p. 22).

My Will Be Done

A few observations about this very insightful quotation: this is one of the few times in which God is acknowledged in the book. And He is acknowledged with a capital G. Ironically, though, when the line appears in the DVD (when subtitles are displayed at the fourteen-minute mark), God is spelled across the screen with a small g.

What is also intriguing in this quote is the reference to "a time delay." Obviously, Lisa Nichols feels the time delay is good because we might initially ask for inappropriate things. She claims the "element of time delay serves you," allowing you to revisit what you really want. How long is that delay? And what if the delay is not long enough for you to align your wants with something that's truly good for you?

As stated previously, a Christian cannot legitimately embrace the major thesis of *The Secret*, in spite of the fact there are occasional Christian themes in the book. A Christian is not one who emits signals in certain frequencies into the Universe for the purpose of his or her wants. A Christian is one who prays as even Jesus Himself did, with one major condition: "If it is Your desire or will, Father God."

The difference is enormous. One is a self-centered, self-serving request; the other one is a desire for our wants to have a healthy external "check" on them, that is, the God of the universe who knows all good and determines whether or not He is to answer this prayer.

Gratitude Is Golden

There are glaring failures aplenty in *The Secret,* to be sure. But as we close this chapter on how to think properly, it's only fair to point out some of *The Secret*'s positive teachings. One of the most noteworthy lessons in the book is the teaching on being grateful. Joe Vitale emphasizes the importance of not focusing on "what you don't have." He admonishes readers by saying, "start to be grateful for all the things that you feel good about" (p. 74). That is not merely advice from *The Secret*. It is straight from the heart of the Christian Scriptures.

When we were complaining children, our parents would notoriously admonish us, "Be thankful for what you have rather than focusing on what you don't have." Grateful people simply receive more in life. Nobody likes whiners. It has been said that whiners are not winners. Ungrateful people are turn-offs and they drive people away. People are drawn to those who have a spirit of gratefulness.

Dr. John Gray wisely wrote, "Every man knows that when his wife is appreciating him for the little things he does, what does he want to do? He wants to do more. It's always about appreciation. It pulls things in. It attracts support" (p. 75). Joe Vitale's advice to "[make] a list of things to be grateful for" (p. 74) is sound counsel for all of us.

Why is gratefulness so important? Because gratefulness is much more than simply saying "thank you." Saying "thank you" means that you're acknowledging someone has provided something wonderful for you. It's a way of acknowledging that you are not the epicenter of your universe. Someone else has provided for you. In other words, gratefulness is actually a form of humility.

Humility is not saying, "Oh, I'm nothing. I'm really nothing." That's *false modesty*. Humility is having a spirit of gratitude for all that's been given to you and the blessings of life. Humility is expressed by gratefulness, and gratefulness results in, or finds its source in, humility.

We all appreciate humble, grateful persons. And that is precisely what God calls us to be. *The Secret* properly acknowledges that we have the capacity to choose in life (p. 20). It is called free will. You can choose to have thoughts of gratefulness. You'll be happier if you do. Everyone around you will be happier if you do.

Chapter 6

BRIDGE OUT

Delusion: Avoid Make-Believe

Lois, a high school classmate of mine (Jim's), loved doing what every high schooler longs to do, drive a car. Excited that she was old enough to drive, she took the car for a spin—in the country. She came to some road construction, where there was a sign placed annoyingly in the middle of the road. Lois, not to be deterred by some pesky warning, buzzed around it. What she did not realize was the sign said "Bridge Out!"

She soon discovered the reality of that sign, even if she had neither read it nor heeded its warning. She approached a large ravine, fortunately at a very slow speed. There was no bridge. Due to her snail's pace, the car did not plunge into the creek bed. But it did high center, hanging precariously on the edge.

What is the moral of the story? Read the signs. And this chapter is a warning: "Bridge Out." I will yell as loudly as I can. I will even flail my arms. But it is up to you whether or not you will stop. Rhonda Byrne's *The Secret* is dangerous. It will harm you.

Deluded Deities

One of the most obviously overstated claims of *The Secret* is that our "thoughts are the primary cause of everything" (p. 33). This must be patently untrue for two reasons: before you were born you didn't exist, and evil exists in spite of you.

Cogito, Ergo Sum

First of all, there is the rather obvious reality that something existed before our thoughts. Presumably most of us wouldn't lay claim to having eternally existed in the past. So our thoughts cannot be primary.

The great seventeenth-century French philosopher René Descartes—called the "founder of modern philosophy"—is perhaps best known for his argument for existence: *cogito, ergo sum* ("I think, therefore I am"). Descartes doesn't make the logical leap *The Secret* wants to—"I think, and everything is." Rather, he makes a much more logical connection that often goes unnoticed when philosophy is taught in contemporary schools.

To put it simply (if not simplistically), the argument goes: I know I exist (I'm not the product of some *Matrix*-style dream) because I can think. But there's a second fact as well—something lesser cannot create something greater than itself. So...if I can even conceive of a being infinitely greater than me, then it must exist independently of me. That being is generally known (and by some, personally known) as God.

Hence: I think, so I know I'm real. And I can think of God, so God must be real; and despite what *The Secret* suggests, I couldn't create a superior God. So...I'm not God. Behind and before our thoughts there must be a primary cause of all thought. That primary has a name. It is called God.

THE SECRET AND *THE MATRIX*

The movie *The Matrix* has a scene in which Morpheus shows Neo two pills—one red and one blue. Neo must choose a pill to take: one offers truth and reality, the other will allow Neo to stay in the delusion of the Matrix.

The Matrix "reality" fools the human mind into thinking it is real life, which is wonderful and desirable. The vast majority of those trapped in this delusion offer no resistance to their captivity because they believe the Matrix *is* reality. *The Secret* offers such "reality."

The Problem of Evil

So some of us begrudgingly have to admit that our thoughts are not the primary cause of all that exists. And honestly, it's just as well—history bears out that humans playing God isn't all that it's cracked up to be. Things usually end badly when we do.

In fact, considering the state of our world, we can be relieved we're not responsible for all that goes badly in this world. Our thoughts could not be the cause of everything, because sometimes evil itself is the cause. But where does evil come from?

Christians believe it comes from being separated from the originator of all that is good—God. If God is good, then guess where evil comes from. Ever since humans took the path of being their own gods (that story of Adam and Eve and original sin), we've all been born separated from God. So even evil didn't really originate from us any more than we create darkness by leaving a lit room. You're just caught up in the absence-of-light reality, and evil comes about from not being in the Good.

That's arguably a simplistic response to a fundamental question the greatest philosophical and theological minds have been grappling with for millennia. You'll forgive us if we don't presume to solve that problem in these pages right now, anyway.

But we can agree this world is trapped in evil, and there are times when people face horrific situations, not because they've had thoughts that caused them, but because we're in a very broken world (separated from God) that includes heartache, suffering, and pain. You didn't create the darkness, but you're in it and part of it.

Perhaps we can disabuse some of their troubled thoughts, then—those who may struggle with guilt after reading *The Secret*. You did not attract evil to you, despite what Byrne claims (pp. 27–28). Consider: does anyone honestly think for a moment nine-year-old Jessica Lunsford actually attracted the evil incarnated in John Couey when, in February 2005, he kidnapped her from her Florida home, raped her, and then murdered her by burying her alive?

It should not take much thoughtful weighing of *The Secret*'s theory against any number of such examples of real-life evil in our world to realize the delusional nature of such a belief system. Does any rational person believe JonBenet Ramsey attracted her own horrific fate by thinking and feeling murder?

These ludicrous ramifications are *The Secret*'s logic carried through. This kind of thinking not only fails any kind of logical scrutiny, but it must necessarily place upon suffering people a great deal of personal guilt for failing to prevent, or perhaps for even attracting, evils that are in truth far beyond their control.

Be Anything You Want to Be

Furthermore, you cannot simply think and feel your way to "creating your future" (p. 32). While it is important to acknowledge that thinking and feeling have enormous impact upon your present and future, they are not the defining forces.

While no one need act as if he is a victim of his circumstances, at the same time not every person starts in life on an equal footing. For example, fans can't simply think and feel their way into becoming LA Lakers team members. For most, no amount of wishful thinking is going to change the fact they simply do not have the body makeup, the mental skills, the muscle development potential, or the height to be on one of America's better known basketball teams. You cannot think and feel your way to everything.

It is true, however, that by proper thoughts in your mind you can either significantly improve your station in life or learn how to better accept and cope with the situation you find yourself in. But it is just not true that "everything that is coming into your life you are attracting into your life" (p. 4). To be sure, some things we bring upon ourselves by virtue of our thoughts, beliefs, words, and actions. But we all live in a world in which we sometimes receive blessings we did not deserve, or we feel the impact of pain we did not cause. That is the reality of the world, the real world in which we live—a world (you remember) Christians call "fallen" by virtue of its being separated from God and under the dominion of fallen would-be gods.

You Can't Always Get What You Want

Whatever the "Universe" is, it is not some grand mechanism forced to deliver "pictures" of a "new frequency" (p. 19) as you might demand. As bitterly judgmental and condemning as this worldview must end up being, it also is one destined to put many on a road to deep disappointment. Succinctly stated, your "transmission" does not create your life and create your world.

Thinking good thoughts is important. Acting on those thoughts is paramount. Being willing to sacrifice for a worthwhile cause is to be applauded. But don't rely on some miraculous "transmission" to create your world.

Not Getting Any Younger

Perhaps the most insidious of *The Secret*'s flaws is its capacity for denial—denial of reality. A glaring example is Joe Vitale's assertion, "I'm not getting older, I'm getting younger" (p. 167). Vitale, like the rest of us, is getting older; and there's nothing wrong with that. A newborn baby two minutes old is also getting older. We're all getting older, and it's nonsensical to be in denial and to say we're getting younger.

We can say we feel younger. Some people, for a short time, may even look younger. Some people may get their bodies in better condition and be able to perform better athletically than years before. But the reality is, even if some of us are able to get our bodies into a better state of being than they had been for years previously, we are nevertheless getting older—it's a simple matter of chronology.

Yet if Rhonda Byrne is to be believed, any understanding of aging is strictly in our minds (p. 139). We are expected to experience eternal youth. If that is true, why have some of her leading proponents died? Wallace Wattles, whose 1910 book, *The Science of Getting Rich*, influenced Rhonda Byrne, died in 1911. He's not getting any younger. Prentice Mulford, who is cited frequently in *The Secret*, also did not seem to get a handle on this growing younger phenomenon: he died in 1891 at age fifty-seven. Charles Haanel died in 1949. Robert Collier died in 1950. In fact, to date, no one has lived forever.

The fact is the Bible takes a very different view regarding this age-old phenomenon of getting older. It is simply called "the glory of aging."[1] Aging is a spectacular thing. That's not to suggest that some of the physical aliments often accompanying aging are wonderful. They are not. Bodies hurt. Bodies wear out. People die. (Again, from the Christian worldview, the ailments of old age are another one of those nasty consequences of the Fall—of humanity's state of being separated from God.)

Aging Gracefully

But the Bible does attach great significance to the knowledge that comes from experience, especially for those people who walk through life in true wisdom. Gray hair is supposed to be a credit to a person, not a reason for dread and loathing.

I (Jim), due to weight loss and vigorous exercise over the last three years, am far more healthy than I was a decade ago. After not exercising for almost two decades, I now exercise almost every day. At the time of the writing of this book I am running a race, and not just any race: a mud race—literally a 5K race through mud pits. I could not possibly have done that three years ago. But in spite of my newly increased physical vigor, I cannot honestly make the claim I am getting younger. The fact is I'm three years older than I was when I went through my behavioral change involving weight loss and physical exercise.

But *The Secret*'s faith in your power goes further than offering to reverse time: with regard to disease, it insists, "You cannot 'catch' anything unless you think you can. And thinking you can is inviting it to you with your thought" (p. 132). Again, there is a grain of truth in these exorbitant claims: certainly there are significant parallels between one's thinking patterns and disease. Healthy thoughts help produce healthy bodies, without a doubt. But do not fall into the trap of assuming you can do *anything* by self-suggestion.

A safer foundation upon which you can build your life is who God says you are. In His Word He says you are His child, He loves you, and He cares deeply for you. He says he has "purchased" you with a price (see Acts 20:28). He can offer you forgiveness, healing, completeness, and, in Him, wholeness. Everything you long for, that is right to desire, these good things—healing, wholeness, health, prosperity, the blessings of life—is available in Him.

However, you will not get them by suggesting to yourself how badly you want them or emitting frequencies into the universe. You'll get them when you come into agreement with the wonderful statements your Creator says about you.

DELUSIONAL DENIABILITY

In 1975–1976, Senator Frank Church conducted an investigation of U.S. intelligence agencies. The Church Committee, as it came to be known, attempted to establish a linkage between John F. Kennedy and the attempted assassinations of several foreign leaders, including Cuba's Fidel Castro. Although the president clearly approved such actions, it could not be established that he was directly involved. Thus the term was developed: "plausible deniability."

The Secret offers people a stark opportunity of what might well be called "delusional deniability." Consider phrasings from several quotations from *The Secret*: "act as if" (p. 117), "acting as if" (p. 115), "feels like a lie" (p. 106), "got myself into feeling as if" (p. 105), "make believe" (pp. 50, 98), "seeing it as done" (p. 85), "a holographic experience—so real in this moment" (p. 83), "believe you have it already" (p. 49), "feels like you have it already" (p. 83), "put yourself in the feeling place of really being" (p. 84), and "feel…even if it's not there" (p. 35).

What do the expressions have in common? At their core, they're all about make-believe.

Imagine yourself graduating from college, being married with children, living in a nice home, or driving a nice car. In and of itself this is not harmful. Those may be honest expressions of legitimate desires of your life. But "imagining" such into existence? Even characters populating fairy tales, even superheroes, have some limitations.

THE DANGERS OF "OUT OF CONTEXT"— FOR THE AUTHOR, FOR THE READER

1. Proper Context—for the Author

One of the great challenges for any writer is to use quotations carefully and accurately. In fact, a legitimate fear of any author is that he or she would take a statement out of context. In this book and in previous books I have written, my editors and I have checked and rechecked quoted statements, desiring to make certain that they were well within their original context.

I (Jim) was so concerned about this that, many years ago, I actually used too many quotations in my master's thesis. And they were too long. The reason? I was concerned about misquoting a writer, unintentionally distorting someone's viewpoint. Thus I erred on the other side: simply listing long quotations without much comment on my part.

Rhonda Byrne apparently lacked any such concern with quotations' context. If someone uses similar language, Byrne carelessly assumes that the writer is referring to what Byrne so endearingly calls "the Secret." (For examples, see the Winston Churchill and Martin Luther King Jr. sidebars.)

Allow me to be facetious for a moment. One might expect that with such sloppy scholarship, Byrne might claim that Victoria's Secret is really about emitting to the Universe—simply because both Rhonda Byrne and the highly visible retail chain store both use the term *secret*. All joking aside, the task of a writer is to make certain that quotations are used as the original writer intended them.

The prime example of this (discussed at length elsewhere) is Byrne's misuse of "Ask, Believe, and Receive" from the New Testament. She completely misapplied the text, abusing the intentionality of the writer. I shudder to think what might have happened had Ms. Byrne read one of my books—*God Still Heals*—and decided to use it. She could have taken isolated phrases—legitimate concepts about faith and believing for good things—and have transferred them into her "emitting to the Universe" language, thus abusing my intent.

2. Proper Context—for the Reader

The out-of-context concern is not only an issue for the author. It is an issue for the reader as well. Readers must be discerning enough to *read* the book in proper context—i.e., what the author is really saying.

Due to the fact that Byrne's book appeals to persons already conditioned to the self-help motifs of "think it, act on it, and it will happen," they read *The Secret* through that lens. They mistakenly assume that her writing is within the standard fare of "positive mental attitude" literature. It is not. It is well outside of that—from its foundation up.

During my graduate school days (admittedly, long ago), I was a door-to-door book salesman. I learned a lot, grew a lot, made lots of money, and became the number one rookie salesman in the company, out of some two thousand new salespersons. We were trained to demonstrate a "positive mental attitude." (Who would prefer a negative mental attitude?) Unlike Byrne's thesis, however, this PMA was not based upon distinctly anti-Christian, antibiblical moorings. It was, in keeping with the teaching of such persons as Zig Ziglar, biblically based.

Certainly not all PMA teaching is biblically based. There are essentially three sources for such teachings:

- Biblical or Christian, as demonstrated by Norman Vincent Peale and Robert Schuller. Their positive attitude emphasis could, in some cases, be a substitute for confident faith in God (although some of his critics are far less charitable and consider his ideas nonbiblical).
- Humanism, based upon one's own innate human ability; this view may appear harmless, but it is destined to lead to long-term disappointment.
- Non-Christian sources, which can include a wide array of sources, even (from a Christian viewpoint) power from demonic

forces. This source of "believe and receive" may have short-term results, but it is painfully destructive in the long term.

The readers of *The Secret* owe it to themselves to know the "context" from which Byrne is writing.

If you are accustomed to *healthy* self-help literature, do *not* assume that *The Secret* fits with that reading genre. Succinctly said, "Buyer beware!" Just because the can you are drinking from is shaped like a Coca-Cola can does not mean that you have not reached unknowingly for a can of arsenic.

In summary, authors should quote others in context. And readers should understand the author's context, the author's nuances.

Alternating Realities

Perhaps one of the most dangerous aspects of *The Secret* is its call to change reality; in fact, to alternate "your current reality" (p. 71). Once more, there's the grain of truth: the desire to improve one's lot in life can be a healthy desire. In fact, people should desire to improve not only themselves but to improve this world for those around them.

But an altered state of reality can be lethal. Thinking persons should be seeing warning lights whenever they read phrases like, "That's when you see how you create your own reality" (p. 39). The next assertion is even more disconcerting: "That's where your freedom is. That's where all your power is" (p. 39).

Your freedom is not in creating some kind of a fantasy reality. No real power is located there, and in fact obsession with such fantasy world living can ironically prove to be enslaving to some. No—true freedom comes when you know how to have the capacity to do what is right, whether it feels good or not. That's freedom.

To a sexual addict who habitually violates the covenants of his marriage, the power to break free of his sexual addictions is freedom. Obsessive fixation upon a fantasy world is not power. True power is the ability to alter or improve this world for yourself and others...and to graciously accept those things you cannot change.

For that matter, altered reality can be achieved rather easily and commonly by various means of substance abuse. Most would agree that such altered realities are the antithesis to freedom and power. Drug and alcohol addiction actually renders people either inert or inept, and it remains the method of choice in contemporary culture for the ever-popular practice of slavery. Far from altering reality, drugs and alcohol reduce one's ability to understand or enjoy reality.

Turning "fantasy into fact" (p. 53) is self-serving and delusional, especially when you are attempting to "build bigger and bigger fantasies" (p. 53). That is not a "creative process" (p. 53); rather, it is a destructive process.

It should be pointed out that there is a profound and fundamental difference between, on the one hand, the would-be god who denies the reality of this God-created world and would presume to believe into existence his or her own preferred reality and, on the other hand, a follower of the true Creator who will be used by Him to change this fallen world for the better. The latter can have a God-given vision of that which is truly good, noble, pure, and right; that one truly has access to omnipotence and can be privileged to be an agent of change.

But using some form of delusional thinking to turn fantasies into facts is a dangerous form of narcissism.

Weightier Matters

Let's look at one specific application of the so-called creative process: specifically, Rhonda Byrne's advice on losing weight. She reports she weighed a "hefty 143 pounds" all because she was thinking "fat thoughts" (p. 59). She now maintains her perfect weight of 116 pounds (p. 62).

As one who has struggled with weight loss, let me [Jim] be quick to compliment Ms. Byrne. In fact, if I were privileged to meet her, I would say, "Rhonda, way to go. That is impressive. I'm proud of you!"

But it is the next few paragraphs after her testimony of weight loss that would be cause for pause for almost every medical doctor in the nation. She states that "food cannot cause you to put on weight unless you think it can" (p. 59). In other words, the only thing that causes weight to come on your body is your *thinking* food causes you to gain weight.

My own experience attests to just the opposite. In all my years of gaining weight, I thought precisely the opposite. I was rather convinced food could not put weight on me. I kept eating and kept eating, hoping and believing I wouldn't gain weight. Guess what? I did. Lots of weight, in fact.

I have news for all would-be weight losers. Food has calories (there's a thought). If you eat 3,500 calories, and burn none, you will gain one pound, regardless of what you think about it. Especially menacing is the statement that "the definition of the perfect weight is the weight that feels good for you. No one else's opinion counts" (p. 59).

Let me tell you what feels good for me—eating an entire package of Oreos. That feels very good, at least while I'm eating them. (It doesn't feel too good a couple hours later, I'll admit.)

Of course, once again (predictably), there is that element of truth in Rhonda Byrne's promise that it will feel better to have the weight off. But that future promise of feeling better is cold comfort at best to the person to whom it simply feels good to eat the comfort food that puts the weight on.

And what is the perfect weight for you? It is not whatever makes you "feel good." Medical science has studied and created formulas to help establish the approximate weight for someone of a particular body build, height, and gender. Those are helpful for determining what a proper weight is, and they should be consulted. They don't have to be our map "masters," but they may be of service...that is, if we're willing to listen to someone else's "opinion."

As one who has to watch caloric intake and has to exercise faithfully, let me give you this warning: simply thinking food causes weight does not make you overweight. Eating it does.[2] You can pray and attempt to "cast the calories out of the food" all you want, but for every 3,500 calories of intake, you are going to gain a pound. For every 3,500 calories burned off in exercise, you are going to lose a pound.

Loser Thinking

To be sure, your mind is very important in the weight-loss process. In fact, your mind is the single most important factor in the weight loss process. As I journaled during my weight loss phase I wrote some guidelines for myself, called "How to Think Like a Loser."[3] By *loser*, I meant one who is losing weight.

I followed this mental discipline carefully. I thought a certain way. My mind was keyed to weight loss. So in that sense, *The Secret* confirmed my own reality. But it wasn't simply because I thought thin thoughts alone. I made sure those so-called thin thoughts resulted in a controlled caloric intake with proper foods, primarily fruits and vegetables, along with a vigorous daily regimen of exercise.

Another way in which my mind played a key role in weight loss was the aspect of "vision." I truly envisioned a healthy body. I purchased a suit some twenty years earlier when I was on a trip in London, England. I was now many sizes beyond that suit, but I kept it hanging in my closet in a highly visible place with a dream and a desire I would once again be able to wear it.

Finally, that day came. Admittedly, I looked a bit ridiculous in a suit that was beyond out of style. But I didn't mind on the one day I wore it. I was so happy once again to be able to wear it. The mind does play a key role in appropriate weight loss and health issues. So much of this is true that Charlie Shedd wrote a book called *The Fat In Your Head*. In other words, how you think affects your weight.

But you cannot wish the pounds off by thinking thin thoughts. Accompanying those thoughts must be special attention to what you eat, how much you eat, and how much exercise you get.

To all the would-be *Secret* followers (including *Secret* dieters), I hope this chapter will serve as one more reality check. Remove yourself from the "delusional deniability" of *The Secret*. Face reality and accept the fact that what you think is important, is powerful. But the key is to see yourself as God sees you. That is a wonderful blessing, and you'd be surprised how freeing it is. You won't have to wear yourself out emitting transmissions into the Universe.

Instead of the cold comfort of being your own pathetic god, feel the embrace of a God who loves you for who you are and lets you know how special you are!

Chapter 7

"BUT WAIT,
THERE'S MORE"

Scams: Be Discerning

In a previous chapter we visited some of *The Secret*'s remarkable statements about attracting awful ailments and thinking them away. Elsewhere in *The Secret* is Rhonda Byrne's astonishing proposition—the supposedly false belief that food was responsible for her onetime weight gain. She now holds such views as "complete balderdash.... Food is not responsible for putting on weight. It is your *thought* that food is responsible for putting on weight that actually has food put on weight" (p. 59). Not appearing in the book, but possibly coming to an upcoming *Oprah* segment near you, could be these comparably pithy insights: "Guns don't kill people...it's those little bullets"; "The twenty-three-story fall didn't kill him...it was that nasty pavement."

"SHAME ON OPRAH," WRITES COLUMNIST FROMA HARROP

"Shame on Oprah Winfrey for promoting [*The Secret*]. Thanks largely to Oprah, *The Secret* sits at No. 1 on the so-called nonfiction list. The companion DVD is also flying off the shelves.... There's really something evil about *The Secret*, and that's call to civic passivity.... *The Secret* holds that thinking about bad things happening in the world actually makes those bad things worse. I've respected Oprah Winfrey for her tough mind and seemingly genuine interest in bettering the lives of women.... But then she goes out and hypes a book in which Ms. Byrne writes, 'When I discovered *The Secret*, I made a decision that I would not watch the news or read newspapers anymore, because it did not make me feel good.'... The summons to cast off civic responsibility pollutes the whole enterprise. Oprah should know better."

(Froma Harrop writes for *The Providence Journal*, a Belo newspaper. Originally published April 10, 2007.)

There is a superficial, iconoclastic, perhaps even refreshing logic to the Law of Attraction's satellite concepts...until you actually think about them. Rhonda doesn't say thinking about eating leads to immoderate consumption. No: if you believe that food puts on weight, those thought frequencies evidently scatter calories throughout your organs and flesh before they pirouette toward the "Universe."

We have also examined several aspects of the phenomenon known as the Law of Attraction and its latter-day face to the world, *The Secret*. We will take a few moments to look at it—as it seems largely to regard itself—as a commercial project. Not "profit-making" for Rhonda Byrne (as we have said, everyone is entitled to compensation for the sweat of his or her brow), but a cash-centered enterprise, which is a different thing. And to the extent this is a component of *The Secret*, the public should know it, and the public should be aware of similar schemes in the past.[1]

THE LAW OF ATTRACTION: WHERE SHE GOT IT

There are several books, the oldest about a hundred years old, that form the foundation, such as it is, of Rhonda Byrne's *The Secret* program. In her DVD and book (p. ix) she tells of receiving the old book *The Science of Getting Rich* by someone with the name of Wallace Wattles that shook off her funk. She suddenly knew that several famous people in history knew the same secret she and Wallace Wattles did, and she determined to tell the world, something that evidently hadn't occurred to the smart and famous keep-away crowd. Wallace Wattles, on the other hand, did share his secrets, but the world seemed uninterested a century ago.

Following are summaries of Wallace Wattles's book and several others by other writers who contributed to the Law of Attraction. Not all of them attracted large followings—otherwise, presumably, every literate person in America would be filthy rich today. We offer them here as a sort of milk-carton pix of sound thinking gone missing.

We earlier cited Santayana's dictum about history—not learning its lessons dooms mankind to repeat them—yet in this day of well-written textbooks and a twenty-four-hour History

Channel, the public still acts as blindly and gullibly as did the public of earlier, less-sophisticated generations. Each generation seems to need the truth of the gospel told in a new way, so perhaps it is an aspect and not fully a flaw of human nature that we need to learn for ourselves. Children can be told a hundred times not to touch a hot stove, but invariably it is the first burn, not the hundredth warning, that teaches them.

So in this chapter we are going to review a few of the most famous (or most surprising) schemes of the past, many of which prefigured *The Secret*; we will deconstruct some of the "metaphysical" scaffolding erected around this so-called Law of Attraction; and shed some light on the cults and cultists that have immediately preceded and inspired *The Secret*.

THINK AND GROW RICH BY NAPOLEON HILL, 1937

Napoleon Hill parlayed an interview with steel tycoon Andrew Carnegie a century ago into a decades-long association with Carnegie, an assignment to interview five hundred other fabulously wealthy businessmen, and eventually a charter membership, so to speak, in the American dream machine: the formulaic, glad-handing, push-for-success ethos that has driven many personal fortunes of the past century.

First published in the midst of the Great Depression, Hill's *Think and Grow Rich* has been a bestseller. It contains many phrases that pop up in *The Secret*.

Basic to Hill's argument is the assertion "thoughts are things" and whatever we think we can bring into being. "All achievements, all earned riches, have their beginning in an idea." Persistence pays! If once we grasp the fact that a "success consciousness" begets financial prosperity, we will, with the poet William F. Henley, know that "I am the master of my fate: I am the captain of my soul." Everything depends upon me and my mind-set. "Both poverty and riches are the offspring of thought." The book is replete with such sentiments, which have had lives of their own as mottos in companies' break rooms ever since.

Hill leads the reader through thirteen principles of success, devoting a chapter to each of the following: desire, faith, auto-suggestion, specialized knowledge, imagination, organized planning, decision, persistence, the master mind, the mystery of sex transmutation, the subconscious mind, the brain, and the sixth sense. Hill also reckons there is a "magnetic force" in the universe. "Whatever the mind can conceive and believe, it can achieve."

With a plan in hand, persistence is mandatory, a blister-raising aspect that Rhonda Byrne apparently rejects. "A Quitter Never Wins—and A Winner Never Quits," Hill declares. Strongly sexual people succeed, Hill says, insofar as they rightly control and successfully "transmute" their energies in worthwhile ways. Such energy works through the subconscious mind, building up positive emotions and overcoming negative ones. This enables one to develop a discerning "sixth sense" and exercise the creative imagination necessary for success. "Man alone has the power to transform his thoughts into physical reality; man, alone, can dream and make his dreams come true." In sum, a Rotarian, middle-American sort of pep talk for achieving sales goals that very carefully eliminates God from planning and priorities.

(Hill, Napoleon. *Think and Grow Rich.* Reprint of the 1937 edition, edited by Ross Cornwell. Clemson, SC: Aventine Press, 2004.)

PUBLIC AND PRIVATE DELUSIONS

The first major writer who sought to warn the public of "hot stoves" was Charles Mackay. His 1841 book *Extraordinary Popular Delusions and the Madness of Crowds* was not so much an exposé of scams themselves, whether wealth, health, or "self-help," but an observation of human nature: What makes people suspend disbelief and ascribe to bizarre propositions? More, why does a rash of enthusiasm for weird schemes every generation or so, pass like a fever from individuals to large numbers of people? Mackay wrote that people "think in herds; it will be seen that they go mad in herds, while they only recover their senses slowly, and one by one."

Since mass acceptance is an aspect of *The Secret*, the appearance of rational discussion masking a Declaration of Incoherence, it is instructive to visit a few of Mackay's reports. "In reading the history of nations, we find that, like individuals, nations have their whims and their peculiarities, their seasons of excitement and recklessness, when they care not what they do. We find whole communities suddenly fixing their minds upon one object and going mad in its pursuit; millions of people becoming simultaneously impressed with one delusion and running after it, till their attention is caught by some new folly more captivating."[2]

Critical Mass of Delusion

In the eighteenth century, a remarkable example from French history illustrates the power of mass delusion—the hysteria on this occasion was in response to a scheme invented by John Law, who alleged treasures beyond imagination in the American Louisiana Territory. Dubbed the "Mississippi Bubble" (see sidebar), the scheme eventually burst, resulting in widespread misery and many riots. Remarkably, it's at times like these that many people put aside their better judgment because there appears to be "safety in numbers." In today's culture the Pied Pipers are the likes of Oprah, Ellen de Generes, and Larry King.

THE TALE OF THE MISSISSIPPI BUBBLE

Mackay's own words still evoke the public infatuation: "At the commencement of the year 1719 an edict was published, granting to the Mississippi Company the exclusive privilege of trading to the East Indies, China, and the South Seas, and to all the possessions of the French East India Company.

"The wild enthusiasm that swept France was due in large part to descriptions and promises published by the transplanted Scotsman John Law of the Mississippi Company. He described the Louisiana Territory as a landscape of gold mountains and silver plains. His writings and appearances—not unlike going on TV talk shows today—even made reference to an enormous emerald rock in the middle of the Arkansas River.

"The public enthusiasm, which had been so long rising, could not resist a vision so splendid. At least three hundred thousand applications were made for the fifty thousand new shares…. The price of shares sometimes rose ten or twenty per cent in the course of a few hours, and many persons in the humbler walks of life, who had risen poor in the morning, went to bed in affluence….

"[Predictably, soon] value of shares in the Mississippi stock had fallen very rapidly, and few indeed were found to believe the tales that had once been told of the immense wealth of that region…. The bank stopped payment in specie; Law was dismissed from the ministry.

"What has come to be called the "Mississippi Bubble" burst, and countless people suffered horrible losses: money was worthless; the government continually minted new coins, arbitrarily set values, and announced rules against owning things of value. There was widespread misery and many riots. Law fled the country at the end of 1720."[3]

But as Mackay notes, though the very similar scheme—close in fallacy and in failure—was unfolding before British eyes, across the Channel in France, the London public nevertheless followed in mass after its own will-o'-the-wisp fantasies, chasing one more bearer of great promise and grand prosperity, John Blunt. His set of impossible promises is known to history as the "South Sea Bubble."

In America, less than a century ago, there was a comparable mass delusion—a multitude following a dream and believing an obvious fallacy, though it was right before their eyes. Its name has gone into the dictionaries as an example of too-good-to-be-true schemes. It was a financial chimera that required a readiness to suspend disbelief. The Ponzi game is probably the closest America has come to a Law of Attraction mentality stripped of its costume-party adornments of pseudo-science and pop philosophies.

Charles Ponzi was also an immigrant to America. He came from his own context of "down under"—southern Italy—and despite the (literally) unbelievable nostrums he peddled, he was a beloved figure who seemed secondarily involved with amassing baubles. He talked wealth, but more as a way to gain adherents than to show it off. No doubt, if he were around today he would be a popular talk-show guest. If his life were a movie, Danny DeVito would play Carlo Ponzi.

While he was flying high, convincing people they too could "imagine wealth" with a minimum of work, someone called him the greatest Italian who ever lived. "You're wrong," replied the smiling huckster. "Christopher Columbus discovered America. And there's Guglielmo Marconi, who invented the wireless!" The answer shot back: "Yeah, Charlie, but you discovered money!"

What Ponzi discovered, actually, was a way to parlay international postal exchange coupons into profits. The coupons, in the days following World War I, were then common ways for nationals, especially displaced people, to communicate, and even to transfer funds between countries. You could buy International Postal Union coupons in one country, mail them to another, and they'd be redeemed for cash. But Ponzi noticed that drastically fluctuating exchange rates presented the possibility of losing—or making—money on the transaction.

The transactions depended on moving massive amounts of coupons around the world, reliance on exquisite timing, and participation of people to fill the coffers, as Ponzi foresaw a huge operation involving more than himself. But he was obliged to depend upon more. You see, Ponzi actually explained his system, out in the open. Bankers and government officials—even the *Boston Globe*, his local paper—warned the public. Yet people invested, in astounding volume; and Ponzi never had to kick in his Postal Union coupon plan.

That was because he depended upon the essential factor in any of these schemes, whether "unlimited" rising values of stocks and currencies, as in the Mississippi and South Sea Bubbles or promises that "feeling happy now is the fastest way to bring money into your life" as *The Secret* pledges today (p. 111) or initial favorable publicity, word-of-mouth endorsements from a few people that multiply in effect.

Once again, we see in history the component of people who simply *want* to believe in these schemes. What developed with Ponzi was this: a feeding frenzy of "investors" gave him enough money to promise returns (even without the postal coupon operation) of 50 percent interest every ninety days. In the beginning it worked. This was because he paid out from the incoming investments; when, quickly, those investments rose to two hundred thousand dollars a day, it was easy. Bankers, regulators, and newspapers warned the public that nothing but rising investment funds enabled Ponzi to pay out...for the moment. Logic and hard truth played no role: the streets around Ponzi's Boston office soon resembled John Law's neighborhood at the height of the Mississippi Bubble frenzy. "Lie to me," the people seemed to be saying. As long as investors outnumbered withdrawals, everybody *felt* happy.

The Ponzi Game collapsed eventually, partly under its own weight—there are a finite number of investors, gullible or not, in Paris, Rome, and even Boston—but the surprise is more that it succeeded as long as it did. And once again we see an example of a gullible public defying common sense, economic facts, and even legal warnings, and following a fallacy.[4]

In the case of *The Secret* and the so-called Law of Attraction, "wealth" and "feeling good" are promised at the end of the rainbow despite the questionable credentials and the self-serving statements of a curious cheerleading squad. The Bible has a term for this tendency in people: "For the time will come when they will not endure sound doctrine; but after their own lusts shall they heap to themselves teachers, having *itching ears*" (2 Tim. 4:3 KJV, italics added).

Let's Go, Metaphysics!

What allows theories like the so-called Law of Attraction to slip into overdrive is the sloppy state of contemporary culture's standards. Precision of thought and lucidity of speech are endangered species in America today. When a president of the United States, caught in a lie, equivocates about an earlier assertion: "It depends what 'is' is"—and he is not laughed off the national stage by people whose intelligence should have been offended—we witness the depreciation of both honesty and communication.

Here's an illustration of *The Secret* marketers' ethos at work: to put over a concept that might evince skepticism, "wrap" it in an exotic label like *metaphysical*. Remember, again, that *The Secret* is a marketing colossus, introduced by an "us *versus* them" premise, sold by appeals to selfish impulses, promising great riches, and wrapped in terminology arcane enough to persuade any doubter outside the circus tent. "Quantum physics" and other nifty concepts we will turn to next, but consider the movement's *metaphysical* basis, and how—thanks again to America's sloppy attention to details—the word can cover a multitude of sins.

In other words, before turning to "science" to attempt an explanation of the secret Law of Attraction, the Byrne Unit flashes some psychology and philosophy before your eyes—much of it avant-garde enough to dazzle, new enough to have a short history of scrutiny, borrowed in parts enough from recent fringe movements to have a patina of plausibility. Step right up, folks!

Do you want to lose weight? Be rich? Be richer? Metaphysics explains it all!

THE SCIENCE OF GETTING RICH

The Science of Getting Rich is based on the "monistic" theory of the universe that "One is All, and that All is One," derived from the Hindu. This "science" is presented as the most important of all knowledge, for a person cannot develop, contribute to society, help others, or attain happiness without possessing material things. Thus, it is of "supreme importance to him that he should be rich."

This is presented as an "exact science," in that there are certain laws defining the process, which will work "infallibly" for anyone who properly applies them.

The universe is made of "Formless Substance," of which there is an inexhaustible supply. "Formless Substance" is controlled by thought, and man is a "thinking center" who can cause it to take on whatever form is desired. Good thoughts create good things, such as riches, health, and greatness; bad thoughts create bad things, such as poverty, disease, and failure.

The following steps are basic to the "Science of Getting Rich":

- Believe there is one "Intelligent Substance," which gives you everything you desire,
- Create a clear mental image of what you want, with a certainty it is yours,
- Never allow doubt, failure, or negative thoughts to enter your mind,
- Use the power of your "will" to keep your attention fixed on the image you desire, keeping it continually in your thinking,

- Maintain an unwavering "faith", combined with "gratitude",
- Claim it as yours and it will come to you.

(Wattles, Wallace D. *The Science of Getting Rich, or Financial Success Through Creative Thought*. Reprint of the 1912 edition. New York: Penguin Group, 2007.) ∞∞∞

The Metamorphosis of Metaphysics

Very significantly, the very word *metaphysics* is misapplied—a mistake from its earliest days. Many people think its Greek origin means "beyond physics," that is, "the science of what is beyond the physical." Hence, *metaphysical* came to be used in the sense of "legitimate speculation; abstract." Literally, however, it meant the writings "after *The Physics*," the title assigned to the collected thirteen essays by Aristotle appearing after those on physics and natural sciences. So the word, originally referring to an indexing arrangement, was coined by Andronicus of Rhodes, around 70 BC.

Although Aristotle addressed the origins of things (teleology: contemplating causes, or "final causes"), and even the possibility of a relationship between the universal and the particular, he likely would not recognize his illegitimate child, modern metaphysics. In common parlance today, *metaphysics* has come to mean the studying of ideas about the first causes of things.

But even more, it amounts to philosophic speculation on the nature of reality, including the relationship between mind and matter, substance and characteristics, fact and value. Included, and invariably of highest concern, are questions unanswerable to controlled experiments, scientific observation, and analysis.

In discourse, *metaphysical* has even experienced a metamorphosis similar to the misapplication in Aristotle's works.

These days a "metaphysical discussion" usually connotes extremely subtle reasoning, abstruse arguments, and obscure rhetorical points. And the focal points have indeed gone "beyond" physics! Before the first herbal-tea break at your local metaphysical conference, you can find yourself visiting the worlds of religion, philosophy, epistemology, Freudian and Jungian psychology, parapsychology, astronomy and astrology, mysticism, reincarnation, meditation, UFOs and ESP, Eastern meditation and yoga, self-help, positive thinking, dreams, and more. Maybe it should be called meta-meta-metaphysics.

THE CLIMATE FOR NEW THOUGHT

As metaphysics has moved far beyond its origins in physics, a long American tradition of quasi-mystical Transcendentalism moved well beyond some ironically Puritan roots. The evolution from a God of justice to a religion of universalism, and then to the ultimate assertion that God (if there is one) is a spiritual pathology, might well be the inevitable result of Pluralism in America.

If everything is allowed, in other words, and nothing (short of, say, cannibalism) is condemned, then everything is equal or must be equally valid. Right? Who are *you* to say? What's right for me, say a growing tribe of Thought Police, is my business, and you can't impose your ideas on anyone else. This is all said with a militancy, bigotry, and arrogance that has the New Thinkers trying to impose their view of life and reality—that is, their secular religion—with all the muscle they ascribe to the old "rocked-ribbed Puritans." The allegedly "tolerant" are in fact profoundly intolerant.

As we say, perhaps the seeds were always there, just under the surface of the soil that was American Pluralism. As the nineteenth century witnessed great evangelical revivals—camp meetings, mass conversions, missionary movements at home and abroad (critic Gilbert Seldes called it the "stammering century" because of the plethora of ecstatic worship experiences) there was a bifurcation.

The "other" side of American Christianity was rushing to cohabit with secular philosophies, even Buddhist and Hindu beliefs, as well as social movements like communal living, socialism, universalism, and varieties of deification of the mind. This deification—finding God in oneself, not in the biblical sense of inviting God's Spirit into one's life, but declaring oneself equal to, and indistinguishable from, God—was like a vine, spreading out in many directions and attaching itself everywhere: to established denominations, to social movements, to university faculties, to urban intelligentsia.

Then Came New Thought

William James, the Father of Pragmatism, called himself a "Methodist minus a savior," capturing in a phrase an entire movement that eschewed traditional biblical Christianity, often with clever-sounding slogans and propositions, and sometimes retaining the trappings of traditional denominations.[5] For instance, New Age movements met in "churches"; religious science groups gathered on Sundays; philosophies called themselves religions (and some religions called themselves philosophies).

"New Thought" became a formal and unifying name for movements addressing social organization, healing, scientific advances and speculation, optimism, and a curious American amalgam of business-modeled success paradigms and socialist and Marxian critiques. Hand-in-hand with these "Mind" and "Universe" teachings were dozens of experimental, communistic towns established across the nineteenth-century American landscape. Phineas Parkhurst Quimby is generally acknowledged as the "Father of New Thought."

Quimby's New Thought was similar to the views of the Transcendentalists like Ralph Waldo Emerson, whom *The Secret* quotes on page 107—one of its few accurate representations of a historical figure's actual ideas. It is, however, an innocuous quotation about self-reliance (one of Emerson's pet subjects), and not about Emerson's role in larding American spirituality with Hindu mysticism. The Indian connection was a pantheist, Hindu-like denial of worldliness...ironic, given the excessive greed and hedonism of New Thought's granddaughter of sorts, *The Secret*.

Quimby overcame a case of tuberculosis and began practicing and teaching forms of what he called spiritual mind healing. He relied on writings of Emanuel Swedenborg, a Swedish mystic who lived one hundred years earlier and claimed to speak with spirits; in turn he influenced, among others, Mary Baker Eddy, the "Mother" of Christian Science.

Avatar Babies

With the influence of Eastern mysticism, not only concepts but terminologies were grafted onto Western traditions. Quimby referred to "avatars"—and so, in fact, does *The Secret*. In fact there are more references in the book to avatars than there are to Bible prophets or Christian saints; more references to Buddha than to Jesus. What is an *avatar*? In Hindu traditions, an avatar is the incarnation of a supreme force (or incarnations of Vishnu) on Earth. In informal parlance, it also means "prophets"—and

Jesus would be described as a mere prophet, on a level with Mohammed or various teachers, not God.

The avatar concept was central to Theosophy, which maintains that creatures have attained the human state through many reincarnations, bouncing through the mineral, plant, and animal stages since before life appeared on Earth. Helena Petrovna Blavatsky founded the movement in New York City in 1875.

Another figure is even more eccentric than these people, and possibly more directly related to the Law of Attraction and the *Secret*istas of today. The similarities between the works of William Walker Atkinson (also known as Theron Q. Dumont, Magus Incognito, Yogi Ramacharaka, Swami Panchedasi, and Theodore Sheldon—for some reason he wrote under many pseudonyms) in the early 1900s are striking. Atkinson might have been the man who conceived the phrase "Law of Attraction," and is another father of the New Thought movement. He wrote on the Rosicrucians, a secret society; Hermetic philosophy (*The Kybalion*); and probably his most famous (although all were about as obscure as they were understandable): *Thought Vibration or the Law of Attraction in the Thought World* (1906). Oddly, though it seems to be the clearest progenitor of *The Secret*, Rhonda Byrne never mentions Atkinson, nor any of his multiple identities, in her book.

THOUGHT VIBRATION OR THE LAW OF ATTRACTION IN THE THOUGHT WORLD

Two of Atkinson's legacies are a W. C. Fields–like address book of colorful assumed names, including those of swamis, under which he wrote many books; and, evidently, the honor of coining the phrase "law of attraction."

The universe, he says in *Thought Vibration*, is governed by law: one great law, the Law of Attraction, a working principle of nature that is in full operation whether you know it or not, whether you believe in it or not.

Few people realize, but Atkinson assures us that he does, that the will may be developed, disciplined, controlled, and directed just as any other of nature's forces. Your will does not need training, but your mind does. The mind needs to be trained to receive and act upon the suggestions of the will. The will is the outward manifestation of the "I AM"…yet again, an usurpation of the biblical term, employed in a strictly personal sense.

When we think, Atkinson says, we send out vibrations of a fine ethereal substance, which are as real as the vibrations manifesting light, heat, electricity, and…magnetism. That these vibrations are not evident to our five senses is not proof that they do not exist, he maintains.

We are largely what we have thought ourselves into being, the balance being represented by the character of the suggestions and thought of others, which have reached us either directly by verbal suggestions or telepathically by means of such thought waves. A positive thought is infinitely more powerful than a negative one, and if by force of will we raise ourselves to a higher mental key we can shut out the depressing thoughts.

The conquest of fear is the first important step to be taken by those who wish to master the application of Thought Force. One must proceed to cast out fear and worry and replace them with confidence and hope. In order to attain a thing, it is necessary that the mind should fall in love with it, and be conscious of its existence almost to the exclusion of everything else. Mental force operates best when it is concentrated.

You are entitled to the best there is, for it is your direct inheritance. So don't be afraid to ask, demand, and take. The good things of the world are not the portion of any favored sons. They belong to all, but they come only to those who are wise enough to recognize the good things as theirs by right, and those who are sufficiently courageous to reach out for them. The best the universe holds belongs to you as a divine heir, according to Atkinson.

(Atkinson, William Walker. *Thought Vibration or the Law of Attraction in the Thought World*. Chicago: The New Thought Publishing Co., 1906.)

From the Fringe

In 1912 Theodore Roosevelt ran for president as an independent candidate because the Republican party purloined and denied delegates he won in primaries, thwarting the clear will of the rank and file. His risky campaign confirmed the truth of these situations and validated his personal popularity: he came in second and ran ahead of the Republican incumbent. But in this amazing undertaking he was obliged to call on volunteer workers and recruit others.

Among his followers were a committed band of reformers, social workers, crusaders for various causes, vegetarians, and pacifists. He was grateful for their assistance, but he knew the affection of such liberals would be short-lived: he looked over the movement, assessed the "types," and wrote of them, "They are the lunatic fringe that are the votaries of any forward movement."[6]

The same might be said of the people we have profiled in this chapter: the ancestors and prophets of this generation's breathless fad. It seems all the ingredients of the stew known as *The*

Secret can be found in these mass delusions like the financial "bubbles" that amazingly shook people of their judgment as well as their money; the schemes like the Ponzi game that succeeded despite authoritative warnings to the public; and the spiritual, philosophical, and mystical fads—always growing more extreme in their claims, forever growing less coherent.

But wait: Larry King says *The Secret* "is supported by science." And Grand Ol' Oprah, arbiter and avatar herself of pop culture, said she has been practicing the Law of Attraction for years (without knowing it).[7] As Greg Beato said in *The Reason* e-zine, *The Secret*'s real secret is that it "gets people to behave irrationally.[8] For most of the 20th century, self-help charlatans labored under a common constraint. Their primary medium was books, but their targets—the lazy, the impatient, the credulous—were exactly the kind of people who didn't read books. In the mid-1980s, the advent of the infomercial helped liberate the charlatans from the tyranny of print…"

Hence the densely visual *Secret* book, and a production-rich DVD with dark imagery, tense music, and glowing backdrops.

HADDOCK'S MASTERY OF SELF FOR WEALTH, POWER, SUCCESS…

Haddock was the son of a Methodist preacher. Following in his father's footsteps, he started going into ministry himself but left in order to practice law. Haddock taught many of the ideas later known as the Law of Attraction found in *The Secret*.

A key word to Haddock is *magnetism*. He urged people to become more familiar with "the unused portions of our nature," thus leading to health, wealth, power, and success by "acquiring magnetism."

"Acquiring magnetism is a constructive effort. It is a building process. You are rearing a structure," which supposedly connects us to the magnetism of the universe, or Universal Forces and their Eternal Thoughts. It will garner benefits of which most people are unaware. "Physical Magnetism is indifferent to TRUE Moral Health; Psychic Magnetism assists Moral Health; Psychic Magnetism assists Physical Magnetism."

He explains mind, body, and psychic connections through the picture of a pyramid. He labels the four sides of the pyramid: 1) magnetic concentration; 2) the relation of the divisions of self to the whole of self; 3) a better understanding of your personality; 4) the supreme importance of psychic righteousness. Haddock maintains that when your pyramid aligns itself properly, "You are looking down from the 'I AM.'" In both the virtuosic inventions of new meanings for magnetism and the use of "I AM," Haddock presages the Law of Attraction and "secret" ideas of Rhonda Byrne. He also blasphemes God by appropriating the term "I AM" used by Father and Son in Scripture.

(Haddock, Frank C. *Haddock's Mastery of Self for Wealth, Power, Success: Courage and Power—a Scientific Course of Proven Methods in Thirty Books and Sixty Lessons*. Meriden CT: Pelton Publishing, 1923.)

To borrow Rhonda Byrne's term, it's all complete balderdash.

Chapter 8

QUANTUM LEAPS OF FAITH

Science: Seek Reality

In a couple of places in *The Secret* book, author Rhonda Byrne writes about "hundreds" of letters (pp. 99, 104) she has received from people who have seen the DVD or read the book. None of these are quoted or summarized, but we imagine that at least one might read something like this:

Dear Rhonda:

Please excuse the fact that I am contacting you through traditional means. I know you must be receiving a lot of messages these days, so I thought that one sent by mail would stand out, and you would see it.

I wanted you to know that I have read *The Secret* frequently, and have absorbed all of its thoughts. I am positively thinking and emitting a lot of waves all day long. I strictly observe the Law of Attraction at all times.

But the magnetism is what I like the best. I think about magnetism all the time, and I am trying to make "likes" attract like the book says. But magnetism is for me, and I don't care if the whole Universe knows it.

I have become so magnetic, in fact, that every morning when I wake up, I find that I'm lying in bed pointing north.

Scientific Inquiry

There is science in *The Secret*—not all of it good science, not all of it even real science. Some terms are dropped—just as the book engages in name-dropping—and we can suspect that the sci-babble matches the psychobabble, as spurious disciplines are called. Magda Healey, on the book site BookBag.uk, recently wrote: "Calling [*The Secret*] pseudo-scientific is an insult to pseudo-science. Most 'scientific sounding' sentences there are not only not true; they don't even make sense."[1]

For instance, as we mentioned earlier, "Dr. Joe" Vitale writes, " 'I'm not getting older, I'm getting younger.' We can create it the way we want it, by using the law of attraction" (p. 167). Many readers and bloggers, gazing on the photo of Dr. Joe in the book, have observed that the photo looks rather like a "before" photo in lifestyle commercials and wonder why the Law of Attraction is not put to uses more in line with the recommendations Dr. Joe and his colleagues make to readers.

Dr. Joe calls it "creat[ing] it the way we want it"; others would call it *denial*. And by the way, in those numerous blog replies he has stated he's perfectly happy to be bald. Indeed it is a noble state; "Hair today, gone tomorrow" is a condition visiting many people. Yet even in his responses, Dr. Joe reveals a lack of faith in his own Law of Attraction. He states that, if he wanted to, he could attract wigs, toupees, even "plugs" to himself, but he decides not to. Interesting how "attracting new, real, growing hair" doesn't even make it to his list of skullduggery.[2]

We're going to look at some of the scientific claims in *The Secret*. By now, after all our other focus points in this book, science, scientific claims, and Rhonda-approved scientists might have us ready to step through yet another rotting floorboard on *The Secret*'s dance floor.

Failing Logic

Many of her scientific postulates beg for some responsive reasoning: "When a patient truly believes the tablet is a cure, he receives what he believes and is cured" (p. 139). If that's the case, can we dispense with pharmacists, insurance, and Medicare? Can we remove those misleading warning labels on poison substances? If so, maybe they should be affixed instead to copies of *The Secret*.

ON THE ORIGIN, SCIENCE, AND PHILOSOPHICAL IMPLICATIONS OF QUANTUM MECHANICS: DOES A LEAD TO B?

The branch of physics known as Quantum Mechanics represents a formal, mathematical recognition that the description of the properties of matter cannot be successfully extrapolated from the macroscopic world to the atomic world. The classical physics of Isaac Newton was so successful in describing the visible world that physicists reasonably tried to extend these laws to the world of atoms and subatomic particles. Up to a point, these efforts were quite useful. Examples of the successful application of classical physics to atomic theory include the kinetic theory of heat and the development of a theoretical understanding of the gas laws.

Efforts to extrapolate classical physics to the properties and behavior of individual molecules, atoms and subatomic particles failed. Well before the twentieth century, physicists and chemists demonstrated that the atomic description of matter helped to make sense of many important observations and natural laws. By the year 1900 the atomic description of matter was universally accepted. However, the classical view of energy as continuous remained the dominant view, in spite of the fact that evidence to the contrary (from the study of light produced by excited atoms) had been accumulating for several decades. It was the German physicist Max Planck who first proposed that energy, like matter, also comes in tiny packets called quanta. In other words, both matter and energy are discontinuous or quantized; that is, they can be extremely small but discrete increments.

In 1897, the English physicist J. J. Thomson discovered that the simplest element, hydrogen, is actually composed of a proton and an electron, and that these subatomic particles have equal but opposite charges but very different mass values. In 1911, Ernest Rutherford announced a new theory of the atom—the nuclear model—based on a series of experiments conducted several years earlier. This in turn led the Danish physicist Niels Bohr to apply classical physics to a simple model of the hydrogen atom...while the Bohr model worked amazingly well for hydrogen, attempts to extend the model to more complicated atoms were an utter failure. Clearly a new approach was needed.

Twentieth-century physics overturned the sharp distinction between matter and energy, between particles and waves, and between space and time. Virtually all attempts to extend the laws of classical physics to describe the behavior of atoms and subatomic particles failed.... Albert Einstein received the Nobel Prize in Physics, not for his work on Relativity but for offering an explanation of the photoelectric effect, whereby light, which is usually described as a wave, can also behave as if it has momentum by ejecting electrons from the surface of certain materials.

Strangely, the type of property observed for subatomic particles depends on the type of experiment done. So by choosing the experiment, a physicist observes either the particle nature, or the wave nature, of either light or subatomic particles. This fact has led to a range of philosophical speculations about the extent to which the observer determines the outcome of experiments by the process of observation. Wild speculations by some have carried this idea way beyond the realm of physics to suggest connections between mind and matter that are not really supported by physics itself.

The Quantum Mechanics approach describes a universe that exhibits a measure of unpredictability at its most fundamental level. According to the Uncertainty Principle developed by Werner Heisenberg, it is impossible, even in principle, to determine simultaneously both the precise position and the precise momentum of any subatomic particle. The more precisely we determine one property, the more we change the other property in the process, and the less precisely we are able to measure that property.

Although the classical physics of Newton still provides a very satisfactory way of looking at the macroscopic world, quantum physics provides a superior and more accurate description of the behavior of matter and energy on the atomic level. But the theories of quantum physics do not imply that the universe itself generates mind or that it responds directly to human thoughts, as some New Age proponents suggest. The truth is that Quantum Mechanics does not support such a notion.

R. L. Daake, PhD, professor of chemistry, Oklahoma Wesleyan
University.   ∞∞∞

Another of *The Secret*'s scientific principles appears on page
130: "Declare and intend. 'I think only perfect thoughts. I see
only perfection. I am perfection.'" To a degree, this is true: it is
perfect nonsense. Even people who deny the existence of God
or an absolute truth know from memories of, say, five or ten
minutes earlier in the day that they are not perfection. *Striving*
for perfection is a great motivator, but even that has no part in
The Secret's science class.

"The Universe does everything with zero effort. The grass
doesn't strain to grow. It's effortless" (p. 63). This science is not
supported by an informal poll we conducted, though ironically
the majority of people we asked to read *The Secret* confessed to
expending great strain and effort! Seriously, though, the statement ends with, "It's just this great design." Well, this is *not* great
science, logic, or consistency. *The Secret* nowhere acknowledges a
creator God...yet if there is a "great design," there must be a
"great designer."

Michael Bernard Beckwith further "clarifies" on page 22,
"It has been scientifically proven that an affirmative thought
is hundreds of times more powerful than a negative thought."
Translated, this means, *The scientific method allows for verifiable,
statistical, measurable results. Because we offer no proof, cite no studies, weigh no accumulation of "thoughts," and don't define "positive,"
"negative," or even "thoughts," we admit to peddling junk science.*

Yet Byrne insists, "Henry Ford knew much more than the
people who ridiculed him. He knew the Secret and he knew the

law of the Universe" (p. 169). Unfortunately, he also knew the *Protocols of the Elders of Zion*, a discredited anti-Semitic tract, which was among many of his smears against Jews in his own publications for many years.[3] This "science" must be challenged: is the Secret all truth, or is a percentage of it corrupted error? What happened to the "perfection" Ford possessed as legatee of the Secret?

OXFORD UNIVERSITY PRESS SCIENTIST ON *THE SECRET*'S QUANTUM PHYSICS

There is no scientific basis of any sort to suggest that the mind or brain can influence the external world by quantum physics or any other kind of interaction. Basic physics has established that all interactions are either gravitational, electromagnetic, or one of two types of nuclear interaction. All four interactions are well understood and measurable. The brain does not interact with the external world by any of these interactions—plain and simple. If it did, we could measure the result.

Because quantum physics is mysterious, it has been invoked to explain other things that are also mysterious. For decades, people with no understanding of quantum physics have been making claims like those in *The Secret*. Such claims are so laughably silly that scientists rarely bother to comment.

But the silly claims are often widely believed because they describe a world that we might wish to exist. If only we could shape reality around us with our minds, and not at the mercy of an unknown external world. Who does not want to play God and control the world? But quantum physics provides no such tools for human beings to control the world.

"The mystery of quantum physics, which bothered Einstein, was its deeply random character. Some events have no cause and are completely unpredictable. The essence of quantum physics is this essential unpredictability. To suggest that quantum physics can be used to "control" something is to completely miss the point. How can something that is unpredictable and random be used to control the world around us? If our brains could exert quantum effects on the world, the result would be chaos, not harmony.

Can the author of *The Secret* write down the Shroedinger equation —the basis for quantum physics? College freshmen can. That's why they know that quantum physics can't be used by humans to shape the world around them.

Karl Giberson, PhD, professor of physics, Eastern Nazarene College, Quincy, Massachusetts

Those who read *The Secret* or saw the DVD, however, know these examples of scientific legitimacy are neither taken out of context or are isolated examples. Besides, whether it's junk science or get-rich-quick promises, "as a book and marketing exercise, *The Secret* is self-reflexive," observed Oliver James in TimesOnline (London). "Write a book quoting other people who have written books about how, if you write a book or advise others about becoming rich, you will do so. It's like pyramid selling, hocus-pocus."[4]

Expert Opinion

Bob Proctor is a primary advocate of *The Secret* and all of its science, which is claimed to be founded upon quantum physics. But when Cynthia McFadden of ABC News' *Nightline* told him that Dr. Brian Greene, professor of physics and mathematics at Columbia University, questioned the application of quantum physics in *The Secret*, Proctor's only defense was that he didn't know anything about Dr. Greene.[5] But Brian Greene (PhD, Oxford) is a noted physicist who has written several books including *The Elegant Universe* and *The Fabric of the Cosmos*, discussing subjects like string theory, nonlocal particle entanglement, special relativity, spacetime and cosmology, origins and unification, and reality and the imagination. That Bob Proctor confessed to not having heard of Dr. Greene alone speaks volumes.

Dr. Greene attacked *The Secret*'s claims on several levels— misapplication of the roles of gravity and electromagnetism in physics, even something that could be called a law of attraction, but nothing like the representations in New Age movements like *The Secret*. Also, addressing *The Secret*'s invocation of Newton and Einstein, he found them completely misunderstood and misrepresented: "They worked *hard*!" and didn't parlay a secret into wealth and fame. Dr. Greene explains his point of view on his field of expertise, which parallels *The Secret*'s self-defined scientific basis:

My area of research is superstring theory, a theory that purports to give us a quantum theory of gravity as well as a unified theory of all forces and all matter. As such, superstring theory has the potential to realize Einstein's long-sought dream of a single, all-encompassing theory of the universe. One of the strangest features of superstring theory is that it requires the universe to have more than three spatial dimensions. Much of my research has focused on the physical implications and mathematical properties of these extra dimensions—studies that collectively go under the heading "quantum geometry."[6]

Who knows, though? When all is said and done, maybe Proctor is smarter than Dr. Brian Greene of Oxford and Columbia University. Because, brilliant as he is, there are at least a handful of people around the world who can fully understand Dr. Greene's impressive research. In Proctor's case, on the other hand, it might fairly be said that *nobody* can understand what he's talking about.

The Science of Karma

Ingrid Hansen Smythe, in *eSkeptic*, confronted *The Secret* and the Law of Attraction and reminds us of an Eastern term much used in the sixties but still referred to and widely believed today: "The Law of Karma":

> Besides scientific gibberish, *The Secret* DVD props up faltering dogma by relying on charismatic representatives and a lot of smooth talk, which is so expert and cleverly edited it is easy to miss the false premises, tautologies, red herrings, straw men, *non sequiturs*, and other varieties of fuzzy thinking. However, even if The Law of Attraction was logically consistent and scientifically sound, the moral implications of a Law such as this are alarming. Interestingly, some of the difficulties with The Law of Attraction are similar to those encountered by believers in the Law of Karma, and comparing and contrasting the two yields some curious insights.
>
> It is the business of both laws to explain why good

and evil befall us, and both laws come to the conclusion that the fault is exclusively ours. In neither system can there be accident or coincidence—we are all at all times getting exactly what we deserve, and what we have attracted. The Law of Attraction seems particularly suited to the modern temperament though, given that with karma, you might have to wait a thousand lifetimes to get the good things you deserve, whereas with The Law of Attraction *everything* is possible in *this* lifetime. No waiting! Better service! The Law of Attraction might be said to be the lazy person's karma, since karma is based on doing, whereas the Law of Attraction is based on *feeling*. This is also handy for the modern American, who is quite busy enough as it is. In addition, karma is concerned exclusively with morality (specifically good and evil deeds), but The Law of Attraction is concerned only with positive-feeling vibrations, which needn't necessarily be connected to pesky morality at all.[7]

There are greater problems than silliness and the ultimate embarrassment to a culture persuaded by bogus science. Spiritual harm and actual physical harm can come to misguided members of the cults and fads. Professor John Norcross of the University of Scranton, who has extensively studied the self-help movement, voices concern for the consequences after *The Secret* and the Law of Attraction don't work. "It's pseudoscientific, psycho-spiritual babble. We find about 10 percent of self-help books are rated by mental-health professionals as damaging. [*The Secret*] is probably one of them. The problem is the propensity for self-blame when it doesn't work."[8] According to Byrne, if it doesn't work for you, the problem is you.

REPEAL THE LAW OF ATTRACTION?

Dr. Fred Alan Wolf, one of the team members of The Secret, *wrote the following in his own Weblog,* The Yoga of Time Travel *and Dr. Quantum's World. In it he appears to achieve the anatomically challenging feat of simultaneously embracing the Law of Attraction and keeping it at arm's length. Is it woo-woo or why-why?*

For those of you who wish to market a new self-help book on "the new Secret" of the "law of attraction" I hope you read these thoughts before you go ahead. There are many books out there, even more than I can imagine, written by people who have seen "the secret" or "the bleep" and think they have a unique insight to teach others techniques for personal growth.

I give a lot of seminars, and I personally don't teach people techniques for realizing their potentials and other such ideas as I have found that they simply don't work and are in their own way spiritual "diet books" which may work for a while but in the end fail. Spiritual techniques advocated by people who have never made a serious study of spiritual teaching or base their books on quantum physics principles without studying the subject at length and who really don't know enough to teach others techniques based upon these deeper "secrets" make me really wonder why such people write such books other than the obvious one to make some money. Does your book do other than that? Or are you just another person trying their own hand at writing another imitation "think and grow rich diet book"?

It appears to me that any author who does not understand the quantum field and is only quoting what has been written by others who do understand it and have written for others from the point of view of knowledge, will create a lot of noise and little light. Should your book appear to be written from such a point of view, I would rethink it. Come from your own experience. For example are you a financially successful business person? A book which explains how you made it would be good, but a book advocating spiritual quantum physics techniques based on the quantum field by someone who has no such background in quantum field theory rings a little false to me.

A quantum field consciousness-spirituality and growth book may sound wonderful but it is possibly misleading if you think that this field can give you anything you desire. First of all the quantum field is not really an energy field and secondly consciousness cannot exert a force. Nor is consciousness energy. Consciousness and energy are not the same things at all. Thirdly if everyone could just tune into this hypothetical field and just by doing so create anything they wanted to create, the world would be in a [worse] mess than it is right now.

For example suppose my neighbor wanted to tune in and create a fence between our two houses higher than my window or have a million dollars appear in his bank account without taking appropriate actions to do so. Innocent enough? But if his wish did create such a fence and the next instant a fence were to appear between our houses or workmen came out and erected one I would lose my view of the mountains. Then I would have to knock down his fence or make a fence low enough to see the mountains and my neighbor would be [annoyed] at me and on and on our little wish-duel would go. If he just wished for a million bucks to magically appear in his account without appropriate actions, maybe it would appear, but if it did in my account, I would suspect the bank had made a serious error and that someone else was out a million bucks. If I didn't care and only wanted my selfish desires satisfied, the world again would be worse off. Do you get my point here?

The real quantum field has such checks and balances and in fact when it creates from nothing a particle of matter it also creates a particle of antimatter and they cancel each other out in a very short instance. Hence just wishing for things from this field does not make it so.

Our universe works and things are always balancing each other to make it work—such are the laws of nature.

Hence in a world where "wishes were horses" would simply not work. Your creation could very well [buy] another's annihilation. Let me put this another way. Reading a self-help book written by someone who really doesn't understand the nature of reality is like listening to someone play a violin who watched a great master play a violin in a silent movie and decided to play for real by just imitating what she or he saw. Undoubtedly it would sound like something near to what the master was playing, but it would give many false notes. Is your book ringing out false notes? Such books appear to me to be like that. Oh by the way, I get a lot of requests to blurb such books, nearly one a day so the field may be getting glutted.

(Dr. Fred Alan Wolf's blog is http://fredalanwolf.blogspot.com. This posting appeared on Feb 27, 2007.)   ∞∞∞

QUANTUM LEAPS IN LOGIC

Once New Age science—from abstract physics to personal well-being to all forms of self-help advice—started to spread, there were no vaccines to stop it. The runaway success of *The Secret* confirms that. A recent book, *Crazy Therapies*, charted some of these New Age nostrums. Robert Todd Carroll, in a review, wrote:

It is difficult to select the most egregious New Age therapy, but Neural Organization Technique (NOT) developed by chiropractor Carl Ferreri, is hard to top. Ferreri decided, without the slightest hint of scientific evidence, that all mental and physical problems are due to misaligned skulls. Ferreri believes that as you breathe, the bones in your skull move, causing misalignments that can be corrected by manipulation. This theory was put into practice without the slightest proof that cranial bones move or that there is any sense to the notion of "standard alignment" of the cranial bones. Ferreri was not stopped by logic, however, but by lawsuits and criminal charges.[9]

Quantum physics is most often the fallback foundation for science claims in *The Secret*. John Hagelin, who is director of the Institute of Science, Technology and Public Policy at the Maharishi University of Management, an institution that features consciousness-based education, transcendental meditation technique, and organic vegetarian meals on its Web site, says in *The Secret*, "Quantum mechanics confirms it; Quantum cosmology confirms it: that the universe essentially emerges from thought and all of this matter around us is just precipitated thought. Ultimately we are the source of the universe," (p. 160). It's worth noting that this particular authority was a candidate for president of the United States (the Natural Law Party candidate), though he evidently forgot to wish for victory.

"You'd be hard-pressed to find a physicist or cosmologist who would agree that quantum mechanics or quantum cosmology would confirm that the universe emerges from thought," said Bruce Schumm of the University of California–Santa Cruz. "That's something science has not addressed…and scientists wouldn't consider provable at this point."[10]

Thought into Action

Ultimately, the belief that an observer's thoughts can influence the actions or movement or energy of the smallest particles of matter—and, in a grand whirlpool of "significance," vice versa—proves nothing except that the proponents substitute speculation for fact (a practice of primitives and infants). And that the proponents are trying very hard to find any way to deny the existence of an all-knowing, omnipresent creator God. Word games (immediately phrases like "You are God" (p. 164) leap to the lips of Law-of-Attractionists) avail nothing. The Bible teaches that God created mankind separate from Him, in His likeness, but as part of Creation, not indistinguishable from Him. We can seek and know God; we cannot be Him.

The infantlike nature of wish fulfillment and dream projection constitutes a lot of *The Secret*'s appeal. It's comfort food—chicken soup, if you will—for the secular soul. "Why not?" becomes "It's true!" Especially if Oprah tells millions of followers that she's known it all along, even though she didn't actually know it.

Oprah aside, why has *The Secret* seduced so many people? We can have sympathy for the emotionally needy, and we can discern the clever mass-marketing techniques of Rhonda Byrne's growing colossus. But let us not pass by too many mirrors without examining ourselves too. "Knocking on wood" or "wishing for luck" is only lower-hanging fruit of the same tree. If *The Secret* incites your suspicions—if what we are revealing is persuasive—be careful to take your new convictions to their logical conclusions.

Final Equation

Finally, on the subject of science, we all know that most of the great ideas of science and philosophy can best be explained by a sentence, summarized by a phrase, or represented by a formula. We all know $E = mc^2$, for instance—or we have all heard that Einstein promulgated the theory of relativity behind it. Now, just say *"The Secret"* and if you have read at least this book you hold in your hands, you know what *it* stands for.

In that regard, maybe "Dr. Joe" Vitale best encapsulates not just the "science" but the entire philosophy behind *The Secret*, specifically the vaunted Law of Attraction. Speaking to Larry King, America's ears of record, he said: "I'll tell you this. I'm 'attracting' a sequel. So we're going to have a sequel one way or another."[11] In other words, even as experts and former colleagues are questioning the first *Secret*, some members of the team are looking to the next version to sell.

A Case Study in the Law of Attraction: The *Titanic*

Many people know the story of the sinking of the *Titanic* ocean liner, the horrible accident of almost a century ago. In April 1912, on a maiden voyage from England to the United States, the brand-new ship, largest in the world and reputedly "invincible," glanced against an iceberg in the dark night and sank within hours.

Scores of celebrities and wealthy notables were on board—millionaires John Jacob Astor IV and Benjamin Guggenheim, Isadore Straus of Macy's department stores, socialite "the unsinkable" Molly Brown—as well as more than a thousand middle-class and "steerage" passengers, mostly immigrants. Only a few hundred were saved, partly because the headstrong Cunard White Star Line failed to outfit enough lifeboats, thinking there was no need for them.

We know the *Titanic* story partly because the James Cameron movie of recent vintage was widely seen. It was a class-warfare flick (was a single upper-class passenger depicted favorably?), but pop-culture history is pop-culture first and history second. Yet the suspicions that the White Star Line executive on board, J. Bruce Ismay, gave "full steam ahead" orders to Captain Smith did exist at the time. Trying to make headlines and break speed records, he might have been motivated by cupidity.

One passenger who was not depicted in the movie offers maybe the most interesting story. Major Archie Butt had been military aide to President Theodore Roosevelt, and then to President William Howard Taft. More than that, he was a remarkable figure in American history—friend, diplomat, riding companion, confidante to both men. Because of the strain on him when Roosevelt and Taft grew apart, resulting in a Republican Party split (Major Butt was sympathetic to TR but loyal to President Taft), the president practically insisted Butt take a European vacation and rest. The *Titanic*'s maiden voyage was his trip home.

All survivors' accounts tell of Butt's leadership, "cool as an iceberg," helping women, children, and the infirm. He firmly calmed hysterical men. A man who survived the sinking later said of Butt: "In the presence of death...there was never any chance of Butt getting into any of those lifeboats. He knew his time was at hand, and he was ready to meet it as a man should, and I and all of the others who cherish his memory are glad that he faced the situation that way, which was the only possible way a man of his caliber could face it." He was lost, of course, at sea.

People of Major Butt's caliber, the Astors' and Guggenheims' and Straus's enterprise, Molly Brown's irrepressible joy of life, the everyday passengers enjoying their time together, and the hundreds of immigrants dreaming of a new life in America for themselves and their descendents—think about them. If you believe the cynical worldview advanced by *The Secret*, you would have to believe the *Titanic* was not only doomed, but that the Law of Attraction pulled the ship toward that iceberg, that passengers somehow desired disaster.

But no one believed it could sink: neither crew nor passengers panicked for a while after the impact. No "negative frequencies" there.

In this story it becomes clear *The Secret*'s Law of Attraction distorts history, insults your intelligence, and impugns pure motives of noble people. It accounts not at all for God, evil, or even coincidence. Its answers are absurd and (in the case of advice about diseases) dangerous. Did the U.S. sailors and Marines at Pearl Harbor "attract" the Japanese attack in 1941? *The Secret* would say so. Did the three thousand plus who perished in the 9-11 attacks "attract" the terrorists? *The Secret* would say so.

By the way, on the previous page we reported the rumor that the White Star Line's executive on that maiden voyage, eager to establish a record, issued "full speed ahead" orders out of cupidity. J. Bruce Ismay did *not* go down with his ship, although many women and children did. If his motives were cupidity, and if that's a word you don't know . . . it means "excessive greed, avarice, aggressive lusting after material things."

It might be the case that the representative of the ship's owners, not the passengers, exhibited more of the "qualities" of the Law of Attraction. . . .[12]

Chapter 9

EPICENTER OF
THE UNIVERSE

You: Surrender Grandiose Delusions

I s it true the earth, the oceans, the singing birds, and the stars
cannot exist without you?" Are you the "master of the Universe"? Are you the "perfection of Life"? All of these are claims
made in the final paragraph of *The Secret* (p. 183). Are those
claims true?

There is some good news for all persons who read Rhonda
Byrne's *The Secret*: ironically, it's not about you. In the "Byrne Universe," You (with capital Y, no less) are the epicenter. That is a pathway to disappointment and, eventually, certain self-destruction.

HUMAN-CENTEREDNESS

The good news is there is a "center" to the universe. The bad
news is it is not you. The great news is the center of the universe
is occupied by someone bigger than you.

But perhaps even that bad news is not so bad. After all, do
you actually want to see yourself as the epicenter of all that

is? You should hope not. Why? Because *The Secret*, if followed, would become quite disappointing. *The Secret* correctly states there is some kind of power beyond you and me. It is referred to in a noticeably depersonalized phrase: "the Universe" (again, capitalized). Ironically, *The Secret*, while avoiding the distinctly personal term *God*, makes a feeble attempt to personalize that power (for reasons that will become clear later).

Personifying the Impersonal

The Secret simply does not acknowledge that there is, in fact, a *personal* God—a divine One with personality. It's not for lack of trying, however. *The Secret*, for example, personifies this abstract force called "the Universe." Ms. Byrne claims, "The Universe has been answering you all your life" (p. 172). Answering? Inanimate objects don't "answer." That requires personhood. Nevertheless, she attests personally, "I ask the Universe" (p. 171). Whatever the "Universe" is, Rhonda wants to talk with him, her, or it.

Not only is the Universe capable of conversation, it's capable of loving. In fact, *The Secret* claims, "You are blocking all the love and the good that the Universe has for you" (p. 120). Apparently you should even be feeling some shame for "dissing" this entity. Here is this loving entity called the Universe that is trying to love you and you won't let it. More so, Lisa Nichols, one of *The Secret*'s cohorts, emphasizes all the "great things that the Universe has for you" (p. 127).

At one point Byrne attempts to expand the understanding of that which is beyond humankind, "whether you call that the Universe, a Supreme Mind, God, Infinite Intelligence, or whatever else" (p. 163). Finally, after all these pages we have an acknowledgment that possibly—just maybe—the name "God" could even be relevant. But is this the God of the Bible—a personal, warm, caring God? Or is it simply a "Universal Mind" (p. 158), some aloof, nonpersonal entity?

One of Byrne's favorite thinkers is Prentice Mulford, who died in 1891. He similarly acknowledged the existence of "the Infinite" (p. 119), but once again we are left to believe this is no personal God, but rather some impersonal force known as "the One Energy Field, or the One Supreme Mind, or the One Consciousness, or the One Creative Source" (p. 162).

I Dream of Genie

Even so, according to *The Secret*, the Universe is your "Genie" (p. 46). "Traditions have called it so many things," Byrne writes, "your Holy Guardian Angel, your Higher Self. We can put any label on it, and then choose the one that looks best for you, but every tradition has told us there's something bigger than us and the Genie always says one thing: 'your wish is my command!'" (p. 46).

Consider this on-the-surface rather attractive proposition—your own personal genie god.

1. *Your Wish?* Is that the way life works? Do you want life to be that way? Do you want to live in a world where every person believes (and experiences) a personal "genie" who grants his or her *every* wish? What does it tell you about those around you if they are constantly searching for a "genie" to grant their every wish? Perhaps at least that their central driving ethos is hedonism and self-centeredness.

2. *A Genie?* Let's keep our perspective here: this is a metaphor, and such a literal genie does not exist (literary, yes). There are

obviously dangerous ramifications for trying to define your reality by fantasy intended to be a metaphor.

3. *Every Tradition?* Most importantly, it just isn't correct that every tradition believes such a thing. It is true that almost every tradition believes there is something or someone bigger than we are. However, "every tradition" does not believe there is a genie who tells us, "Your wish is my command."

One particular tradition (a rather substantial part of the earth's population, and a rather important one, Christianity) does acknowledge there is something bigger than us—namely, God. However, this is the same One who tells us to obey. This is the same One who tells us to, in the person of Jesus, "take up your cross and deny yourself."

Most religious traditions stand against the notion that God is merely a genie who says, "Your wish is my command." The three monotheistic traditions—Judaism, Christianity, and Islam—all call followers to obey God's commands, not submit individual wishes.

THE GOD WHO IS "IT"?

The way this philosophy of an impersonal god can work for Ms. Byrne and her ilk is to not believe there is a personal god. She speaks about any power beyond ourselves as an "it." Joe Vitale notes, "The Universe will rearrange itself" (p. 51). Notice the phrasing. The Universe is portrayed with the capacity of a living being. Yet it is always referred to as a depersonalized "it." Vitale later instructs the reader to "turn it over to the Universe"

(p. 85), again unable to avoid personifying what is supposed to be inanimate.

Is it not at least a more attractive way to seek the Bible's God—a warm, caring heavenly being?

Greater Than the World

Michael Bernard Beckwith uses distinctly biblical phrasing when he states, "the power within you [is] greater than the world" (p. 183). This is an obvious borrowing (and distorting) of 1 John 4:4, which states, "Greater is he that is in you, than he that is in the world" (KJV). Notice how endearingly Beckwith speaks of this "power," but once again, he cannot seem to acknowledge that God might be *personal*.

According to Beckwith, "this something" is "within you" the moment you begin to "think properly" (p. 183). It is important to note the distortion of the biblical meaning. In fact, the use of the Scripture is in direct opposition to the intention of the biblical passage. The verse before it (v. 3) speaks about Jesus Christ. He is the One who is "in you." It also speaks of the "spirit of anti-christ," which is "in the world." The passage is literally saying Christ is stronger than anti-Christ. That is the message. Beckwith has distorted the passage by deleting Jesus and putting "think[ing] properly" in His place. (Even more ironic, the passage actually states that anyone who does not recognize that Jesus came from God is the anti-Christ.)

This book is not primarily about the Bible. Yet, due to the fact that Rhonda Byrne used—or rather abused—the biblical texts, we are obliged to respond with explanations about the actual intention of Scripture. One cannot simply dismiss Byrne's misuse of texts.

So Caring

Beckwith goes on to explain that this universal force "will begin to emerge. It will take over your life. It will feed you. It will clothe you. It will guide you, protect, direct you, sustain your very existence" (p. 183). Look at the great accomplishments of this "power": feed you, clothe you, guide you, protect you, direct you, and sustain you.

How eerily close this is to the personalized God of the Judeo-Christian (biblical) tradition.

- Feed—"I have ordered the ravens to feed you" (1 Kings 17:4).
- Clothe—"If that is how God clothes the grass of the field, which is here today and tomorrow is thrown into the fire, will he not much more clothe you?" (Matt. 6:30).
- Guide—"I will guide you in the way of wisdom" (Prov. 4:11).
- Protect—"The Lord is faithful, and he will...protect you" (2 Thess. 3:3).
- Direct—"In everything you do, put God first, and he will direct you" (Prov. 3:6 TLB).
- Sustain—"I have made you and...I will sustain you" (Isa. 46:4).

Now which is most likely to care for you? An impersonal "machine" or force, or a personal, warm, caring, loving God—the God who defines "personhood"?

Of course, many readers of The Secret might not believe there is a God at all. But it seems as if it would be easier to believe in a God than to believe a mechanistic, deterministic, aloof "force" will treat you so tenderly—feeding you, clothing you, guiding you, protecting you, directing you, and sustaining you (p. 183). So, arguably it takes more faith—truly "blind" faith—to believe in Rhonda Byrne's impersonal force than in the personal God portrayed in the Bible. I just don't have that much (blind) faith.

The Grand Absence

The absence of a personalized God becomes even more inexplicable as one examines the choice of words scattered through *The Secret*.

In the statements below, take a moment to mentally fill in each blank. What obvious word fits into these blanks?

- Praise _____ (p. 61).
- Bless _____ (p. 61).
- "All things are possible when you believe" (p. 137): Believe in _____.
- "Thank you, thank you, thank you" (p. 107): Thank _____.
- "By the time I'm ready for the day, I have said, 'thank you' hundreds of times" (p. 76): Thank you, _____.
- "These men knew *The Secret*. These were men who had utter faith" (p. 82): Faith in _____.
- "Asking is the first step of the Creative Process, so make it a habit to ask" (p. 48): Ask _____.

Bottom line, we all know the answers. Praise whom—God? Bless whom—God? Believe in whom—God? Thank you to whom—God? Faith in what or whom—God? Ask whom—God? Believe in whom—God? Receive from whom—God?

Rhonda Byrne would have us believe when we get out of bed we simply begin the day by saying, "Thank" and "You" (p. 75). Are we thanking ourselves? How utterly self-absorbed. How self-exalting. How disappointing life will be for those who look in a mirror and think they have seen God. What a letdown it must be to live each day. This is not a "secret"! This is self-exaltation.

THE EVIDENCE OF CREATION

The Secret wants us to remember that "everything in this world began with one thought" (p. 143). Thoughts precede words; everybody thinks before speaking (some more, some less, but there has to be thought). This would especially be true of the Supreme Being. God could have certainly "thought" before He "spoke."

According to the biblical record, God spoke the world into existence. In fact, twelve times in Genesis 1–2, the Creation account states, "God said." He literally spoke the world into creation. We can assume He thought and then spoke. So *The Secret* would be correct in its assumption that everything came from one thought—in reality, God's thought.

But *The Secret* has no such understanding of the Creation account. When it declares the world began with one thought (by itself a defensible statement), we must still ask—who thought it? *There can be no thought without a thinker.* Who was here before everything else was who had the capacity to think? It was not you and it was not me. It was not any of us. It was One who always was and is. There is a name for that One—it is God.

Anthro versus Theo

At the core of this chapter is a fundamental issue: either we are anthropocentric or we are theocentric in our understanding of the universe. *Anthropo* means human; *centric* means centered; *theos* means God. We are one or the other; we cannot be both. The Christian faith is unabashedly theocentric—that is, God-centered. And there is good reason why anyone who calls himself or herself a Christian cannot legitimately embrace the principles of *The Secret*.

The Christian faith is also others-driven. That is why the phrase "one another" appears so often in the New Testament: we're instructed to love one another, forgive one another, care for one another, and so on.

Byrne sees life quite differently. In the final paragraph she exclaims: "The earth turns on its orbit for You. The oceans ebb and flow for You. The birds sing for You. The sun rises and it sets for You. The stars come out for You. Every beautiful thing you see, every wondrous thing you experience, is all there, for You" (p. 183). As yourself, O godlike one—is it all for you? Really?

It is true God created the earth for humanity. But not for you individually—rather for *us*, all of us. We are a *community* of human persons. So it is also not about only you, nor is it all about me. It is first about God. Second, it is about us—together. We are in this together.

Designers of Destiny

When *The Secret* states you can "create your life in advance" (p. 65), what does that really mean?

Perhaps rather it's about control. All of us want to be in

control. Being out of control is a frightening experience. Yet we don't really have control of all aspects of our lives. We are able to make only some decisions affecting our futures.

We can truly attempt to instill destiny in our children, just as we would value such in our own lives. We help them dream wonderful dreams. We help them establish discipline. We teach them morals and ethics. We teach them how to make good, healthy, wholesome decisions. We teach them how to sacrifice. We teach them how to avoid self-centeredness. We teach them how to love, honor, and respect other human beings. Some of us even teach them how to love God and honor His principles, which results in a blessed life.

On the other hand, there are limitations. We do not have full or ultimate control over everything. To attempt wise decision making that brings good results is a wonderful and positive goal. In fact, our lives are the results of the cumulative impact of thousands of small decisions we have made through our lives. However, being created equal does not mean our life experiences are equal. We are equal in our standing before God. God loves us. But we don't have identical backgrounds.

The point is, we cannot create *all* of our lives in advance. We can affect many aspects of our lives by making good decisions. However, one cannot exercise total creational control over one's life. To believe that will lead to defeat and disappointment.

Creating: Vocation versus Occupation

There is one sense in which *The Secret* is correct in asserting we are cocreators with God. Every person who is a follower of God has a vocation and an occupation, but the meanings of those two words are not the same.

- One's occupation involves a specific skill set he uses to benefit society. One's occupation can change several times through life.

- One's vocation should not change. The use of the word *vocation* in this sense means to serve God in whatever one does—including one's occupation.[1]

If every worker in America came to embrace the principle "whatever you do, do it all for the glory of God" (1 Cor. 10:31), productivity in this nation would escalate dramatically. In fact, that is one of the outgrowths of the Protestant Reformation in the 1500s. This view of labor caused people to perform their callings at a higher level. In occupation, one in effect becomes a "cocreator" with God.

God designed us with the need to have significance, and that significance includes how we perform our work. In fact, part of what it means to have been created in the image of God (Gen. 1:26) is our capacity to produce—to "create."

In our daily occupational callings, we live out our vocation. Our vocation is to understand that everything can be done to honor God. In our occupational setting, we become cocreators with God. In that sense we do have creational powers given to us by God Himself. *The Secret*, however, appears to use the word *create* in a much more grandiose way.

Manifestor of Heaven?

Ms. Byrne speaks about her friend, Marcie, who is "one of the greatest manifestors" (p. 53) she has ever seen. Byrnes claims Marcie "*feels* everything into existence" (p. 53). One is left to wonder, is there anything she cannot "feel" into existence? Otherwise, why would Marcie and at least a few others similarly gifted not be "feeling" world peace for us all? Are they not doing their part? Considering Marcie's exceptional ability, why are suffering, heartache, sickness, and injustice in this world? Marcie's "feelings" evidently are not working.

"*Feeling* into existence" is also not working for some of the people who embraced *The Secret* and have since died. What went wrong? Did they simply *think* their lives out of existence? The explanation is we live in a broken world that includes such things as heartache, suffering, pain, sickness, and death. Those things are not simply "felt" or "thought" away.

But what about this "perfect world" our thoughts are supposed to be able to create? Rhonda Byrne emphatically declared, "I believe and know that nothing is incurable.... In my mind, and in the world I create, 'incurable' does not exist. There is plenty of room for you in this world, so come join me and all who are here. It is the world where 'miracles' are every day occurrences. It is a world overflowing with total abundance, where *all* good things exist now, within you" (p. 135).

It is hard to reconcile Ms. Byrne's comments with the common experiences any one of us has experienced even recently, if we've just lost a loved one. It's not to say we Christians don't believe in miracles. (I, Jim wrote a book titled *God Still Heals*, because I believe God does heal, having seen what I understand to be a miracle.) But Christians know they have to live in two worlds at the same time: this world with its brokenness, and the kingdom of God where God inexplicably brings His finger to Earth and brings healings and miracles.

The most revealing phrase regarding this topic is found in Rhonda Byrne's admission in what *world* it is that everything could be curable. The world is "in my mind, and in the world I create" (p. 135). And what kind of a world might that be? The hard answer is, this world exists merely between her ears and not beyond.

The irony is that she closes off that same paragraph with these revealing words, "Sounds like heaven, doesn't it? It is" (p. 135). Frankly this way of thinking is bitterly sad. This world—with Byrne's mental gymnastics and denial—is the best her heaven has to offer. Worse yet, it may be the best she and her followers will ever know. To Ms. Byrne, simply denying the pains of life is "heaven."

The central book of Christianity, the Bible, talks about heaven but does not give us as much information as we might want. Suffice it to say Earth is not heaven, and heaven is not Earth. According to the Bible, there will someday be a new heaven and a new earth (Rev. 21:1). But nowhere does it suggest that if we "wish away" this Earth, it becomes heaven. Ms. Bryne's "heaven" is not one to be desired. There is a better way to interpret reality.

The Real Issue: I Am

The real issue is demonstrated in the question, who or what is God? To Byrne, *The Secret* is within you. "The more you use the power within you, the more you will draw it to you. You will reach a point where you won't need to practice anymore, because you will Be the power, you will Be the perfection, you will Be the wisdom, you will Be the intelligence, you will Be the love, you will Be the joy" (p. 182).

It is safe to assume the capitalization of the word *be* is not an accident. Why the capitalized *Be*? (The same conspicuous capitalization occurs with "You"—see page xii.)

Here is the explanation: it is all about You! You will Be all things. Simply put, you are a god. Perhaps it is better said as follows. To Byrne, You are God (p. 164).

If you wonder throughout *The Secret* why God is not mentioned in a biblical sense, you have missed the point. God is mentioned repeatedly... and it is you. Even the play on such words as "I am" is a not-so-accidental reference to a biblical name. At one point Byrne states "It would be a good idea to begin to use the two most powerful words, 'I AM' to your advantage" (p. 168). Though this might be coincidental, this repetitive listing of "I AM" and in capitals can hardly be accidental. It suggests the interplay with Exodus 3:14 in the Bible in which God tells Moses that His name is "I AM WHO I AM."[2]

The reason God chooses such a name is because God is indefinable. If you define God, you confine Him, and whatever you confine cannot, by definition, be God. God is indefinable. He is also the essence of all being—so while He cannot be defined, all that exists is defined by Him.

When Moses wonders how he should explain to the Israelites who have been talking to him, God instructs him to say, "I AM has sent me to you" (Exod. 3:14). When Byrne uses "I AM," though, she is not referring to the God of the Bible. She is referring to her definition of God—you. Remember that in *The Secret*, "all power is from within" (p. 173). You are God. You certainly don't need a God to be outside you.

You Are *Not* God

It must be tremendously disappointing for those who embrace *The Secret* to look in the mirror and entertain the prospect that they are looking at God. Be honest—it has to be a letdown. To the mirror gazers, we have good news and bad news. The bad news is you are not God. But the good news is you are not God—God is God.

In contrast to the grandiose claim that "there are no limits to what you can create for You, because your ability to think is unlimited!" (p. 150), you do have limits. Your thinking has limits. Simply creating your own reality is not "where all your power is" (p. 39). In fact, creating your own selective reality is actually your greatest weakness, not your greatest power. Succinctly stated, when *The Secret* says you have "all the power," *The Secret* lies.

Contrast this with some of the ancient biblical manuscripts, such as those recorded in Matthew 6:13, which says, "for thine [O God] is the kingdom, and the power" (KJV). In short, we don't have all the power. God does.

Now if you are one who believes you have all the power, then please . . . prove it.

THE HEART OF THE MATTER: "YOU ARE GOD"

All those who read *The Secret* have the option to choose Byrne's functioning theology. But make no mistake about it, one cannot claim to be a Christian and, at the same time, endorse *The Secret*.

The core issue is found in one claim in *The Secret*: "You are God manifested in human form, made to perfection" (p. 164).

Christians do believe that there was one who was "manifested in human form, made to perfection." However, that one was not you. It was Jesus. He came as God.

Admittedly, Christianity does teach that you are made in the *image* of God. But you are not God.

So "choose for yourselves this day whom you will serve" (Josh. 24:15). It will be the god of *The Secret*—you—or it will be the God of the Bible. Weigh it carefully. Your decision has far-reaching consequences.

"But as for me and my household, we will serve the LORD" (Josh. 24:15).

∞

DENOMINATIONS AND CHURCHES

Finally, is *The Secret*'s doctrine truly from "all traditions," as Rhonda Byrne claims (p. 46)? Not really. All "traditions" would certainly include Christianity, and as we've seen, it is fundamentally opposed to some basic Christian tenets, such as theism and its "one true God" worldview.

Could it at least be true that "churches of all denominations...are sharing *The Secret* "with their congregations" (p. xi)? *All* denominations? There are thousands of denominations.[3] Are *all* of them using *The Secret*, as Byrne claims?

There are two types of churches that might find *The Secret* compatible or useful: (1) religious science / Unity / universalist churches and (2) liberal churches (that are intentionally, not concerned with biblical teaching). These two groups represent a fraction of churches that might call themselves Christian. Byrne's claim is one more demonstration of her severe overstatements. Of America's approximately four hundred thousand churches, *The Secret* would be used in a tiny fraction of them.

Pagan

Whatever *The Secret* may be, it is not Christian. Some of its readers might not be concerned about that. They see themselves as not being Christians anyway, so why should they care? One answer is intellectual honesty. Rhonda Byrne's teaching is a mixture of a few parts Hinduism and large doses of paganism.

What is paganism? At its core it is monism. *Mono* means one, so it's essentially rooted in the belief that "all is one, and one is all." Whereas theism (upon which Christianity is based) insists that God is separate from and is the originator of Creation, monism insists God simply is (and has always been) creation.[4] The two views are fundamentally opposite, so every person has to choose one or the other. You cannot have both. (For more discussion on monism, see chapter 13.)

- Theism distinguishes between a Creator and a creation, between God and a created order.
- Monism views the creation as being God itself. Historically, it is paganism.

So, true to monistic sensibilities, if everything is truly "from within" (p. 135) and nothing is "from without," then there is no God outside yourself. Rhonda Byrne is very consistent on this point: when she claims "you are God" (p. 164). In the earliest parts of the book she thanks those who helped her for their "wisdom, love, and divinity" (p. xiii). She thanks them for being "divine."

Eternally You

Ms. Byrne is partially correct when she claims you are eternal. Actually she believes you are simply a vibration. But you're more than that. You are an eternal spirit. You are an eternal person.

In reality one cannot become less than eternal. In fact, you technically cannot commit suicide, spiritually at least. That is, you cannot end your true "self." You can end your physical life. But you cannot end your selfhood. You are eternal.

To Byrne, however, you are something other than eternal. In Rhonda Byrne's cosmology (understanding of everything that is), "we are ONE" (that is, in monism or paganism). There is no creator separate from the creation. That is why she says repeatedly, "Everything first comes from thinking and feeling on the inside." Everything, to her way of thinking, is within you.

If there is no God except you, then who is going to be in charge of your life? The obvious answer is you. That's why the claim is made repeatedly, "You are the master of your life" (p. 146). Being the "master of [one's] own destiny" is the desire of "every mind," according to *The Secret* (p. 71).

ATTRIBUTES OF GOD—A MIRROR?

As at the beginning, so at the end. *The Secret* asserts the Law of Attraction throughout, and *The Secret Revealed* has exposed it throughout. The thesis of Rhonda Byrne's book, and the so-called Law of Attraction, is that we all stage an overthrow of God Almighty, because the enablers and destination of the Law of Attraction are ourselves. If we are in synch, we are by definition facets or avatars of the universal: deity.

Here are traditional attributes of God, and passages from pages 4 and 5 of *The Secret* that outline the cosmic keystrokes that "send" them to you:

Transcendence: "Recorded throughout the ages in all its forms, the law can be found in ancient writings through all the centuries."

Eternal: "It has always been there for anyone to discover. The law began at the beginning of time. It has always been and will always be."

Omnipresence: "It doesn't matter…where you are, the law of attraction is forming your entire life experience."

Omnipotence: "This all-powerful law is doing that through your thoughts."

Infallible: "In 1912 Charles Haanel described the law of attraction as 'the greatest and most infallible law.'"

The Lord and Giver of Life: Haanel also claimed that it is "the law upon which the entire system of creation depends."

Master of Your Fate

The claim to be one's own master is reminiscent of poetry by the late William Ernest Henley. In his poem "Invictus" there is a famous and captivating phrase: "I am the master of my fate: I am the captain of my soul." What power one has. What authority— to be "master" and "captain," to control my own fate. To think, I can truly be in control.

In one biographical treatment, Henley is said to have committed suicide. In another, Henley is said to have died after a fall "from a railway carriage [which] caused the dormant tuberculosis germ in his system to resurface."[5] Not at all to diminish the sorrow of his passing, but these causes of death seem to contradict his mastery of fate. You were not designed to be God. You were not designed to be the master of your fate. You were not made to be the captain of your soul.

Without a God outside of yourself you are left truly to try to fix this world's problems—on your own. Regardless what you face you are alone—with just you and your thoughts. That is why Byrne encourages her readers, "Heal yourself" (p. 128).

The Secret does correctly portray one component of healing. Byrne acknowledges the joy and delight of laughter and the fact that laughter is truly the best medicine (p. 129). Many years ago, a wise man observed, "A cheerful heart is good medicine" (Prov. 17:22). In that sense, there are ways in which we are instructed to follow practices that enhance healing. There are numerous things we can do to allow our bodies to experience the healing they need. Ultimately, though, we can never truly heal ourselves.[6]

But there is One who can heal us. One of his names in the Hebrew language is *Yahweh Rophe* (Exod. 15:26). This is translated "the Lord who heals."

In summary, there is a God. You are not Him. He is not you. But He loves you. The fact that you are reading a book such as *The Secret* indicates you have an inner quest or longing. Your search is valid. However, this search can be addressed *only* when you come into close acquaintance with the One who heals. It is not a secret. It is openly displayed—for anyone to see, experience, and feel.

He waits for you.

Chapter 10

LOOKING IN ALL THE WRONG PLACES

Love: Act Kindly

WORLD'S WORST QUOTATION

Okay, it may not be the world's *worst* quotation. But it would surely make it into the final round of competition. Bob Proctor stated, "I wanna kiss myself sometimes!" (p. 121).

Let us hope that "sometimes" is rare.

" Love and gratitude can part seas, move mountains, and create miracles" (p. 128), claims Rhonda Byrne in her runaway bestseller *The Secret*. And she is correct. Love *is* powerful—very powerful.

Unfortunately that is one of her few accurate statements about one of life's most important characteristics. Having begun with poetic flare about love (parting seas and moving mountains), Ms. Byrne's commentary about love sadly and quickly degenerates into science fiction. With no scientific support, she exclaims, "The feeling of love is the highest frequency you can emit" (p. 38)!

Even the most ardent supporters of *The Secret* have to know deep in their hearts when they read the term *love* in *The Secret*, something is sadly lacking. The thesis is clearly stated: "A law of attraction, the study and practice of the law of attraction is just figuring out what will help you generate the feelings of having it now.... Do whatever you have to do to generate the feelings of having it now" (p. 54).

Only our most self-centered instincts could agree with such language as "do whatever you have to do," and only the most childish in us could insist on having whatever we want now. One of the marks of maturity is growing out of having to have *what* you want *when* you want it. The move from childhood to adulthood is leaving behind the self-centered "I want it now." Rhonda Byrne's writing appeals to some who have never grown up or want to revert back to the worst characteristics of childhood: wanting what I want—now.

WHAT'S GOOD FOR YOU?

One of the ambiguities running through the text is the understanding of *good*. We are instructed to feel good. We are expected to receive good things by emitting our transmissions to the universe. But what is good? What determines if something is good? Where is the reality of good versus bad discussed or considered in *The Secret*?

How do we handle the reality that what may be good for some may be bad for others? What if two people are wanting "good"—but those desires conflict with each other? What about competing "goods" between various people? What if something appears to be good for you but is bad for me? What makes something good? And furthermore, on what basis is something bad?

If a pedophile desires to take advantage of a child, he might perceive that as being good because, after all, it makes him feel good. This good feeling helps him, according to *The Secret*, know he is having proper thoughts, because feeling good is such an important indicator that his thinking is right. Thus, he presumably would be "transmitting" at the right frequency.

As the reader will immediately discern, the desires of the pedophile to entrap the child are not good for the child. And for that matter, if the pedophile could see what his actions are doing to his own broken spirit, he would discover his desires are not good for him either.

On what basis do we establish the understanding of good? What I call good, you might call bad, and *vice versa*. A man might aggressively pursue a female, thinking it is good. She might feel threatened, harassed, and stalked. It is not good from her perspective. Could "no means no" be a bad thing if the male aggressor doesn't like that answer?

One of the grand flaws at the foundation of *The Secret* is its failure to provide proper definitions and appropriate boundaries to its claims.

Good Enough?

How is good determined? Do we determine good by what 50.1 percent of the population thinks is good? At the present time a substantial number of Americans feel it is good for alcohol to be legal. Thus it is. There are some who feel marijuana should be legal. But it is not. Is "good" determined by what the majority wants?

It wasn't so long ago in our nation's history that the majority held that slavery was a good thing. More recently in our history, the majority opinion changed on whether it was a good thing for women to be allowed to vote. Most will agree those changes were for the good, but before the weight of the majority shifted, was slavery once a good thing? Was it better in the bygone era that women couldn't vote?

History is replete with many more examples of the majority belief not necessarily being right: consider Nazi sensibilities of the early twentieth century, or more ancient cultures practicing human sacrifice, and to this day, far too many societies still support oppression of minority groups and even genocide. It's hard to escape the reality that the majority has often been prone to get it wrong.

So who determines good? You? Me? Or 50.1 percent of Americans? Or would it require a two-thirds vote—66.6 percent of Americans? Or 90 percent? What should be the standard for determining what is good?

We Do Have Standards

We are in desperate need of an objective standard: A standard not based on you, me, or even the majority of our citizens. A standard not dependent upon the whims of a culture (50.1 percent and holding for today), not dependent upon your whims or upon my whims.

This is, in part, an epistemological question. (Epistemology is the study of how we gain knowledge of something.) On this point, how do we know something to be true? How do we determine the source of truth? How do we know what is good? Some twenty-seven hundred years ago, that question was being asked. The Bible states, "They say that what is right is wrong, and what is wrong is right; that black is white and white is black;

bitter is sweet and sweet is bitter" (Isa. 5:20 TLB). In other words, humans have the capacity to distort things and call good things evil and call evil things good. (This was being observed, by the way, in an era when many cultures thought the practice of child sacrifice to local deities was a good thing.) Thus the question: how can we know good? And how do we determine good from evil?

Remember, *The Secret* admonishes that you want to make certain "only all *good* can come into your life" (p. 28). You are even instructed to "make your last thoughts before going to sleep good thoughts" (p. 16). Rhonda Byrne provides us no foundational definitions. When she writes, "The only thing you need to do is feel good now" (p. 184), what does that mean? Cocaine? Sex? Quit your job? Beat up a mean neighbor? Overeat? Have an affair? Steal a thousand dollars? What is "good"?

LOVE FEELS SO GOOD

What is true of the word *good* is equally true for the word *love.* In the worldview of *The Secret,* "love is a feeling" (p. 122). In fact, if you are not feeling loving, the power of the Law of Attraction will not work (p. 120). You are instructed to base your life on feelings, because happiness is a *feeling* state of being (p. 133). But there is more. The whole cosmos is feeling. In fact, "this is a feeling Universe" (p. 62).

Love Is Action

Readers of *The Secret* are eventually going to be sadly disillusioned. Love, ultimately, is not a feeling. It is wonderful when we feel good. It is wonderful when we have feelings of love. But love, at its core, is generally not feeling-driven, or at least feeling-based. If love is feeling-based, then what becomes of love when your feeling changes? What if a bride and groom have a change of feelings a few hours (or years) after their wedding? Do they simply trash the marriage and go looking for another—based upon their feelings at that moment?

Good feelings are the by-products, the results of authentic love. Byrne's advice to get our minds off of negative things (things we are against) and to "focus instead on love" is good advice (p. 143), so long as you understand the definition of love.

Here is the key: love, by definition, is not a feeling. Love, by definition, is action. It is best used as a verb. Love is demonstrated or expressed by action. Love without action is not love. It is something much less than love.

Lust, Like, and Love

There really is no such thing as authentic "love at first sight," because love is action-based and "action at first sight" doesn't make sense. There may be a feeling called "lust at first sight." It is called "lust" if it is inappropriate attraction. (Lust is being attracted to that which should not, cannot, and will not be yours.)

There can also be such a feeling as "like at first sight." This is not innately bad. Feeling physical attractions is not bad. In fact, physical attraction is extremely important in a marriage relationship. However, never confuse physical attraction with love, which is deed-based. "Like at first sight" needs to be understood for what it really is. It is "like." It is feeling-based. It is not love. Like is based on what I see and can get back. Love is action-based. Love is proved or demonstrated by actions of sacrifice, kindness, nurture, and gentleness. Here is the way to understand the three terms:

- Lust is all about me. It is destructive, because lust wants that which it should not have.
- Like is all about me. It is not necessarily destructive. In fact, it can be very good. We have to "love everyone." But we like certain persons.
- Love is all not about me. It is about others. It calls for sacrifice. It is demonstrated by acts.

Mother Teresa is cited by Jack Canfield in *The Secret*. However, Mother Teresa did not demonstrate love by "feelings." Mother Teresa demonstrated love by actions. How odd to use Mother Teresa in such a book. Can you picture Mother Teresa pouring her energies into "feeling good"? Can you imagine her following Byrne's advice—emitting transmissions to the "Universe" so they would bounce back, giving her whatever she wanted? Mother Teresa's sacrificial life—a bad concept to Byrne—is the counterpoint to everything in *The Secret*. This is why the great woman is really such a *non sequitur* in the book: she loved actively.

The mother of a newborn might not feel like getting up in the middle of the night to care for a crying baby, but her love is demonstrated by actions, not feelings. A wife might be annoyed with her husband because he is not as responsive as he should be. But she does not let feelings consume her. Instead, she demonstrates love for him by actions of love. A father might not feel a lot of love toward a self-centered teenager. Yet he demonstrates his love by actions.

It's crucial to understand that Byrne's popular definition of love is not only inaccurate, it is lethal. A definition of love based upon feelings, ironically, kills relationships.

Acts of Love and Sacrifice

When a person focuses on expressing love by actions, feelings often follow. One of the contributors to *The Secret* touched briefly on this important definition of love. Psychologist John Gray correctly stated, "Every man knows that when his wife is appreciating him for the little things he does, what does he want to do? He wants to do more. It's always about appreciation. It pulls things in. It attracts support" (p. 75). This is one of the rare servant-minded, "others-focused" statements in the entire book.

Love is a wife appreciating her husband by doing something special for him. Love is a husband not only wanting to but doing things for his wife that help her know she is valued. Love is a neighbor doing acts of kindness. Love is an employer surprising a hardworking employee with an honoring gift. All of these are examples of love. Notice they are all actions. They are not feeling-based, though feelings might precede and follow the actions.

As previously stated, Byrne's self-absorbed "love" flies in the face of authentic, sacrifice-based love. According to *The Secret*'s hedonistic message, "Sacrifice will eventually lead to resentment" because "sacrificing does not feel good" (p. 108). As if it is not offensive enough reading it the first time, Byrne repeats it ten pages later (p. 118). Byrne makes a feeble attempt to contrast the definitions of giving and sacrifice, contending that giving is good but sacrificing is bad.

To Byrne, sacrifice means "I will go without." And certainly, we would not want any "it's all about you" adherents to have to "go without."[1]

The entire book rings like a "pamper yourself" ad for a Caribbean cruise, rather than for the qualities we have come to respect and value in real life. A stroll through the Washington, D. C., Arlington Cemetery reminds one quickly of the value of sacrifice that has ensured our nation's freedom. A glimpse of the Iwo Jima Memorial reminds us people have sacrificed to protect what we cherish. One look at the gnarled hand of one's great-grandmother reminds us of the beauty of sacrifice that helps sustain generations to come. Throughout secular literature and biblical literature, the person who sacrificed has been extolled as a model of selflessness. Not so in *The Secret*'s self-absorbed planet.

There is a biblical concept that says, "They that sow in tears shall reap in joy" (Ps. 126:5 KJV). Its central message bears repeating. When people are willing to sacrifice of themselves (sowing in tears, perhaps even pain), they will reap many wonderful benefits from the sacrifice. It is a deeper version of "pay now, play later."

To Byrne, sacrifice is bad. Put yourself first, she says. Apparently not only is sacrifice bad, but so is putting yourself last. Jesus is cited by Byrne on one occasion. Somehow she missed Jesus' well-loved words on this point: "If anyone wants to be first, he must be the very last, and the servant of all"(Mark 9:35). Whom are you going to believe? Admit it: none of us like to sacrifice. But, Jesus' way of life is truth.

The First Shall Be First?

Byrne's narcissism continues: "Many of us were taught to put ourselves last.... You must change that thinking" (p. 119). In fairness to Byrne, she is *partially* correct. For example: if you are on a jetliner at thirty-five thousand feet, and the cabin suddenly decompresses, you are instructed to put the oxygen mask on first before assisting a child. The reason is obvious. If you cannot breathe, you cannot help anyone else.

The Bible affirms having a healthy priority of being able to love your neighbor *as yourself* (Mark 12:31). Love others *as yourself*—this is an appropriate self-love. Self-loathing is unacceptable and does not resemble biblical humility. Learning to be at peace with yourself is an important step toward emotional and spiritual maturity.

We don't love ourselves, however, because we are ourselves. We love ourselves because we are creations of God. He loves us. He designed us. This self-love is not a fundamentally hedonistic "me first." It is having a healthy self-respect, by virtue of the fact I am a creation of God, a child of God, and I have been put on this earth for something special. And that special thing is to be a servant to God and to others. In that sense, self-love is good, wholesome, and healthy. But that same healthy self-love causes us to be so thoroughly secure in ourselves that we can put ourselves last without having the alleged consequence of feeling "unworthy and undeserving" (p. 119).

Byrne's Antidote

What is *The Secret*'s prescription for life? "Make feeling good a priority" (p. 118). Lisa Nichols, one of Byrne's contributors, tells us to focus on joy (p. 132). But that cannot be accomplished as long as you are trying to "focus your thoughts on something you want" (p. 14). Once again, Bryne is operating with a wrong definition—this time—of joy. Joy is not self-absorption.

In the earliest pages of the book, Byrne tells her readers, "There isn't a single thing that you cannot do with this knowledge. It doesn't matter who you are or where you are, *The Secret* can give you whatever you want" (p. xi). "Whatever you want" will never bring you joy. It might bring you temporary happiness. It will not bring you deep and lasting joy.

Byrne does not seem to understand the importance of proper definitions when halfway through the book she announces her intention was to "bring joy to the world," and thus, she chose to "share this knowledge with the world" (p. 80). Her motives are likely pure enough. But, her method of bringing joy is flawed. If she really wants to bring the delight of life to her readers, she needs to help people function in the purpose for which they were created: a relationship with a warm, caring, loving heavenly Father, and giving their lives away for the benefit of others.

The Secret readers are told they "need to go for the inner joy, the inner peace, the inner vision, and then all these outer things appear" (p. 110). That is close to the truth. But it is not accurate. Jesus had a different order of priorities: "Seek first his kingdom and his righteousness, and all these things will be given to you as well"(Matt. 6:33). In other words, seek to obey and love God and be a reflection of His character (which includes true love and authentic sacrifices). And then the delights of your heart will be given to you.

But how do we give our lives away to others? Lisa Nichols correctly observed we were "born to add something, to add value to this world" (p. 182). But how do we do that? We don't add value by focusing on our wants. We add value to the extent that we bless others. The "biggest thing that we have ever come across" (p. 138) is not the Law of Attraction. The biggest thing that any person can ever discover is the inexplicable love of God—and then participate in sharing that love with others.

THE MEANING OF LOVE

Our literal language of love in English is inadequate—we apply the word *love* to many things. The Greek language (the language of the Bible's New Testament) has four distinct words for love. We don't have comparable terms in English. We might say, "I love my spouse, I love my parents, I love my children." Yet in the same breath we say, "I love my new shoes," "I love my car," or "I love my dog." We tend to use the same word to describe very different types of relationships. Consider carefully the Greek distinctions:

Storge means love between blood relatives, like a mother's love for her child.

Phileo means brotherly love, from which we get the name Philadelphia, the *City of Brotherly Love*.

Eros: Many associate this with sexual love (it is the root origin of "erotic"), but that is not adequately defining. Erotic love is sensual, that is, sensory-based. In other words, we love something because of what we perceive with the five senses. It could be sight, hearing, smell, touch, or taste. Erotic includes the sexual, but it is much more than sexual love. It is any sense-based love. *Eros* loves because of what it sees (or physically senses) in the other person. And consistently, erotic love is about what it can get back from that person. Erotic love is not inherently wrong. It is acceptable to love other persons because of what they bring back to you. But, it is far from the ultimate expression of love.

Agape (pronounced ag-AH-pay) is the most profound expression of love, because it values people simply because of who they are. It is a particularly unique word the apostle Paul (author of approximately half of the Bible's New Testament) used to describe God's inexplicable love for humankind. *Agape* is the way in which God loves you. Unlike many of the gods of Greek mythology, for instance, He does not love you erotically (for what He can get out of you, or what you can do for Him). God loves you simply for who you are. *Agape* is a value-adding response: that is, you are valued simply because you are loved.

LOOKING FOR LOVE—IN ALL THE RIGHT PLACES

Love is a much used and often misunderstood word in American conversations. The term is especially abused in *The Secret*. This potent word deserves a proper definition. To do that requires an examination of its Greek New Testament meaning.

Agape is a profoundly rich term. In the New Testament writings of Paul, *agape* can be understood in nine categories:

1. The nature of God
2. Spontaneous
3. Indifferent to value
4. Initiator of fellowship with God
5. Creative

6. The direction of *agape*
7. Eternal
8. Fundamental requirement
9. How to acquire *agape*

The Nature of God

If one word described the very nature of God, *agape* would definitely be in order. Paul instructs his readers that *agape* is given to man by the biblical God and was demonstrated in its highest fashion when God the Father gave to this world God the Son. In Paul's Hymn of Love (I Corinthians 13), the term *agape*, in the minds of most commentators, could be interchanged with "Jesus" without doing injustice to what Paul is saying. Paul becomes overwhelmed at times that God would care for him to such great extent that He should call him to be an apostle, especially when Paul's previous life did nothing to merit this special calling.

Spontaneous

Agape is entirely spontaneous and "unmotivated." Though it is uncaused, it causes much. Very little in humanity makes us desirable. In fact, much about humankind makes us very undesirable. Still God continues loving us. Humans are completely incapable of loving in a spontaneous (unmotivated by what is seen in the one being loved) fashion, but God's love comes with no thought of receiving. That is true love—*agape*.

Indifferent to Value

Of significance is the fact that *agape* is an unemotional love, almost a "disinterested" love as it is described. The term *unemotional* does not imply a lack of warmth. It is a love that can be extended in real concern and compassion to someone the giver of that love may not particularly like. This is not to imply that *agape* specializes in being expressed toward unliked persons. This does mean that *agape* is a love not prompted by what it sees in its object. The recipient's worthiness is completely foreign to *agape.* No distinction whatsoever exists between the righteous and the sinner in receiving God's *agape.*

Initiator of Fellowship with God

This section closely resembles those before it. *Agape* is the initial God-man contact, and through man's awareness of God's loving him, a reciprocal relationship begins. Man is not the initiator. In fact, from man's side, there is no way to love God. It was noted before that everything begins with the love of God, and this is certainly true of fellowship with God.

Creates Value

Agape is not impressed by worth. God's *agape* goes to sinful humans. But the very fact that God loves humans gives them a new value. Humanity is not worthy of anything from God. But we are recipients of *agape.* This creates value in us all. God's love is all that is required to make us valuable. It is a love that, when we fully realize it, transforms us to a state of spiritual productiveness. Other than God's *agape*, we can make no claim to an intrinsic worthiness.

Direction of *Agape*

Agape is that expression from God to man. As was noted earlier, *agape* cannot be expressed by humans back to God. This is expressed in the Greek word *pistis*, meaning "faith." However, as we open our lives to God, we can express this unmotivated, spontaneous *agape* to other persons. This type of love never comes from humans alone, but ultimately from God. In other words, even when a person has *agape* for his or her neighbor, the *agape* comes from God, since persons are a vessel for *agape* and not producers for it.

Eternal

The apostle Paul informs his readers that *agape* never ends. Other gifts and talents from God will serve their purpose and pass on, but *agape* remains forever. Even in the final section of 1 Corinthians 13, when Paul is presenting the "greatest three," *agape* is presented as the superlative. To understand something as never ending is difficult for us.

Fundamental Requirement

Paul writes that *agape* fulfills the requirements of the biblical Law, in that when one loves with *agape* love, he or she will automatically meet every intention of the Law. *Agape* is also present as that "fruit" from which all of the other Christian kindnesses or graces will flow. It is also stated that in our "walking in" *agape*, we become imitators of God Himself. *Agape* is also compared to something we "wear" that binds everything else together. The increase in *agape* in knowledge and discernment will even help to keep one blameless and to establish one in a meaning-filled relationship with God. In 1 Corinthians 13, we are told that without *agape*, our other attempts to be religious are in vain. And Paul finally makes the declaration that of all the things that are important, *agape* is the most important thing.

How to Acquire *Agape*

Paul admonishes his reader to "put on" *agape* as an outer garment, like an overcoat. Putting on *agape*, however, is not quite as simple as putting on an outer garment. It is clear that the persons who are not walking in conformity to God's biblical ways will not only be unable to fully "put on" *agape,* but they will lack a desire for it, for *agape* is given by the Holy Spirit. The expression of *agape* from one person to another is an act of the whole will. It has prerequisites. One must value it, seek it, desire it, pray for it, and pursue it. It even involves a "walking in" *agape*, as one progresses along life's pathway. In this process, one becomes an imitator of God.

This chart lists key New Testament Scriptures of Paul expressing *agape,* along with descriptions:

Text	Characteristic of *agape* portrayed:
Romans 5:5	indifferent to value, spontaneous, initiator of fellowship, God to humans
Romans 5:8	spontaneous, indifferent to value, initiator of fellowship, God to humans
Romans 12:9–13	human to human
Romans 13:8–10	fundamental requirement
Galatians 5:6	initiator of fellowship, human to human
Galatians 5:13	human to human, indifferent to value, creates value, spontaneous
Galatians 5:22	fundamental requirement
Ephesians 4:22–5:2	fundamental requirement, human to human
Philippians 1:9–11	fundamental requirement, human to human
Colossians 3:12–14	fundamental requirement, human to human
1 Thessalonians 3:11–13	initiator of fellowship
1 Corinthians 13:1–3	fundamental requirement
1 Corinthians 13:4	human to human

1 Corinthians 13:5	human to human
1 Corinthians 13:6	human to human
1 Corinthians 13:7	human to human
1 Corinthians 13:8	eternal
1 Corinthians 13:13	fundamental requirement

(James L. Garlow, 1971, "A Motif Study of *chesed* in Hosea and *agape* in Selected Passages of Saint Paul," unpublished M. A. Thesis, Southern Nazarene University.)

God Really Likes You

Imagine I was sitting with a friend, when all of a sudden the president, or the prime minister, or king calls me. My friend would be quite impressed that I received such a call. He would think I was more important *after* I received the call than I was *before* the call, by virtue of my connection with a person with unusual influence.

One more illustration: imagine you are looking at an old house in a small southern town. The houses around it are valued at $150,000. The one at which you are looking has an asking price of $500,000, many times the prices of identical houses on the same street. How could that be? Then you discover the house was the birthplace of one of the most famous country-and-western artists in America. Having the connection with the musical celebrity gives the house nearly four times the value of similar houses nearby.

Let's return to our original point. The fact you are the object of God's love increases your value many times over. You were originally valuable because God created you. Now you have indescribable value because God loves you. Your connection with God increases your value.

However, God does not merely love you—*He really likes you and wants to be with you*. That is the nature of *agape*. The phrase "God loves you" has taken on a bumper-sticker level of impact. Although the concept is quite amazing—the Creator of the entire universe would love you—you have likely heard it enough times that it fails to have the impact it should. Thus, the notion that God *likes* you has a fresh force to it. And the fact that God really *likes* being with you should be both humbling and encouraging.

Human Love versus God's Love

No human is able to love another person with this absolutely unconditional *agape* love. Why? Because we tend to love other people, in part, for what we are able to receive from them. Our love, by definition then, is erotic. Humans don't seem to be able to love each other innately, in a pure *agape* love.

In the New Testament, however, Paul implies we can love another with *agape* love when and if it comes *from* God and flows *through* us. In other words, the love with which we are loving others is not our self-satisfying love. We are loving others with God's pure *agape* love. And for the record, this *agape* is a sacrificial love. This is where you love people, not for what you can get out of them, but *for who they are*. You love them simply because they have personhood, because they exist, because they were created by God. This is radically different from the love referenced in the writings of *The Secret*.

In the Hebrew language in the Old Testament there is a

word similar to *agape*: the word *chesed* (pronounced KESS-id). It is breathtaking love. It is tenacious love. It is "a love that will not let you go," as the old hymn goes. It is God's love for you. More importantly, when people are completely open to God, that same *agape,* or *chesed,* love will flow through them to others. We become conduits, funneling God's powerful love through us to those around us—both friends and strangers.

THE GOD OF THE OLD TESTAMENT

Sometimes people think of the New Testament as being a depiction of a God who is loving, while the Old Testament God is wrathful and angry. Such is *not* the case. One of the most spectacular stories of God's love occurs in the Old Testament book Hosea.

Hosea and Gomer

Hosea, who lived seven hundred years before Christ, was told by God to marry a particular woman—a woman with the unusual name of Gomer. As they began to have babies, Hosea was suspicious that he was not the father of the children. Sure enough, Gomer had been unfaithful. In fact, one of the children was given a name as a reminder that Gomer had been unfaithful. They called the child *Lo-Ammi*, which means, in effect, that some other man had fathered the child (Hos. 1:9–10, 2:23).

Finally Gomer ran away, following the lustful glances of other men. Hosea was alone with his children. Some time later, as he walked through the slave market, Hosea saw a woman being sold as a slave. He was stunned to discover that it was his wife, Gomer.

Her beauty was now gone. Slavery had taken its toll. Just then, their eyes met. In that moment he still saw so much that had originally caused him to love her.

He intruded into the heated bidding and purchased her back as a slave. However, he did not keep her as a slave. He reinstated her to her role as wife and mother. He honored her in spite of her unfaithfulness.

What comes next gives us a glimpse into God. He explains to Hosea that now Hosea knows how He feels. He too has been abandoned by one he loved.

God created humankind. But humankind—specifically Israel—turned its back on God and "ran away with other lovers." However, God came pursuing us, even though we had lost some of our original beauty. He "bought us back" and he reinstates us in the role of honor we once had. The entire book of Hosea is a spectacular portrayal of the depth of God's love. In the book of Hosea, the Hebrew word *chesed* is used to portray this undying love of God.

Yes, the God of the Old Testament is loving.

Hand in hand with this *agape* and *chesed* love is the power—and it is a power—to forgive. At one point *The Secret* comes quite close to acknowledging this profound application of love, and for that Rhonda Byrne is to be complimented. She is at least coming close to helping her readers understand the importance of that vitally important life principle.

Byrne states you should "praise and bless your enemies" (p. 152). Of course Jesus originated the truth to which she is alluding here: "But I tell you who hear me: Love your enemies, do good to those who hate you, bless those who curse you, pray for those who mistreat you" (Luke 6:27–28).

Years ago my (Jim) father gave me some wise counsel regarding this. I had received some mean-spirited letters, and he said to me, "I know you can't throw them away. I understand that. However, if you have to keep them, put them in a file and label it the 'forgiven file.'" I did that and have continued the practice through the years. I have a labeled "forgiven file" both in a filing cabinet and in my computer files. Any time I remember the writers of those critical letters I think immediately, *I forgive them*. By God's power, I refuse to live in a spirit of unforgiveness.

This is the kind of love that builds stable families, healthy communities, strong nations, and a healthy world. This is the kind every human being desires and needs. Only when we receive *agape* love flowing from God Himself to us can we ever have what the human heart most desires to have—the sense that we are truly loved and cared for.

DEALING WITH ENEMIES

At one point *The Secret* comes quite close to saying something profound on this theme. Byrne states that you should "praise and bless your enemies" (p. 152).

She is correct in saying we should bless our enemies, as opposed to cursing them. Blessing people does not mean you are agreeing with them. Blessing means to ask God to interfere with their lives, helping them to become all that God desires them to become. That is the true meaning of "God bless you."

Contrary to the advice of *The Secret,* we are not to *praise* our enemies. If we are going to praise someone, let's praise the right One!

We should praise *God*, the One who loves us and cares for us, the

One who created us, the One who wants to win back our affection and our love. Praise goes to God, but blessing goes to not only God but all those around us.   ∞∞∞

Agape versus Secret Love

The Secret knows nothing about this kind of love. *The Secret*'s love is self-absorbed, self-focused, and self-contained. In marked contrast to the Bible's concept of love is perhaps the zenith of *The Secret*'s ideal in self-worship found in Bob Proctor's statement, "I want to kiss myself sometimes!" (p. 121). *The Secret*'s form of love could best be classified as narcissistic. This is the best approximation of love that can be mustered by a people who are far too self-absorbed.

In contrast to this is God's love. This is the love He wants to flow through all of us in order to help each person realize he or she has value, a purpose and significance. *All persons on Earth matter to God and they should matter to each one of us.* Only *agape* love does that.

The love evidenced in *The Secret* is a ticking time bomb that will destroy, ultimately, every relationship on Earth. No, the "biggest discovery" is not the Law of Attraction (p. 138). The greatest discovery on Earth is the indescribable love of God.

World's Greatest Lovers

Once people discover and experience God's love, they become some of the world's greatest lovers. The world's greatest lovers are not Hollywood celebrities on the big or small screen. The world's greatest lovers are not featured in magazines and on showbiz news shows. The world's greatest lovers are often well below the radar. They are too busy truly loving people to attract much attention.

One of these world's greatest lovers is Cassie, who works with invalid senior adults, changing diapers for people whose minds are so incapacitated they don't even know they are unable to walk to a bathroom anymore. She cares for them lovingly, tenderly during the night hours on the midnight shift. She has never had the benefit of marriage. No man has shown her that kind of attention and she is approaching her fortieth birthday.

Cassie is truly a hero. She is one of the world's greatest lovers because she understands *agape* love. She is not living life to get what she wants now. She's living life to give herself away, and she is blessing many people in the process.

TRUE PROSPERITY

When Byrne speaks of "how to attract abundance" (p. 99), it seems unlikely she has love in mind. She would have done well had she cited Jesus' statement in the New Testament when He said, "I came that they may have life, and have it abundantly" (John 10:10 RSV). Of course, Jesus was speaking of a truly abundant and meaning-filled life, abundant by much higher standards than material prosperity.[2]

The Secret is obsessed with material wealth. And material wealth is not in itself a bad thing; in fact, it can be a good thing when it comes with the full-orbed understanding of God's blessing. This understanding of wealth includes wholeness of spirit, soundness of mind, and generosity of heart and is grounded on an authentic love relationship with God Himself. *That* is abundance!

The abundance for which the human heart longs will never be experienced by emitting thoughts into the Universe in hopes they bounce back with a new BMW, as wonderful as a new BMW might seem. A meaning-filled life means we walk in conformity with the purpose for which we were made, which is not to "get yourself on the feel-good frequency, and you will receive" (p. 53).

Jesus said if you want to save your life you need to lose it, sacrifice it. In fact, he insists whoever sacrifices his life actually finds it (Matt. 16:25). In the next verse He says that even if a person gains the whole world but loses his own soul in the process...he has lost.

If anyone wanted humanity to have fulfillment, it was Jesus. It was not because he understood some *secret* about emitting transmissions into the Universe. It was because He understood what fulfills the human heart, what brings significance and purpose. We experience abundance when we are in alignment with the One who made us and we do what He made us to do.

Admittedly, Jesus stated it in terms that were not and are not very popular. He challenged you and me to deny ourselves and take up our "cross[es]" daily (Luke 9:23). It isn't a fun or Rhonda Byrne feel-good proposal, for sure. One translation of the Bible states it this way: "Anyone who wants to follow me must put aside his own desires and conveniences" (Luke 9:23 TLB).

Jesus, above all, understood how to make life count, and He said it's by loving and caring for others the exact way He designed us to. For those of you who are followers of *The Secret* and have already discovered it doesn't work, God has some wonderful news for you: nothing you can do will change His love for you.

Chapter 11

THE WORD THAT DISAPPEARED

Sin: Know Evil Exists

You have come home from work, having experienced an exhausting day. You have waited for this opportunity to watch the evening news while you reward your hunger with a medium well-done thick steak. You turn the channel to your favorite cable news show, where you see a split screen with two "talking heads." The text under the pictures reveals the debate is about prison reform.

The speaker on the left side of the screen is agitated by the time you tune into the broadcast. You hear him exclaim, "But he should be let out of prison. That's the simple fact!"

The confident woman on the right side of the screen is not about to be outdone and fires back, "Absolutely not! He needs to pay the price! After all, he is a murderer. He killed her." Not the least bit moved by the accusations, the left-screen, balding, fifty-something psychologist retorts, "But his childhood was horrifically tragic, Linda! He was a victim too. Don't you get it? We all know now the story of how his father beat him. How else is he going to respond to society? He's a person too, you know! What would you have become if you had been in a home like his?"

The middle-aged woman, labeled at the bottom of the screen as author of a book on victims' rights, is ready to respond: "Well, that's sad, Dave. It's sad that anybody is reared in a home like that. I feel bad for him. But that does not mean he did not do something wrong. Bottom line, Dave, he *killed* her, and he must pay the price for that. It is unconscionable that he should only serve thirty months for murder."

The psychologist on the left side of the screen, now comparably labeled on the bottom of his screen "Prison Reform Advocate," isn't going to wait any longer. Clearly the "only serve thirty months" comment was the trigger he had been waiting for. "Yeah, and that's what's wrong with people like you. You think the purpose of prisons is to make them pay the price. It's not! It's the rehab. He has demonstrated in two and a half years that he is ready to be released into society. He's a model prisoner! And furthermore, everyone knows—"

The increasingly perturbed woman on the right side of the screen, having been cut off mid-sentence, returns the favor: "Dave, you know better than that! The purpose for prison is both punitive—to make them pay the price—and rehabilitation. You know too much to have made such a statement."

At that point the commentator cuts back into the conversation, saying, "I'm sorry, Dave and Linda, we've got to go. We have to pay the bills. We'll be back in just a moment. Don't go away."

But the commercial is your chance to do exactly that. You reach for the remote.

Anthropology

The key issue in this debate, ironically, will never be mentioned. Whether it's a question of rehabilitation or punishment, there is a more fundamental premise our culture is prone to skirt. The real issue has to do with a basic question regarding anthropology— the understanding of humankind.

At the core of this and any comparable moral discussion is this issue: is humankind fundamentally good or fundamentally bad? Our psychologist friend regards humankind as basically good. At its core, humanity is bound toward perfection. But his opponent sees humankind differently. She understands mankind to be made in the image of God but fundamentally flawed in terms of maintaining that image and thus, impacted by something called *evil.*

Bull's-Eye

The great Bermuda Triangle of Rhonda Byrne's thinking, the great black hole, is that she demonstrates no awareness of sin and evil. Clearly these are unpopular concepts. Most people do not want to hear about sin, as it sounds so "archaic," so judgmental. But unless we have a foundational understanding of the nature of sin, we only deceive ourselves on how to function in the very imperfect world.

There is an entire academic area of study known as harmatiology.[1] *Harmatia* is the Greek word for "sin." It is an archery term meaning to "miss the mark." Sin is missing the mark that you were designed to hit.

A graduate theology student once observed, "Show me a person's harmatiology, and I'll show you everything else he or she believes. One's doctrine of sin determines everything." The wise student continued, "It's like the launching pad of a rocket. If you shift the launching pad substantially east, west, north, or south, it's going to affect where that rocket goes. A launching pad of the correct understanding of harmatiology will help you end up with an overall correct theology."

He was right. If you have the correct understanding of the nature of sin and evil, it will discern how to put the rest of life together. And it's exactly at this point *The Secret* leaves its readers both misinformed and personally vulnerable. Succinctly stated, there is no understanding of sin and evil anywhere within the pages of *The Secret*. That absence is a lethal void.

Something Is Missing

In 1973, noted psychiatrist Karl Menninger wrote a book with a most revealing title. The founder of the famed Menninger Clinic in Topeka, Kansas, titled the book *Whatever Became of Sin?* The psychiatrist noted the disappearance of sin and even pinpoints the time: 1953.

In 1952 President Truman began the tradition of the National Day of Prayer. The following year, President Eisenhower issued a proclamation continuing the tradition in which he quoted Abraham Lincoln's thoughts on this subject, stating that Americans are coming together, in part, "to confess their sins." Although Menninger was not a theologian, he was astute in noting that was the last time the word "sin" appeared in a proclamation, from then till he wrote his book in 1973. In later proclamations, Eisenhower never mentioned sin, nor did Presidents Kennedy, Johnson, or Nixon. Menninger mused, "As a nation, we officially ceased 'sinning.'" Menniger's observation applies to more than presidential proclamations. It applies to much of contemporary life, including *The Secret*.

Why wouldn't *The Secret* discuss such a profound topic? Doesn't everybody acknowledge evil exists, that there is such a thing as sin? With a quick review of the headlines in the newspaper or listening to the night's evening news, one realizes how much abuse and mistreatment exist in our broken world. The fact is, sin and evil are present.

The quandary of this is represented by the title of a popular book a few years ago by Harold S. Kushner: *When Bad Things Happen to Good People.* It bothers us that bad things would happen to good people. Equally offensive is the reverse of this, that good things happen to bad people. Whether we read the book title properly or if we pose the statement in reverse, those statements presume we are aware that certain things and people can be bad. We acknowledge there is such a thing as "bad."

What is bad? What is evil? What is sin? Those are questions about which Rhonda Byrne shows no awareness.

TWISTS IN DEFINITIONS: CONSERVATIVE AND LIBERAL

It is obvious that my coauthor and I (Jim) feel that Rhonda Byrne's concepts are both wrong and harmful. However, we are not advocating book banning or book burning. On the contrary, we believe that Christian concepts, if on an even playing field, fare well in the marketplace of competitive ideas.

I attended several graduate schools. Some would be considered conservative while others might be considered liberal. In the process of graduate-school education, and in the process of dialoguing with many persons since then—both within and without my theological comfort zone—I have discovered that *liberals are conservatives* and *conservatives are liberals.*

Liberal is supposed to mean "open" to new thinking, new ideas. *Conservative* allegedly refers to one who wants to "conserve" the present, thus not to be open to dialogue.

However, I have discovered that many conservatives—those supposedly on the right wing—both politically and theologically are quite secure and are unthreatened by dialogue. At the same time, I have discovered liberals, who are supposed to be open-minded—those on the left wing—are, in fact, stridently intolerant.

Faculty members in conservative universities are sufficiently secure to assign reading that has been written by liberal thinkers. Professors in liberal universities are often far too intolerant to assign conservative writings.

Therefore, who is truly liberal—that is, open-minded? It is the conservatives.

And who is truly conservative—that is closed, and not open? It is the liberals.

Thus, I say, *liberals are conservatives* (close-minded) and *conservatives are liberals* (open-minded).

I have encouraged people to read *The Secret.* (I believe people will quickly see its errors.) Will followers of *The Secret* return the favor—and recommend the reading of this book: *The Secret Revealed*? I hope so.

IF IT FEELS GOOD

In *The Secret*, we are repeatedly told to feel good. But the implication is this: if there is such a thing as feeling *good,* then there must be such a thing as feeling *bad.* What is bad? We're even told to want good things. To be instructed to want *good* things must mean there are *bad* things. According to *The Secret*, it is desirable for *good* things to happen to us. Apparently, bad things can happen to us.

So where does bad come from? Where does evil come from? Where does wrongdoing come from?

Nowhere to Be Found Here

Remember Rhonda Byrne's weight-loss advice? Food doesn't cause calories. "Fat thoughts" about food cause you to gain weight. Bad exists only in your mind, so you have to get rid of those bad thoughts. But where does such thinking come from? What are Byrne's sources? Where does *The Secret* get such an idea that there is no such thing as evil?

In the next chapter we will discover that *The Secret* is taken from five related, though not identical, schools of thought: New Age thinking, Hinduism, Paganism, occultism, and New Thought. It is important to understand that none of these foundational worldviews has an understanding of sin or evil that is remotely close to the biblical definition.

A closer look at New Age writing alone reveals that sin is largely regarded as an illusion. This is one of the great weaknesses of *The Secret*. It fails to acknowledge basic human sin. It denies the existence of evil. So when we are instructed by Rhonda Byrne to emit thoughts into the Universe for what we want, there is no perceived need to entertain the question, what if what we want is actually *not* good for us? What if our wishful thoughts are, in fact, harmful for ourselves or for others?

All must acknowledge that the human heart has at least the capability of doing wrong, of being evil. If we can simply have anything we want by transmitting thoughts into the Universe, what are the checks and balances to make sure we are wanting things that are truly good?

Rethinking Good

And what is the basis of *The Secret* for knowing when something is good? How do we know when something is good or something is bad? If there are no reference points to tell us what is wrong, what is evil, what is sin, then how would we know, on the other hand, what is good? A great tragedy was inflicted upon the people of Virginia Tech: thirty-two students and faculty were murdered by a madman. Friends, loved ones, the entire nation grieves and asks the ever-present and profoundly difficult, if ambiguous question, "Why?" It's doubtful we'll ever know in this lifetime the exact answer.

The especially bitter reality that *The Secret* would propose to us at times like these is, if the young murderer wanted to inflict this atrocity upon his fellow humans, then he got what he wanted. So presumably that was good for him. Can anyone seriously entertain the question of whether it was a good thing or a bad thing he did? It was a horrible thing, as we all know. Evil is, regardless of how anyone feels about it.

Byrne's failure to acknowledge the existence of sin in the human heart and its capacity for evil means there are no boundaries or parameters upon your wants. There is no moral governor to help guide you into proper decision making. The failure to understand sin and evil ultimately is destructive for individuals, families, and society at large.

A Needed Reference Point

Ironically, the question about the existence of sin is the very same as discussed in the previous chapter in terms of knowing what *good* is. Likewise, we must determine whether we need an objective standard beyond ourselves. Can we simply determine truth for ourselves? If we can determine truth for ourselves, then what if someone else's truth is different from my truth? Who is right? And how will we know?

What if one person standing before you claims it is raining, yet another person claims it is not raining? How do you know which one is true if you both think truth is whatever you want it to be? You need an objective standard—a way of measuring whether or not it is actually raining.

Our concern, however, is not with weather. The concern is with moral judgment. What if I say it's okay for me to kill those I don't like? Do I get to do it simply because I want to do it? Or should there be a standard outside me, beyond me, that says murder is fundamentally wrong and I must refrain from it?

This is precisely why *The Secret* is so lethal in its actual, practical application. Show me a person who does not have a grasp of the nature of evil and wrongdoing in the world, and I will show you a person who cannot possibly have a grasp of what is good. Humans desperately need an objective standard outside themselves to determine what is good.

The Bible offers precisely that. When the Bible says, "Do not steal," it means do not steal—ever. It does not mean don't steal when you don't feel like it, or don't steal when you don't want to, or don't steal when it's inconvenient for you to steal. It says, "Do not steal," ever. It's an objective standard, not based upon my whim or desire to try to bend the law.

We Who Have Chosen Evil

If one is capable of believing in God and all that is good, then one should be capable of believing in an evil one and all that is evil. The Bible indicates there was one named Lucifer who was once beautiful (see Ezek. 28:11–19 and Isa. 14:12–15). But he became self-absorbed. In fact, the very definition of sin is self-centeredness, as we will learn later. Lucifer called attention to himself instead of focusing attention upon the One who really deserves it—God. Consequently, according to the biblical record, Lucifer was cast out of heaven. He is also known as Satan or the devil.

Following the Lucifer disaster is the momentous incident involving Adam and Eve. They originally lived in a spectacular paradise. They could have continued to experience paradise. They chose not to. They were given permission to enjoy the wonderful fruit of all the trees in the garden (except one). They even enjoyed the tree of life. In other words, they savored life itself.

However, there was one tree from which they were instructed not to eat. It was the tree of the knowledge of good and evil. They were essentially (in a sense, perhaps even arbitrarily) instructed not to eat of this tree as a way of saying they were not to make themselves God. God was God; they were not. He would determine what was good. He would declare what was evil. They should not.

Tragically, they chose to violate the prohibition. In violating it, in the eating of the fruit from the tree of the knowledge of good and evil, they attempted to make themselves God. They attempted to define what is good and what is evil, what is bad, what is right, what is just, what is true. Adam and Eve attempted to exalt themselves as God and dethrone God Himself.

When one places the Lucifer account alongside that of Adam and Eve, one has the explanation for evil on the planet. If one understands that the human heart is drawn toward that which is wrong, because it is separated from the only good God (being a god unto itself), then it brings to the fore the reality that any truly authentic good can come only from a reconnection with and submission to God, the source and definer of all that is good.

Ever-Present Sin

The tough question that is on every parent's lips is, why do you not have to teach a child how to do bad? Why is it you never have to teach a child to lie, cheat, or steal? Why does a child instinctively know how to do what is wrong, yet has to be painstakingly instructed in how to do what is right?

It is because there is within the human heart a proclivity or tendency toward evil. We were not originally made that way by God. We were made perfect. We were made beautiful. We were made in the image of God. We were tainted by the fall of Satan and the tragic decisions of Adam and Eve, which led to all of humanity being separated from God—the definer of all that is good. In fact, this separation into being our own gods tainted us so severely that it is much harder to do right than it is to do wrong.

Two Distinct Views

Recall the debating psychologists' view of humanity: Dave believed humankind is basically good and does not need correction. Left to themselves, humans will do well. In fact, they should simply be encouraged. Humanity has the potential for perfection. Education will bring that about.

Linda believed in sin—that it exists. Humans were originally made in the image of God, but due to a fallen nature, they have the propensity to sin. Thus corrective measures are needed in order to place parameters around human activity. People are to be held accountable for wrongdoing. Government has an obligation to protect its citizenry from other citizens who might harm them. In other words, they believe in sin and the human capability for evil.

Dave saw humanity as fundamentally good, even inclined toward perfection.

Linda saw humanity as having been:

- created in the image of God,
- but having been profoundly tainted by sin,
- yet, God not leaving humankind in that condition,
- made provision through the person of Jesus Christ for people to be set free from the power of sin over their lives,
- thus giving them the capability to receive forgiveness, receive healing, and to begin to reorder their thinking,
- so they could long for that which is truly true, righteous, and just.

The difference between the two viewpoints is an anthropological one. Anthropology comes from *anthropos* (humankind) and *ology* (the study of), thus anthropology is the study of humankind. Here is the key question: what is your functioning anthropology? In answering that question you will need to have a well-developed harmatiology, a doctrine or understanding of sin or evil.

In other words, a failure to have a grasp of the nature of sin keeps a person from having a grasp of a healthy anthropology—the doctrine of humankind. If you do not understand humankind, you cannot know how to properly order your life. *The Secret*'s Bermuda Triangle is its inability to articulate any awareness of the capacity of the human heart to do what is wrong. If you don't know the problem, you cannot find the solution.

Chapter 12

SURVIVING TODAY

Life: Cope with Circumstances

If you've observed or participated in many conversations regarding *The Secret*, you probably have noticed many of them going something like this:

"Have you read *The Secret*?" inquires the first.

"Yes, I have and I know why she's writing it."

The first, with raised eyebrows: "Why is that?"

"Aw, she's just out to make money," replies the other, with a knowing nod and smile.

TRUE MOTIVES

Anyone who has written a book has to chuckle . . . most of us with a hint of irony. That's because most books don't make any money. Writing a book is hard work. No one likes writing a book. Everyone likes *having written* one. There's an enormous difference.

Writing a book has some similarity to birthing a baby. Obviously, I (Jim) have never given birth, nor will I. However, when writing a book, there is a conception and a gestation period and then a very painful birthing process. For most authors, the success of a book is simply too uncertain a venture for making money to be their motive. All the writers I know do it primarily for the same reason: to influence others.[1]

Nevertheless, in all honestly there is another reason we're chuckling at the knowing appraisal of Byrne's motives—probably to hide a wee bit of our own discomfort. Because the reality also is that every author hopes to make some money from the hard work.

It's actually unlikely that Rhonda Byrne set out to produce *The Secret* DVD and the accompanying book solely for the purpose of making money. There is simply too much work involved. When one is writing and producing, one has no idea if anyone is going to view it or read it. The DVD represents an enormous amount of work. She had no idea if anyone would ever watch it. The book, since it followed the DVD, and is largely a transcription of it, would have been considerably easier to produce, admittedly. But writing her off because of a supposedly mercenary motive is unjustified and unfair.

We (the authors of this book) have never met Rhonda Byrne, though we did try to contact her when we started writing this book. But it seems her motives were noble enough. She seems to have written for exactly the reasons she *said* she did. She wanted to help people and, as she said, bring joy to the world.

What's the Reader's Motivation?

So why do people read *The Secret*? They likewise read because of good and appropriate motives: they need help. Life can be stressful. Living can be difficult. Finances can get overextended. Dreams can be crushed. Relationships can wound. People want help. We all want meaning, purpose, significance, and love; and some of us find any one of those especially lacking in our lives.

Some critics of *The Secret* have similarly written of the motives of those who read Byrne's book to being filled with greed. That may be the case in some situations, but many people simply want life to make sense. They want life to *work*.[2]

There's far too much disappointment, heartache, pain and suffering in life for people *not* to try to figure out how to make it work better. There's far too much dysfunction in the workplace, in the family, and within our own hearts and minds for people not to be drawn to that which promises "something better." That internal tug for something better is a good motivation that causes us to step up, to attempt to attain the next level. It is a healthy motivation.

Both Rhonda Byrne's motivation for writing and the reader's motivation for reading are, for the most part, appropriate and healthy human drives. And it's to those needs we want to respond authentically. Our concerns are pastoral.

COPING

This chapter ultimately is about facing difficult circumstances in life, and how to cope—how to make it through life when things are challenging. We would all agree it is good to seek help when trying to face life's most difficult challenges.

To many traumatized and discouraged readers, *The Secret* seems to offer a way out. However, *The Secret*, in spite of its engaging ways, will prove to be theologically and emotionally bankrupt. It simply will not work, pragmatically speaking, very long in the lives of honest, reflective, clear-thinking people. It will prove to be a disappointing and a potentially disastrous dead end.

Our goal in this chapter is to take people from the flawed message of *The Secret* to the timeless *Mystery*. It is when we understand the mystery of life—God Himself—that we are able to move through life.

Prepare for Impact

All of us desire to control our lives. That is actually the primary focus of *The Secret*. However, we *cannot* control life. We can *impact* much of life—and well we should. But to claim that one totally controls one's life is to suffer from delusions.

God did "wire" us, however, with the need and the capacity to truly *impact* our lives and the lives of others. In fact, He invites us to do exactly that, and it happens through an exercise called prayer.

As has so often been the case, Rhonda Byrne and *The Secret* come very close to at least the language of Christian tradition and Scriptures. But a bridge that comes close to reaching the other side of a canyon still falls effectively as short as does no bridge at all—the car can't cross over, regardless of the good intentions of the builders. It's that same dilemma with Rhonda's purposefully spiritual language—it still falls short.

Here are the essentials of the message of *The Secret*: Have good feelings so that you know that your thoughts are good, and then emit those thoughts into the "Universe," from which they will bounce back and give you what you want. Let's unpack that. It would break down as follows:

- have good feelings
- that indicate our good thoughts
- that we emit
- the "Universe" receives them

- your thoughts bounce back
- you receive
- specifically, what you want.

What would happen if we redefined these steps, without the egocentricity and with greater appreciation for the full spectrum of life's emotions? Following the same pattern, it would look like this.

- Have good feelings: What would happen if we took feelings seriously but also recognized the natural ebb and flow to feeling? Let's admit it, sometimes we feel good; sometimes we feel bad. That is acceptable. However, we will not base reality on how we feel. Admittedly, there are times when we feel good when things are not quite as good as we feel. And, conversely, sometimes we feel bad when things are not nearly as bad as we might feel. Reality vacillates very little. Our feelings vacillate a great deal. What if we determined not to be so severely tied to our feelings? We could appreciate them, value them, and thank God for them but not make them define reality. Likewise:
- instead of "our good thoughts," let's substitute the phrase "His Word."
- instead of "emit," let's substitute the word "talk" or "pray."
- instead of "Universe," let's use the word "God."
- instead of "bounce back," let's use the word "respond."
- instead of the word "receive," let's use a word or concept pertaining to "relationship."
- instead of "what we want," let's substitute "what He wants."

Now let's go through that entire sequence and see how it would sound with these new definitions and terms. It would be something like this:

- Regardless of how we feel (bad or good)
- let's spend time
- talking with God
- praying His Word
- to Him (God, our loving Father)
- and He will respond to us
- so that we can have a relationship with Him
- so that He can bless us with that which is His will and His desire for us—all the good things He has for us.

Speaking His Word

Again, Rhonda Byrne actually comes fairly close to the truth when she asserts that words have power. They have power in the realm of the invisible, the spirit realm. The Bible affirms that fact. But the source of those words also makes a difference. There is a reason why we used the term "praying *His* Word" as opposed to simply "praying *some* words." The key to coping in life's circumstances is understanding the nature of prayer.

Consider two different ways of understanding prayer. Paul Bilheimer's book *Destined for the Throne* assists us in underscoring this understanding of prayer.

• Method A: Picture yourself facing God and talking to Him. Sometimes you're asking for things, saying to Him, "God, I need this, I need that" or "Please help me with this." (At other times you're praising Him, blessing Him, and simply declaring to Him what a great person He is, and how much you love Him.) That's one important view of prayer, and there are several examples of persons in the Bible praying just that way. In fact, there are times when life's experiences are such that we find ourselves praying just one word, "Help!" God hears and responds to that type of prayer of desperation as well.

• Method B: This is a different way of understanding prayer. The New Testament of the Bible clearly takes prayer to another level. In Method B, you don't face God. Instead, you face life's circumstances. God is behind you, backing you up, while you declare "over your circumstances" God's will, His perfect way, His Word. In other words, instead of facing God and asking for things, we are turned around with our backs to God, while God is supporting us. In fact, He is giving us the authority to make the statements.[3]

What kind of declarations do we make? We declare His Word, His way, His will. We do not declare our way. Why do we declare His way? Because He tells us He will watch over His words and make sure they are carried out (Jer. 1:12; Isa. 55:11). More importantly, since God is a loving, tender, perfect Father, He has our best interest at heart. He knows what is best for us much better than we do.

As a point of comparison, picture a child praying, asking to have chocolate ice cream for every meal and to stay up late every night watching television. These prayers may be sincere, but they're sincerely wrong. If that child would pray words based on the maturity of a wise, loving father or mother, then the child might pray for an acceptable dessert (as opposed to a steady diet of chocolate ice cream) and to see the favorite TV show (as opposed to watching TV late every night). The father and mother know what is best for the child, thus they have instructed the child how to pray. Such it is with God. He truly knows what is best for us—thus we pray His Word, His way, His will.

PLEASE REPEAT YOUR REQUEST

The Secret states, "You do not have to ask over and over again. Just ask once. It is just like placing an order in a catalogue. You only ever order something once. You don't place an order and then double the order...you order once" (p. 48). Yet Rhonda Byrne contradicts that advice when she references her mother buying a new house. She stated that her mother "sat down and wrote her name and the new address of the house over and over. She continued doing it until it felt as though it was her address" (p. 92).

Why would Ms. Byrne say that her mother could write the address over and over as an attempt to reinforce the response of the "Universe" and yet when you ask for something, you say it only once? That contradiction was never addressed.

Regardless, it is acceptable to ask God for something (or declare His will regarding a situation) more than once. That's because there is a significant difference between *The Secret's* portrayal of "ordering from a catalogue" and the biblical por- trayal: a child talking to a father. Certainly, it is true you don't need to place an order in a catalogue more than once. And, in all honesty, you don't *need* to ask God (or declare His will) more than once.

However, we are people—with human fears, concerns, and

emotions. We are not "ordering" from an impersonal catalogue. We are sharing our hearts with a loving Father, or as the Hebrew word *Abba* denotes, "daddy." We are His children. He is our heavenly daddy.

But we are limited in our understanding. As a result, we, as children, may go to the Father many times. Although we don't need to repeatedly ask, from God's perspective, we feel the need to ask multiple times, due to our limitations.

Anyone who has children knows what it's like to be asked frequently for the same thing. It is not because they think you lack authority and power—if they didn't think you could provide the solution, they wouldn't be asking. Actually, their repeated coming to you can be a sign of confidence in who you are in their lives. They might even be coming because they love and trust you. They have the hearts of children and are expressing their intense feelings about a particular issue.

When my (Jim) younger son reached driving age, he asked me about getting a driver's license multiple times, in fact several hundred times. In addition, he often brought me descriptions of potential used cars that were within the preagreed price range. He asked repeatedly. I was not offended by that. I did not scold him for it. I understood he was a child who felt strongly. The best way he could emphasize how strongly he felt was by repeatedly asking me. I respected his need to ask.

In the same way, God respects that childlike trait in us. He fully understands we don't *need* to ask more than once. However, since we are (His) children, He fully understands when we ask for things over and over again. We are not asking because we think He does not hear or that He lacks power to respond. We ask because we know He hears and we know He has power. In our asking, He does not condemn us. In fact, He probably smiles, puts His arm around us, and says, "I understand, My child, why you're asking repeated times."

DECLARING THE TRUTH

Recall the two methods of praying:

- Method A: Facing God and telling Him things about our needs or about Himself.
- Method B: With God behind us, backing us up, we declare His Word over the circumstances of life.

He wants us to conform to His Word and His way, because His way is *always* best for us. Once we conform to His ways, He gives to us His authority and power. It is for this reason Christian prayers close with the words, "In Jesus' name, I pray." The reason for this choice of words is the confident belief that Jesus is truly God. Thus we are praying by *His* authority, not our own. Our words have no authority. But praying His Word or will gives one tremendous authority. Why? It's good to repeat it—go ahead: because He is God, and we are not.

An Appeal

To those who initially might have been inclined to follow *The Secret,* take a close look at what the Bible really says about praying. You really should not be "emitting" to the "Universe." Rather, you are invited to enjoy a close, conversational relationship with a tender, compassionate, loving Father. The heavenly Daddy (*Abba* in Hebrew, as noted earlier) wants to be with you.

Candidly, He likes you. His desire for you is the very best. There is a better way than "emitting" to get "whatever you want." You may end up wanting some things that will ultimately be harmful. He doesn't want you to harm yourself. He loves you far too much for that.

You may be facing a very painful situation. There is hope for you. There is hope for your situation. You can make a difference. You cannot control or determine your destiny, but through prayer you can have an impact.

Admittedly, coping with some of life's blows can be difficult, but God has designed a way for us either to (1) move the mountain, (2) climb over the mountain, (3) go around the mountain, or (4) just dig our way right through the mountain. In other words, either God will give you a miracle by changing the circumstances, or He will give you supernatural coping skills to live with the circumstances. Either way, you win!

The central message of *The Secret* overstates the powers and potential of human thought. Consequently, those who are converted to believing this exaggeration of the capabilities of the human mind are at risk for experiencing false hope and needless guilt when examining the circumstances of their lives. Furthermore, for those with serious physical, mental health, and relationship problems, a committed belief in the Law of Attraction could serve as a hindrance to seeking and obtaining effective treatments, and thus contribute to the worsening of their conditions and difficulties.

—Joseph M. Price, PhD, professor of psychology, San Diego State University

Praying "Kingdom Come"

On one occasion, a group of Jesus' closest buddies came to Him and said, "Teach us how to pray." He said, "Here is the way I want you to do it. Pray, 'Your kingdom come.'" Whose kingdom is clear: God's. But what is the kingdom? Clearly the kingdom refers to God being King—that means God rules. So to pray "kingdom come" simply means to pray that God's will or God's way prevails upon the land.[4]

Why doesn't God just do it without us? Why should we even need to pray? After all, He's God, isn't He? God knows what He's going to do. Frankly, we'd be better off with just accepting whatever He thinks best, wouldn't we? So why bother praying at all?

Dominion and Stewardship

God could do anything without us, to be sure. But He chooses to use us in the process. We are not told entirely why this is the case, except that in the early pages of the Bible (Gen. 1:26) we are told God chose to give humankind dominion or authority over the earth. The word *dominion* means to manage something that is not yours, to have stewardship over it. It means being the manager without being the owner.

For whatever reason, God gave us authority over Planet Earth and he said, "Here's the way I want you to change Planet Earth. Here's the way I want you to manage it. I want you to pray, 'Kingdom of God, come on Earth!'" In other words, with God backing you up—you with your back turned to God as He is standing behind you to support you—you are to declare over the circumstances of life, "Kingdom of God, come."

"Will Be Done"

The next line in this famous prayer, known as the Lord's Prayer, is "Your will be done." In other words, the will of heaven (meaning the will of God) is to be done on Earth. The prayer continues, "on earth as it is in heaven." That raises an obvious question: how is it in heaven? The answer: it is great! Heaven is wonderful. The Bible doesn't reveal much about it except to say that it is most desirable. Whatever it is like in heaven is what we are to declare to happen on Earth. That means we are to declare that people experience a taste of the kingdom of God. Here are some of the marks or evidences of the kingdom:

- People come into conformity with God and enjoy His blessing.
- People enjoy a wonderful relationship with Him.
- People experience healing.
- People have emotional health.
- The downtrodden, disenfranchised, and poor are cared for.

Praying on the offense, we are to declare over the planet His healing, His power, and His authority. Praying on the defense, we are to declare over the planet deliverance and protection from the evil one.

If people discovered the spectacular mystery of authentic, biblical prayer as Jesus taught it, they would immediately abandon the precepts of *The Secret*. God calls His people to pray in a manner that declares His will. Doing so acknowledges you cannot control your world, but you can impact it because God has ordained you to do exactly that.

Our Words, Our Thoughts

God never established you to declare your words or your wants. He established you on Earth to pray His Word and His will. Furthermore, as we mentioned before, He watches over His words and will to make sure they happen.

Contrary to what *The Secret* would have you believe, you were never designed to "transmit" your wants. On that note alone, *The Secret* should be renamed *The Lie*. Instead of "emitting your thoughts into the Universe," God tells us to do exactly the opposite. The apostle Paul stated it this way: "We demolish arguments and every pretension that sets itself up against the knowledge of God, and we take captive every thought to make it obedient to Christ" (2 Cor. 10:5).

Instead of emitting thoughts, we take them captive. What does that mean? We take control of our thoughts. We draw them in. We focus them on what our compassionate, tender, loving Father desires, because He loves us more than we do ourselves. He has far more understanding of us than we do. Consequently, we are to bring ourselves, not into *The Secret*'s "alignment with the Universe," but into compliance with His ways, which is in the best interest of our future.

Can you control your world? No, you cannot. Impact it? Yes, you can. But you will never, long-term, positively impact it with *your* words or *your* thoughts. You will only impact your world positively, long-term, by stating words—not yours—His! Embrace the mystery of a close relationship with God and the power of prayer He has given to you. Then you will be able to face the circumstances of your life.

PART III

WHAT NOW?

"...Who understood the times and knew what [they] should do."
—1 Chronicles 12:32

Chapter 13

WHAT WAS SHE THINKING?

Origin: Comprehend Secretive Sources

The Secret, it seems, has something of an uncertain lineage. It isn't particularly forthcoming with specifics of its heritage, but you can look it up and down (as it were)—size up its features, style, and genetic codes—and you'll have a pretty good sense of its roots. But getting down to those roots of the family tree can take some digging, and that's the challenge of this chapter.

Frankly it's tough work—tiresome. But if you're going to understand a belief system such as this, you have to know where it comes from. We have found that *The Secret* actually borrows from several streams of thought. These are difficult to define because they are not necessarily distinct from one another—the roots get tangled. The sources we will list below are considerably more interrelated than they are distinct.

Making the genealogical charting more difficult still is Byrne's knack (knowingly or unknowingly) for being a "cafeteria thinker"; that is, she likes taking what she wants from whatever system of thought she wants.

The Secret is a combination of several overlapping concepts:

- New Age thinking
- New Thought or "mind science"
- suggestions of Hinduism
- hints of classical paganism
- a subtle admission of occultism (by virtue of its opening page), and
- a dose of positive mental attitude thinking thrown in.

All of these streams (except for the positive mental attitude category at the end) have one thing in common: a distinctive anti-Christian, antibiblical core. We will look at these five thought systems as if they are separate, but the overlapping is substantial. For instance, New Agers draws from Eastern religions, especially Hinduism. Yet they'll also employ occultic practices—thus those two streams are confluent. While acknowledging the areas of overlap, we will treat them as distinct in the sections that follow.

Good Old New Age

New Age draws on classically Eastern (that is Eastern hemisphere of the globe) mystical thinking as opposed to Western rationalistic thinking. New Age (realistically very old age, not being new at all) has become a relatively recent (last fifty years) phenomenon of Western fascination with Eastern religions.

Foundationally, New Age thought redefines God. It is less a system of consistent thought as it is an amalgamation of constructs. In part, it advocates that you have all power and you are divine. Christianity, in contrast, speaks about a God who is transcendent (a God who is above all He has created). In Christianity you have two entities: a Creator, and a creation. But New Age thought holds that god is all, and all is god. That is often labeled pantheism (*pan* meaning "all," and *theos* meaning "God"). Thus all is God.

What is obvious is the wide disparity between New Age and orthodox Christianity. Some New Agers consider the Bible to be a wise book; however, they redefine most of the Bible's classic Christian terms. Central to that process is the redefinition of Jesus Himself. Some in the New Age movement contend that Jesus was an avatar—a wise teacher—in contrast to the distinctive role of Savior. Others contend Jesus traveled to India as a youth to study Eastern religions (although no such evidence exists). Still others within the New Age movement reduce the person of Jesus to a "cosmic Christ," which is apart from the biblical, historical person of Christ.[1]

From a technical standpoint, of the five distinct yet related streams mentioned in this chapter, New Age is likely the least of the influences from which Rhonda Byrne drew. However, numerous components of New Age thinking do spring up from time to time in *The Secret*. One was just mentioned—the tendency to play fast and loose with the historical accounts of the life of Jesus.[2]

HINDUISM

New Age springs from several spiritual traditions. Similarly, *The Secret* finds its root system not only in New Age thinking (not to be confused with New Thought), but it also draws from a stream of Hinduism.

Hinduism recognizes many gods and goddesses. Followers worship as many as three hundred thousand different gods. In Hindu belief, the earth is personified, that is, regarded as if it were an actual person with its own emotion and intelligence. The earth is sometimes viewed as having, effectively, its own spirituality and deity. At this point, New Age thinking borrows heavily from Hinduism.

Hinduism was founded between 1800 and 1000 BC in India. Its sacred writings consist of the *Bhagavad Gita, Vedas, Upanishads,* and others. In Hinduism, God is an absolute. He is a universal spirit, known as the Ultimate Reality. True Ultimate Reality is to experience oneness with God. If you experience this oneness (also called *Braham*), you will come to understand that circumstances in life are not real. Individual personhood or individual selfhood is merely an illusion. Only Oneness is real.

Hinduism's view of personal experiences of suffering, regardless of its nature, is due to that person's own evil actions, quite possibly in a previous lifetime. If you experience a tragedy, pain, suffering, sickness, or starvation, it is because you have brought it on yourself.

The Secret and Hinduism

In case that sounds familiar to readers of *The Secret*, it is for good reason. *The Secret* draws occasionally from the ancient religious system. Although Rhonda Byrne does not specifically refer to Hinduism, *The Secret* frequently uses the word *avatar*, which is distinctly Hinduistic. It is a Sanskrit (language of Hinduism and Buddhism) word. As we've mentioned, an avatar is an incarnation, a human form of a deity. In some writing it can simply mean an enlightened teacher.

However, the definition of avatar is less important than the fact that Byrne consistently uses that term. By employing that word, she has revealed some of the root system—her Hinduistic bent.

Some of *The Secret*'s fans may be quite unconcerned that they are embracing New Age and Hindu philosophies. But for those who care about belief systems, they need to know with what they foundationally identify. Even those who do not see themselves as Christian would want to know the underpinnings of their new belief system.

SMOKING GUN #1

For those who may doubt the Hindu foundation to *The Secret,* let us take it a step further. These next few paragraphs are included for those who enjoy connecting the historical dots. Rhonda Byrne speaks openly that her introduction to the Secret was through Wallace Wattles's book *The Science of Getting Rich*. In his preface, Wattles speaks candidly of the Hindu origin:[3]

> It is expected that the reader will take the fundamental statements upon faith.... Every man or woman who does this will certainly get rich; for the science herein applied is an exact science, and failure is impossible.... Those who wish to investigate philosophical theories and so secure a logical basis for faith, I will here cite certain authorities.
>
> The monistic theory of the universe is the theory that One is All, and that All is One; That one Substance

manifests itself as the seeming many elements of the material world—*is of Hindu origin*, and has been gradually winning its way into the thought of the western world for two hundred years. [italics added]

The key words "is of Hindu origin" make the case quite clear. Bear in mind, Wattles is said by Byrne to be her source for understanding this thinking.

Reality

If you are a *Secret* adherent, are you likewise ready to embrace the idea that nothing exists outside what you think exists? Are you prepared to abandon all reason and rational thought and claim that what is in your mind is the only reality? That nothing exists outside of you? That there is no objective truth or reality?

If so, then you have truly found a soul mate in *The Secret*. And it would be well for you to understand that you have embraced a combination of New Age thought, Hinduism, with portions of other beliefs (New Thought, for example) thrown in.

In New Age thinking, there is virtually no reality outside what a person thinks is reality. It is for that reason proponents of *The Secret* can make such claims as "I'm not getting older, I'm getting younger." Presumably, if such a person, regardless of age, weight, or height, *thinks* he or she is an Olympic champion, then that person *is* an Olympic champion. Reality is whatever one thinks is reality.

Consider a humorous anecdote as an illustration of this principle. Several years ago, I (Jim) was flying home to San Diego, seated next to a remarkably muscular male in his early twenties.

Impressed with his bulk, I asked him what he did for a living. I discovered he was training for the Olympics in the hammer-throw competition. Not being familiar with the sport, I received a superb education during our flight.

Wanting to follow his athletic progress, I asked his name, which for our story will be Bill Benson. Bill explained that he was going to meet his teammates who were at the Olympic Training Center in the Eastlake portion of San Diego. He indicated he had never met them, and he was eager to know who they were.

We continued visiting as we landed and walked to the luggage carousel. My luggage came in first, so I exited the terminal.

Curbside were three male twenty-somethings, clearly as muscular as my new friend, standing by a van marked "Olympic Training Center." By the expressions on their faces, you could tell that they were anticipating meeting Bill Benson, their new teammate. At that moment, an idea hit me. Acting on it, I walked over to them, put out my hand, and said, "Hi, my name is Bill Benson."

I wish you could have seen their faces! In a nanosecond, they went from shock to disappointment to incredulity. One of them, looking at my build, conspicuously different from theirs, exclaimed, "Wait a minute, you are *not* Bill Benson!" We all laughed, and I went on my way.

But what if I really believed that I was an Olympic hammer thrower? Could that make me one? What if you believed you were Elvis Presley? Does that make you a famous singer? The obvious answer is no. Simply thinking something does not make it so.

Likewise, as discussed in previous chapters, a distinctive feature of *The Secret*'s (and therein, New Age's) belief system is its understanding of "god." New Age thinkers affirm self-divinity. Thus *The Secret* blatantly states "You are God" (p. 164). And as also examined previously, New Age thinking refuses to acknowledge the normal hurts and sufferings of humanity. Such things as sadness, failure, anger, and wounding are considered illusions. They simply don't exist.

Thus far we have talked about the New Age foundations to *The Secret* and the ways in which it has drawn from the teachings of Hinduism. We need to identify one other source from which Rhonda Byrne is consciously or subconsciously drawing, and that is paganism.

Paganism

In 2003, Dan Brown released the book titled *The Da Vinci Code*. In 2004, I (Jim) was asked to write a response to it. While contemplating writing that response, I talked with my good friend Dr. Peter Jones. As a result of that conversation we coauthored a book titled *Cracking Da Vinci's Code*. I knew Peter fairly well before we wrote the book together, but I became much better acquainted with him, his thinking, and his intellectual acumen during the process of writing the book. What I did not realize before we coauthored the book was that he was one of the foremost scholars on paganism.

Born and reared in Liverpool, England (and a grammar-school chum of John Lennon), Peter completed his schooling at Harvard Divinity School and Princeton Theological Seminary. He became a topflight New Testament scholar. However, his intellectual journey took him far beyond the New Testament—

into the intricacies of paganism. Consequently he founded an organization known as Christian Witness in a Pagan Planet or CWIPP. I am indebted to him for an understanding of this highly visible, yet rarely recognized, religion in America.

Pagan means "of the country," similar in meaning to the way one might use the contemporary and pejorative "country bumpkin" label. The term *pagan* has often been used to describe any belief that is not Christian. However, that is not the way the term is being used here. *Pagan* has a formal, though sometimes ambiguous, definition. Like New Age, pagan is less a highly sophisticated and consistent system as it is a collection or historically merged combination of many primitive and superstitious thought patterns.

Monism

What is this new paganism, sometimes referred to as neo-paganism? What does it refer to? In part, it is a vision of everything being one, not unlike New Age thought and Hinduism. Monism comes from the root word *mono*, which simply means "one." Paganism scholar Peter Jones states, "When you think monism think of 'one-ism.'"[4]

MONISM: A PAGAN CONCEPT, NOT CHRISTIAN

Monism is basically "one-ism." Monism is, however, more complex than the word may sound. There are essentially three types of monism:

1. *Substantial monism* means one substance or "one thing."
2. *Attributive monism* refers to "one category"; although there is

only one kind of thing, there can be many different individual entities, beings, or things within this "one" category.

3. *Absolute monism* refers to the fact of only one being and only one substance.

There are three ways of understanding monism:

1. *Idealism*—only the mind is real.
2. *Neutral monism*—the mental and the physical together form a third substance, or energy.
3. *Physicalism* or *materialism* is the opposite of idealism in that only the physical is real, and the mental can be reduced to the physical.

Which definition is Byrne embracing in *The Secret*? At times, she appears to be an "absolute monist." In terms of category, she is certainly an "idealist," believing that only the mind is real.

However, that seems to be true only theoretically in *The Secret*. Functionally or practically, her writing, due to its obsession with gaining financial wealth and material goods, hints not of monism but of a form of dualism—distinguishing between mind (unseen) and physical reality (seen).

∞∞∞

The Secret consistently utilizes monistic categories of thought. Furthermore, Byrne appears to embrace idealism, believing that only what is in the mind is real. (Note the sidebar on monism.) Byrne's "all is One" claims verify her—theoretical, at least— monism. Practically speaking, Byrne appears to be a functional dualist (spiritual and physical realm both exist) with her emphasis upon not only the mind, but her consumptive obsession with wealth and the material realm. (See chart on *The Secret*'s Worldviews. *The Secret* is listed two different places on the Worldviews chart in an attempt to accommodate the disparity between the monistic (New Age and New Thought) and dualistic themes (occultic) in the book.

The Secret's Worldviews*

Relationship of the Seen and Unseen	Monism – Oneness "One is All, All is One"		Dualism Spiritual and Physical			
Epicenter	The Divine	The Mind	The Creator			The Creation
Relation to All	The Absolute power/being is the essence of all things	All things are the same as Absolute power/being	Absolute Power is source of meaning for creation (in the image of God)			Created Order gives itself meaning (makes god in its image)
Perceived Reality	A person's awareness of the Absolute defines one's state of existence	No god(s) and no objective reality apart from one's perceptions	Physical world was created by the Absolute Power(s)			Physical world is self-creating or created by spiritual force
Examples	Hinduism Pantheism	New Thought New Age Unity *The Secret* (theoretically)	Impersonal Deity Islam (fatalistic) Deism Unitarianism	Personal Diety Judaism Christianity (theistic, providential)		Secular Humanism The Occult Atheism *The Secret* (practically, functionally)

*Categories are broad generalizations and not intended to deny the complexities of these systems of belief. Several of these movements and religions may be properly placed in more than one category.

by James L. Garlow and April Williams

What is significant about the "all is one" mentality? Simply this:

- There is no need of God as an independent, transcendent, beyond-this-earth entity.
- If you have no need of God, you have no revelation from Him.
- If you have no revelation, you have no Bible.
- If you have no Bible, you have no authority.
- Then what is the authority? You, because you (and all the rest of creation) is one and is God itself.

This is, in part, is what paganism advocates. Rhonda Byrne's writing is, religiously speaking, consistently pagan. (Remember, it is not simply something that is non-Christian. It is, in reality, a *bona fide* religion.)

Once again, some who follow Byrne may not have any problem acknowledging they are pagans, and thus we must admit they are theologically and philosophically consistent. However, there are others who probably have embraced *The Secret* thinking it is merely another positive mental attitude book. In fact, it is not.

New Thought

We have seen *The Secret*'s reliance on New Age thinking, Hinduism, and paganism. Now we identify the most prominent of the source streams of Byrne's writing, New Thought. The New Thought system is even more ambiguous and difficult to define. In what is destined to become an intellectual classic, *A Republic of Mind and Spirit, A Cultural History of American Metaphysical Religion* by Catherine Albanese, professor of religious studies at the

Santa Barbara campus of the University of California, is a six-hundred-page, exhaustive analysis of New Thought and other closely related but historically unwieldy movements.

The dust jacket's phrasing demonstrates the difficulty in identifying the various movements as a cohesive whole. It states:

> The book follows the evolving version of metaphysical religion, including Freemasonry, early Mormonism, Universalism, and Transcendentalism—and such further incarnations as Spiritualism, Theosophy, New Thought, Christian Science, and reinvented versions of Asian ideas and practices. Coming into the twentieth century and after, the book shows how the metaphysical mix has come to encompass UFO activity, channeling, and chakras in the New Age movement and a much broader new spirituality in the present.

In the introduction, the author breaks it down for us very clearly. There are basically three major theological and religious streams in America, the first two being quite recognizable:

1. Mainline Protestant liturgical denominations—with emphasis on form
2. Evangelical groups or denominations—with emphasis on life transformation
3. Metaphysical groups—with emphasis on "mind science" (this is the least-recognized and -known of the three categories)

This third, less-definable group contains many movements, including New Thought.[5]

IDENTIFYING THE WEAKNESSES
OF NEW THOUGHT

A young man wrote his doctoral dissertation on the emerging New Thought movement at Yale in 1933. One year later, he wrote an article on the vacuous movement in a sociology review. Alfred Griswold's insightful words still have relevance some seventy years later:

> New Thought had its main roots in the mesmerism [hypnotism] of [Phineas] Quimby and the transcendentalism of Emerson.... It is a system of high-powered mental telepathy which held that matter could be spiritualized and brought under the complete domination of thought, and, conversely, that all thoughts become matter.... It had no church and was essentially a metropolitan religion. Its adherents were impelled mainly by the motive of profit, and few were masters of its theology and metaphysics.
>
> Like Puritanism, it recognized the law of prosperity as a cardinal statute. By personal magnetism the adherent could attract, persuade, influence, or control his fellows, and success in business was assured. The writings of New Thought accord with the traditional American philosophy of success. They banish luck and reaffirm the economic potency of character. Faith in equality of opportunity is sustained. The bulk of the literature contains little but esoteric directions for making money. The very novelty of New Thought gave it popularity.
>
> The adage that money-making has been a religion to Americans has a literal truth unperceived by many who repeat it. There was a native American religion devoted precisely to that end: a cult of economic success.... New Thought.
>
> Although the ideological family tree of New Thought has a gnarled trunk and many branches, its two principal taproots

may clearly be discerned. One of these extends into the historic teachings of P. P. Quimby, the great mesmerist [hypnotist] of Portland, Maine, who had healed (and taught) Mrs. [Mary Baker] Eddy [founder of Christian Science]. The other was fed by the transcendentalism of Emerson and the Concord Group. But New Thought was neither Transcendentalism nor Christian Science. It is often confused with the latter, largely because of their common relationship to Quimby. Barriers hazy to a layman but real to an initiate separate the two.

According to its tenets, the individual was actually divine, a reflection of Emersonian transcendentalism. Its God was this "Supreme Power-Universal Presence-All Mind," who could be addressed, alternatively, as "Mind, Spirit, Law, The Absolute, First Cause, Nature, Universal Principle, Life."…

As to the appeal of New Thought, thousands made use of its teachings who were never in any sense masters of its theology and metaphysics. These were the property of the small, striving minority, and a few writers who explored its mysteries. But the great majority were in it for what they could get out of it, and that was money. They wanted to succeed, to grow rich, to rise in the world, rather than to commune with the All-Mind. For New Thought was a get-rich-quick religion, a something-for-nothing religion; that was the secret of its appeal. No rigorous discipline compelled its followers' worship. What most of them worshipped was not New Thought but success. New Thought, to them, was a new way to pay old debts.…

Because "thoughts are things" the New Thought priesthood instructed neophytes that they might think their way to wealth. As you think, so you are, they said. But this was thinking with a difference—personal magnetism, the "subtle thought waves, or thought vibrations, projected from the human mind," which travel along "like a ray of light," serving their masters. Since "a personal magnet" was in this manner able "to attract, persuade, influence, or control his fellows," how could he possibly fail in business unless, of course, he wanted to?

Here, indeed, was the secret. Even the authoritative teachers of New Thought affirmed its magical properties, so far as success in business was concerned. It might help a man to achieve distinction in other fields, "in art, scientific research, invention, literary work, et cetera," and then again it might not. But these were fields the harvests of which "are reaped by others of a more worldly turn of mind." Because the "personal magnet," with "push, energy, force," is needed to turn works of art and science into money, he "usually reaps the lion's share" of the profit. Therefore, the teachers of New Thought are justified in regarding success as meaning the attaining of financial reward, and *that* must depend largely upon the "Personal Magnetism of the seeker after success." And, if the lion's share of the profit went to the business man, so did the lion's share of the glory.

(Alfred Whitney Griswold, "New Thought: A Cult of Success," *The American Journal of Sociology* 40, no. 3 (November 1934): 309–318.)   ∞

Meet Mr. Quimby

Since this book is not a formal study on New Thought, a cursory overview will suffice. As we mentioned in chapter 7, the intellectual father of New Thought is generally regarded as Phineas Parkhurst Quimby (1802–1866), a watchmaker, clockmaker, and scientist, who resided in Maine. Some trace the New Thought further back to Emanuel Swedenborg, born in 1688. Quimby is the primary identifiable source for New Thought, even though many later New Thought leaders and writers had major differences with the "founding father."

"Dr." Quimby, as he was called due to his emphasis on mental healing, advocated a relationship between the mind and the body in which the mind exercised unique control over the body. To Quimby, all diseases and sicknesses were caused by faulty reasoning. Disease was not the cause of illness; rather it was the result of conflict within the mind.

Some accused him of saying sickness was merely imagined. Actually he believed pain to be real but thought it was caused by errant thinking. To Quimby, disease was an error of the mind that could be alleviated by getting the mind to accept "the Truth." Disease was not independent from the mind, he taught. Sickness is a deception people believe. By accepting "the Truth," the mind brought an end to sickness of the body.

This teaching took on a distinctly more religious tone in the years following, with considerable more visibility, in the form of religious science, science of mind, or later Christian Science and the Unity Church. After a lifetime of teaching and practicing his healing practices, Quimby died of exhaustion on January 16, 1866.

Post-Quimby New Thought

The movement quickly grew well beyond the personality and even the concepts of Quimby. New Thought as a movement is difficult to trace, mainly because it was not cohesive. Instead, there are numerous nonconfluent streams. These streams are similar but clearly not identical. Time and space do not permit us to investigate the list of New Thought leaders during the late

1800s and early 1900s, but the list would include Warren Felt Evans, Julius and Annetta Dresser, Mary Baker Eddy, Emma Curtis Hopkines, William Atkinson, and Charles Fillmore, the latter being often quoted in *The Secret*. Wallace Wattles, who inspired Rhoda Byrne to discover the Secret, is among this group.

In attempting to trace who learned what from whom, there was much cross-fertilization taking place in the rise of New Thought in the nineteenth century. If we combine it with the other influences we've mentioned above—New Age, Hinduism, Paganism—and one more influence to be mentioned below—occultism—then the flow of ideas to *The Secret* has a basic "genealogy" in the Law of Attraction, as illustrated on the facing page.

[*text continues on page 234*]

Basic Genealogy of the "Law of Attraction"*

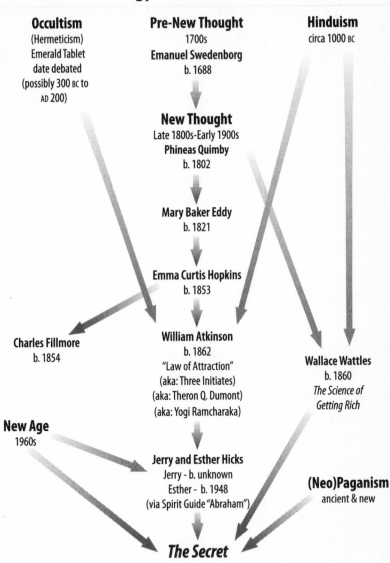

Occultism
(Hermeticism)
Emerald Tablet
date debated
(possibly 300 BC to
AD 200)

Pre-New Thought
1700s
Emanuel Swedenborg
b. 1688

Hinduism
circa 1000 BC

New Thought
Late 1800s-Early 1900s
Phineas Quimby
b. 1802

Mary Baker Eddy
b. 1821

Emma Curtis Hopkins
b. 1853

Charles Fillmore
b. 1854

William Atkinson
b. 1862
"Law of Attraction"
(aka: Three Initiates)
(aka: Theron Q. Dumont)
(aka: Yogi Ramcharaka)

Wallace Wattles
b. 1860
*The Science of
Getting Rich*

New Age
1960s

Jerry and Esther Hicks
Jerry - b. unknown
Esther - b. 1948
(via Spirit Guide "Abraham")

(Neo)Paganism
ancient & new

The Secret

*Actual interactions and influences of movements and persons are considerably more complex than demonstrated on this chart. This is designed to provide only a most basic understanding of influences on *The Secret*.

by James L. Garlow and John Debus

In capsule form, this three-hundred-year lineage provides an insightful history of heresy. The lines get more complex and have much greater intrigue than the straight-lined chart can portray.

William Walker Atkinson (as noted prominently in the chart) was a key leader of New Thought. A man named Ramacharaka was born and raised in India and was influential in bringing the teachings of Hindu to America. Ramacharaka had a student named Baba Bharta, who instructed William Atkinson. The two of them began to write books, using the pseudonym of their mentor Ramacharaka. Atkinson, likely the major American proponent of the Law of Attraction in the late 1800s, used many pseudonyms.

SMOKING GUN #2

When an author writes a book, the first sentence—though often written last—is a significant indicator of the book's leanings. Even more so is any quotation that might be used on the opening page. Such is the case with *The Secret,* which opens (unnumbered page) with only these words: "'As above, so below. As within, so without.'— *The Emerald Tablet,* circa 3000 BC." This fully reveals what Rhonda Byrne believes, and the philosophical basis of what she has written. The reader deserves to know exactly what that basis is.

The Emerald Tablet

The Emerald Tablet was allegedly discovered in a cave used as a tomb, gripped in the hands of the body of Hermes Trismegistus. His name, when translated, means "thrice great Hermes" referring to the Egyptian god Thoth, the Egyptian god of learning and magic, later known as the Greek god Hermes and still later known as the Roman god Mercury.

In art, Hermes Trismegistus is portrayed as holding an emerald (actually a green stone, as opposed to an actual emerald) upon which he inscribed Egyptian philosophy. Who actually found the tablet is debated. Theories range from Sarah (the wife of Abraham) to Apollonius of Tyana (a teacher and miracle worker in southern Turkey in the first century).

The writings on the stone, believed to contain the "secrets" of the "universe," are in the Phoenician language. The all-important phrase, which states in full "That which is above is like that which is below and that which is below is like that which is above, to achieve the wonders of the one thing," is the foundation of astrology (belief that the order of celestial bodies impacts personalities and human affairs) and alchemy. The abbreviated phrase "as above, so below. As within, so without" holds the key to all mysteries, it is believed. All systems of magic allegedly follow this formula.

The Emerald Tablet (sometimes referred to as the *Emerald Table*) is only a portion of the *Hermetica* (often referred to as Hermetic writings), which consists of as many as forty-two different books. Clement of Alexandria divided thirty-six books of the *Hermetica* as follows:

- four books—astrology
- ten books called the Hieratic—law
- ten books—sacred rites
- two books—music

- six books—medicine and the body
- the remainder—writing, cosmography, geography, mathematics, priest instruction.

Many of the Hermetic books were lost when the libraries in Alexandria, Egypt, were burned. Supposedly some books survived because they were buried in the desert. Of those that survived,

- the first part is known as *The Divine Pynander,* consisting of seventeen fragments.
- A second book is known as *Poimmandres* or *The Vision.*
- The third work is *The Emerald Tablet,* the one referred to by Rhonda Byrne.

In that document, one finds the reference to the "One Thing," once again showing the shared worldviews between Byrne and this ancient occultist document.

The Dating of *The Emerald Tablet*

What is the significance of *The Emerald Tablet*? Was it written in 3000 BC? But more importantly, why did Bryne choose to begin her book with this citation? And equally important: why has she not discussed the significance of this "tablet"?

The exact time of the writing of the tablet is not known. Adherents date it at 3000 BC, as antiquity tends to add the notion of authenticity. Others date the writings much later:

- Isaac Casaubon, a Swiss philologist (student of the origin of words), in 1614 stated that the Hermetic writings came after the time of Christ's birth.

- Scholar Walter Scott dates them after AD 200.
- W. Flinders Petrie dates them between AD 200–500.
- Others claim as early as 300 BC, and still others claim, without proof, 3000 BC.

Some Hermetic writings, as they are called, were among the famous 1945 Nag Hammadi (a town in Egypt) discovery, which consisted primarily of Gnostic texts.[6]

HERMETIC WRITINGS AND GNOSTICISM

In the Bible—in the New Testament's first letter of John, specifically—John, closest friend of Jesus, in approximately AD 90 wrote vigorously against a movement called Gnosticism. Gnosticism comes from the word *gnosis*, which means "knowledge." Gnostics taught that an elaborate system of secret knowledge was the key to life and eternal things. Gnostics, though flourishing alongside early Christians, did not believe that Jesus was the provision for sin and for life issues. Knowledge—specifically *secret* knowledge—was.

Gnosticism has many expressions, and thus again it is difficult to define. Flourishing during the second and third centuries AD, it varied from being somewhat close to biblical Christianity—so it was mislabeled Christian Gnosticism (although, in reality, a teaching is *either* Christian *or* Gnostic—but *not both*)—to being more blatantly and conspicuously antibiblical—thus a distinctly pagan Gnosticism.

Until the much-publicized discoveries of ancient documents in Nag Hammadi, Egypt, in 1945,[7] the only Gnostic-related writings were those of early Christianity writing against the belief.

With the Nag Hammadi texts discoveries, Gnostics were allowed, for the first time in nearly two millennia, to speak for themselves. Among the most known components of Gnostic belief is the fact that the spirit world is good, while the physical, seen world is inherently bad or evil. The goal of a Gnostic was to escape this evil world—including one's physical body—thus allowing the experience of being totally and completely spiritual. One could achieve salvation through a series of ever-ascending levels of secret knowledge.

Hermeticists (followers of the writings of supposed author of *The Emerald Tablet*) were close spiritual "siblings." Among their commonalities, both groups valued a particular kind of esoteric knowledge, a very *secret* knowledge only they possessed. This allowed them to enjoy an elitist self-perception. One of the few differences was the fact that Hermeticists saw Hermes as a part of their salvation story. But fundamentally, Gnostics viewed salvation as tied to their secret understandings.

ANTI-CHRISTS

The conclusion is important. *The single primary source upon which Rhonda Byrne based her entire book is distinctly, overtly anti-Christian.* I am not making this point for the benefit of those who consider themselves non-Christian. They have a right to worship as they choose, and they have chosen not to identify with Christianity.

I am making this point for those who might be unsuspecting of Bryne's covert methodology. Those who consider themselves Christian should recognize that *The Secret* is distinctly antibiblical and anti-Christian.[8]

It might surprise the reader that we do not discourage people from reading *The Secret*. And, for the record, we are not in favor of book-burning or censorship. In fact, we have encouraged Christians to read *The Secret* so they would understand occultism and paganism when they see them. Several years ago, I (Jim) coauthored *Cracking Da Vinci's Code*. During a few media interviews, the radio talk show hosts mistakenly assumed I was fearful for Christians to read the anti-Christian *The Da Vinci Code*. They were quite surprised when I responded that I encouraged Christians to read the book and see the movie. Why? Reading the book, and to a lesser exent seeing the movie, accomplished two things: (1) it put them on a journey to pursue truth more vigorously, thus their faith in Christ would grow, and (2) it would make them more prepared for conversations with their unchurched neighbors and friends.

DECEPTION

In the end, *The Secret* is a covert, nondisclosing book. My objection to it has less to do with its content (which Ms. Byrne has the right to present), as much as to the dishonest nature of the book.

- It present theories as fact (quantum physics).
- Most offensively, it quotes the Bible and cites Jesus Christ in historically dishonest ways. The attempt to ride the coattails of Jesus is sloppy scholarship at best, or intentional deception at worst.
- It distorts the viewpoints of deceased celebrities.

Rhonda Byrne's blatant use of *The Emerald Tablet* puts the proverbial nail in the coffin: she and the entire underpinnings of

The Secret are occultic. The open citation from *The Emerald Tablet* is the most recognized phrase of occultism.

Occult

Occult, as a word, comes from the Latin term *occultus,* which means "secret." (Is this a potentially secondary reason for the selection of *The Secret* as Byrne's title?) The occult, with a touch of melodrama, thrives on its highly clandestine nature. The occult promises "deeper" truth, or "hidden" wisdom. Over the years, it has come to mean knowledge of the paranormal.

Paranormal refers to phenomena that, according to accepted scientific observation, go beyond acceptable physical limitations. The paranormal, studied in parapsychology, includes such activities as telepathy, extrasensory perception, reincarnation, magick (intentionally spelled with a *k*), and the fascination with ghosts and haunted places. Persons who practice the occult are referred to as occultists. The additional *k* added to *magic*, making it *magick*, occurred through the influence of a well-known occultist named Aleister Crowley. Magick spelled with a *k* is the correct spelling for any magick that is occultic and ritualistic in nature, achieved by invoking demonic forces. (This is not to be confused with sleight-of-hand magic that illusionists use in entertaining "magic" performances.) The occult practices of which we speak are expressly forbidden in the Bible, in the tradition of Judeo-Christian faith.

Full Disclosure

Byrne never speaks of her sources. Her opening page, with its quotation from *The Emerald Tablet,* could have included forthright explanation of her presuppositions. A simple explanation about *The Emerald Tablet* would have been appropriate. Byrne openly stated the extent to which she was influenced by Wallace Wattles (pp. ix, 76). Why was she not candid about his Hindu, New Thought, or occultic presuppositions? It would have been appropriate to announce that she is influenced by neo-pagan witchcraft rather than try to stay under the radar, occasionally invoking Jesus and biblical passages.

Rhonda Byrne is bright, probably quite articulate. It would seem unlikely that she could produce a DVD and book without knowing the streams of thought from which she was drawing. Why did she not "own" the sources? Why would she not admit to New Age teachings and pagan philosophy? Why not discuss, at least once, the fact that her opening words—"As above, so below. As within, so without"—are the primary source for occultism and witchcraft?

Could it be she does not want the unsuspecting reader to know? Does she simply want the reader to think *The Secret* is an innocent self-help book, a positive mental attitude book? Why were readers not forewarned? Byrne is the only one who can answer that question.

Chapter 14

A PASSIONATE APPEAL

Culture: Look What's Coming[1]

Lewis Mumford wrote in *The Transformations of Man*: "Every transformation of man, except perhaps that which produced the neolithic culture, has rested on a new metaphysical and ideological base; or rather, upon deeper stirrings and intuitions whose rationalized expressions take a form of the new picture of the cosmos and the nature of man."[2]

There was a time, not so long ago in America, when the so-called Law of Attraction and other notions wrapped up in *The Secret* would have been laughed off the stage. These ideas would have been relegated to urban tenements where "thinkers" stared at the ceiling all day and argued with passersby at night. Or they would have found root only in the outskirts of small towns, in utopian farms.

But they did take seed. Obscure journals gave way to larger publications. Rants in the town square morphed into lectures in major cities. Angry pamphlets found new life as college curricula. Some—obviously millions of people, now—would call this progress. But as we have shown in this book, the warmed-over philosophies and heresies masquerading now as the Law of

Attraction have been around for a long, long time. Where they have gained an audience, societies have either rejected them, ultimately, or died from their effects. Which will be America's choice?

For the Law of Attraction to take hold, and for entities like *The Secret* to be popular, there has to be a corresponding decline in tradition, in our cultural heritage, in the influence of Christianity, in trust and knowledge of the Lord, and in agreed-upon standards of values as a nation—the fabric of morals and ideals that used to hold us together. The so-called Law of Attraction, so ridiculous, so alien to our traditions, and so subversive, could *never* take root unless the ground had been disturbed—never.

THE RISE AND FALL?

If America is to climb onto the trash heap of history, how ironic that its foe would not be a conquering army or a deadly plague. Certainly other societies have fallen from within because they surrendered to greed and selfishness and loss of spiritual moorings. God forbid—if this is America's twilight—that a grab bag full of self-evident nonsense, dangerous as it might be, should be one of the final daggers.

Just as (according to the aphorism) history is written by the victors, so do the great movements of history gain ascendancy not so much by winning the hearts of a majority, but by winning what is now called the public-relations war. Only a third of the colonists supported separation from Great Britain, and military victories were hardly numerous or decisive, but General Washington prevailed partly because an air of inevitability overtook the revolutionary cause.

In the Roaring Twenties, artists like novelist F. Scott Fitzgerald and cartoonist John Held Jr. (who drew the famous flappers) basically deplored the Jazz Age, yet their vivid chronicles both left enduring impressions and created a feeling that the Establishment applauded the mores of the time.

The point: in cultural movements—the fads, fashions, and follies of society—the vast, impressionable middle of the public usually is swept along when outlooks and opinions change among the few "influentials." People go along, and don't always deeply process the things that seem to be persuading their neighbors and appearing on newsmagazine covers. Soon, history dictates and institutionalizes the ideas that prevail among the hustle and bustle of the marketplace of ideas.

This is not to say that ideas, even fringe theories, can automatically or even easily rise and take root in societies where they are totally foreign. There must be a predisposition in the culture.

THIS IS NOT A GAME

All of this means we must be particularly careful that New Age heresies are not treated with benign neglect. Christians—indeed, even secular traditionalists—should be alarmed at movements that question values and standards that have operated in our cultural traditions for countless generations. Speaking abstractly (not specifically of what *The Secret* represents), cultural skepticism in and of itself is not bad: the unfolding dispensational periods of history have been replete with correctives. But we must be aware of what we are doing, what implications follow the transformations we allow . . . or encourage. This is not a game.

These sorts of trends—the seemingly trivial inklings of

change, the minor details of life that carry clear implications, if we see them correctly—is what drew me (Rick) to the study of popular culture. This kind of study is also called low art versus high art. Its validity rests on the idea that, eventually, you can learn more about a society from, say, its fashion ads than its economic statistics; more from the nature of its grade-school textbooks than its military victories; more from its TV sitcoms than its Nobel Prize–winning poetry. Not that the pop culture is better or more refined; it's just more revealing than high art. It was not always so in world history, but it is a hallmark of American culture.

CATHEDRALS AND DYNAMOS

Henry Adams, a writer, diplomat, and descendent of two presidents, wrote two impressive books toward the end of his long life. Both were privately printed, meant for personal reflection and the eyes of close friends and relatives only, but they made their way into general distribution. They make points about the relation of popular attitudes to the general culture, and trends of history—especially how we "see ourselves" affects how we "become," and not just in historians' eyes. This model is not "cart before the horse"; it is the nature of organic societies.

In *Mont-Saint Michel and Chartres*, Adams built upon a late interest in architectural history when he studied those two magnificent thousand-year-old cathedrals in France and came away with profound observations about the era in general, and the nature of human interactivity. Interlacing the book's treatment of architecture and art, we learn about the arrangement of relative size of chapels in the cathedrals, and the symbolic theological importance. We learn that stained glass windows and sculpture taught lessons to the illiterate, as comics or slide shows might, even to the use of colors and "signs."

We learn that people in the vast areas surrounding cathedrals put service to God (assisting the construction of the churches in every way possible) before their professions and daily activities. Adams realized that the time around AD 1100 was the last time in Western culture that on-the-ground communities were truly organic, unified, and cohesive. Even the humblest peasant understood his life, his priorities, and his basic security—despite poverty and other ills—and was enormously comfortable about these things.

The average person of that time, illiterate, might have known more of, say, basic theology than many seminarians today. Of course error and superstition were mixed in, but Adams made the point that what cathedrals *taught* and *meant* played a role in dispelling the error and superstition: from the ground up. If Adams's book could be given a subtitle, it might be: *The Dark Ages Were Not Dark After All*. (What a contrast, by the way, to today, when in America, a "Christian nation," there is a cacophony of contradictory viewpoints and violent disagreements about basic values.)

Adams's other startling book fast-forwards our attention to the turn of the last century. *The Education of Henry Adams*, an autobiography written in the third person, presents the possibility (although he doesn't put it in these terms) that such cultural unity is returning. However, it is not a vision most of us would embrace. Adams was impressed by a World's Fair exhibition called the "Dynamo," basically a monster machine that displayed valves, pistons, and wheels. It steamed and tooted, rumbled and shook for the amazed spectators in the relatively early days of the Machine Age. The Dynamo, however, didn't do anything. It was basically industrial art: it said, "Here I am, the machine. I will do everything, consume everything, and produce everything."

Adams realized that this immodest claim was true, and, more, that the Dynamo was the latter-day Cathedral. Everyone in its sight would work for it, maintain it, and change standards according to its needs. *It*, and perhaps not even God, according to the cynical Adams, would become the basis of everyday life, choices, plans, and even values. We have gone from the Industrial Revolution to the Machine Age, to the Atomic Age, to the Computer Age, and Adams's prediction—horrible in its implications—has become clearer. (And how interesting that, if true, we could dust off that phrase *Dark Ages* again....)[3]

OUR OWN "CATHEDRALS" ARE CRUMBLING

The relation to our study, here, is obvious. There are cracks in our cultural foundations in America. And they should not be sought among statistics of, say, church attendance or the percentage of the population who believe that "under God" should be retained in the Pledge of Allegiance. No! The proof of a major shift—we would call it a coming disaster—in America's spiritual life is instead found in the curiosity about and acceptance of anti-Christian, anti-Western philosophies. It is felt in the virtual renunciation of traditional views about the relationship between man and God, man and man. It is seen in the popularity of, frankly, absurd products and appeals and programs that a less-sophisticated America once would have laughed out of town.

To track history and assess a culture through images,

symbols, and metaphors is not brand-new—it is the basis of intellectual history—but has a special urgency to those who care about America's spiritual health and cultural traditions, because images, symbols, and metaphors proliferate. They have assumed roles of greater importance in American life. Images: we have become a visual society, and the written word, with its rational discourse, is getting rusty. Symbols: a new science, semiotics— the study of signs and symbols—presents a useful road map to sorting out the revolution in communication of which we are yet dimly aware. Metaphor: we can seize upon certain phenomena— such as *The Secret* and what it represents—and realize something (beyond book and DVD sales) is being said about the state of our culture, our souls.

An American tsunami of New Age heresies started with tremors of bizarre fringe movements 150 years ago and currently buffets the shores of our culture, the most recent killer waves being *The Secret.* In between—now almost swept up by bigger waves—was the wave of secular humanism. It is still a factor, with its denial of moral absolutes, its deification of evolution, and its neo-Aristotelian relativism...but it is no longer the flavor of the day.

Thanks a little to Rhonda Byrne and *The Secret* and thanks a *lot* to the enablers like Oprah Winfrey, New Age subversives threaten the very core of Western society and American culture. Secular humanism questioned God's authority; Secret devotees and other New Agers are trying to destroy mankind's sense of uniqueness. We (Jim and Rick) run the risk of being called alarmists on this, but we have a firm conviction that this is a seri- ous matter—what *The Secret* might do to America—and that we *should* do no less, because we *can* do no less, than sound alarms.

DESTRUCTION IN ITS WAKE

The Secret is a fad, yes; but, folks, it is no Sudoko. It has come and it will go, but in the meantime, the way we can document, almost to the point of quantification, the sorry scams and loopy promises of the past, so too will *The Secret* hurt people and infect institutions while it rides high.

In the same way, the Law of Attraction clearly is a fad too. In the days of Galileo, Kepler, and Newton, scientists like them assumed, *a priori*, there was a God, He created the universe, in God's providence it could be better known, and to the extent it was understandable, one could have rational discussions on the subject.

The prescriptions of *The Secret* are not "self-help," no matter what the sign says on the bookstore shelf. These ideas are meant to confront and overturn society's foundations and God's laws, appealing to the masses by substituting for them laws of moneymaking. Maybe the secret of *The Secret* is that the golden calf was melted down and used for the printing plates of Rhonda Byrne's book.

When secular humanists (especially during the fever pitch of anticreationism) elevated science to the only valid religion, it was inevitable a next wave would engulf it: our inheritance from food faddists, communal farmers, free-love advocates, and wannabe dervishes is a fierce campaign, not to find a different way to God, or even find a way to a different God, but to advocate many ways to one, or one way to many gods.

The "oneness" and "unity" that New Worlders celebrate is actually a distant second to God's revealed plan of creation—a planned, glorious diversity of species, landscapes, and events.

The new *Secret*-holders sound just like the old sinners and rebels of ancient days, eschewing an awe-filled appreciation of God's mystery as expressed in Creation and His created beings, and instead focusing on conflicts between nations, or injustice among His children. They curse the darkness yet deny the source of light. They choose to live in the darkness, and when they declare nothing wrong, they assert, without realizing it, that they hold nothing right. We've moved from the Giver of Laws to the pusher of the Law of Attraction...and that's called "an advance in thought."

"As above, so below" is *not* a different way of saying, "Your will be done on earth, as it is in heaven." It is a classic slogan of the occult—used many times in many situations—and the speakers intend *no* reverence or honor to God. "As above, so below" to occultic New Agers means that God and humanity are one. Similar is the Hindu belief that "Atman is Brahman"—the individual is the universal; literally, the one is The One.

MY NEW AGE JOURNEY: A TALE OF THE LAW OF ATTRACTION

My father was an atheist. As far as I know, he never set foot in a church. The only time I remember hearing him mention Jesus was during an argument with my mother. He said: "You're right. I'm not perfect. There was only one man on this earth who was perfect and you know what they did to Him."

When I was seven or eight, I began to notice my paternal grandmother was different from others. "Grandma Mary" spoke about her chiropractor and her reflexologist; she was a strict vegetarian, and she never drank alcohol or smoked. All of this was very uncommon in the 1950s.

I was told that Grandma had her own "temple" in Las Vegas. When she visited us twice a year, she would stay in my room, and three times a day she would enter it, close the door, say "decrees" and meditate. I would stand outside the door, and sometimes I heard her say, "I call on the mighty I AM presence." When I inquired how she was calling someone from my room (we had one phone and it was in the kitchen), she told me it was the same as praying. She made me promise not to mention what she said to my father.

One day when I was about ten, Grandma sat me on the edge of the bed and told me her "secret." She told me that each year before coming to our house she went to downtown Chicago to visit her dear friend, Mrs. Ballard, whom she affectionately called "Mama Ballard." She told me the story of Saint Germain, Guy Ballard's meeting an eternal being while hiking on Mount Shasta, the Ascended Masters, and the Violet Flame, telling me that "everyone creates a vibration"...none of which I understood. She gave me a little book (to hide away), *Original Unveiled Mysteries* by Godfre Ray King. I learned she was a member of the "I AM" religion.

After all of this, it is easy to understand why I gravitated to New Age and not regard it as anything out of the ordinary. I spent eighteen years in the movement, and there were a few times I was truly afraid: once, in a session where my father was "channeled," and another with a psychic who predicted events with frightening accuracy. There were many times that evil spirits would show up at "table-tipping sessions," but they were commanded to leave by the leader.

In 1980 I was at one of the lowest points of my life when my roommate invited me to church. On the first Sunday I was drawn to the positive atmosphere. Everyone sang "Reach out and Touch" while they shook hands and hugged each other. I could hardly believe this was church. But it was Terry Cole Whittaker's "church," home of a weekly TV show. Terri's message was always uplifting and I applauded her along with eight thousand other followers. My life turned around.

I remained a faithful follower at Terry's Prosperity Church, as it was called, until she left five years later. I took Ernest Holmes' Science of Mind classes and began saying "affirmations," writing my goals, and changing my way of speaking and thinking. What could be wrong with being a more positive person?

In one of the early classes we had to make eye contact and repeat the following sentence to a fellow classmate over and over until told to stop: "I can have what I want," and the classmate enthusiastically answered back, "Yes, you can!" It worked. I made the journey from disability to diamonds in two years. I attributed this all to the Science of Mind and other teachings.

At Christmas I "manifested" a diamond watch, a diamond ring, and a new car (with the help of my fiancé). It was the best Christmas of my life. Our relationship and his chain of restaurants, now very prominent in Southern California, flourished.

I was focused on being positive: I listened to positive messages on success and had short- and long-term goals written out for my business, my relationships, my health, and my spiritual life. I taped affirmations all over my house. I attended numerous seminars by Shirley MacLaine, Deepak Chopra, Wayne Dyer, Louise Hay, Dannon Brinkley, Dr. Gabriel Cousens, Tony Robbins, and Marianne Williamson (A Course in Miracles; I learned that "we're all Enlightened Masters").

Throughout the years I was addicted to seeking the "higher" spiritual experience. I looked for it in channeling, automatic writing, Sufi dancing, rebirthing, raw food, fasting, chakra balancing, crystals, Rolfing, Whole Being Weekends, sweat lodges, transcendental meditation, chanting, visualization, out-of-body experiences, contact with my "Inner Christ," table-tipping, invoking spirits, spiritual mind treatments, personal spirit guides, and more.

Next I began attending Wendy Craig-Purcell's Church of Today (she is one of the twelve members of the Association for Global New Thought, with Michael Beckwith of *The Secret*). This is a Unity Church. There is no belief in original sin. Sin is separation from God, the Good, in consciousness. Heaven and hell are states of consciousness, not geographical locations. They believe we make our own heaven or hell here and now and create our life experiences by our own thoughts, words, and deeds.

This seemed odd the first time I heard it: I didn't know you could pick and choose what parts of the Bible you believed in. Sunday services emphasized that all sacred Scriptures, when understood mystically and metaphysically, reveal the path to spiritual maturity and enlightenment. Jesus was quoted along with Buddha, Lao Tzu, the Dalai Lama, and other "enlightened masters."

I can tell you honestly, now that I am on the other side, I was living in a world of denial. I did not understand the profound influence of New Age in my life. I was told that what I saw in the world was an illusion. I did not think anything I did was wrong, because there was no sin. I was not accountable to anyone for anything. I was not living by any morals. I did not believe in Satan or a devil. (I had no idea how he worked in the world.) I liked the idea that "All is God and God is all." That meant everything in the world was good. There was no evil, only what I perceived as evil. I was surrounded by other affluent, well educated baby boomers…they couldn't all be wrong, could they?

Looking back now as a Christian, I see just how dangerous these beliefs are.

When the serpent spoke to Eve in Genesis 3, he told her four lies that are common New Age beliefs: You will not die (you will rein-carnate). You will be like God (belief in the deity of man). You will know good and evil (you will be enlightened, there is no difference between right and wrong). Your eyes will be opened (you will have spiritual powers).

Most people are naïve about the demonic influences of the New Age movement. It seeks to change our thinking. *The Secret* suggests we must raise our consciousness to a higher vibrational level through mind-altering techniques. The New Age idea that man is equal to God is a very old lie.

How could I ever have believed that man is God? It is not scriptural. This is America's brand of Hinduism. It destroys the deity of God. It took me eighteen years to find my way out and close to a year of studying the Bible daily and attending a Bible-believing church to learn the truth about how deceived I was during those years.

I am eternally grateful to the Lord, who helped me out of the occult. I pray that anyone reading this would believe my words and find strength in them to avoid the occult and New Age movement.

—Christine Demery

Christine Demery is a businesswoman and mother living in Southern California.

THANK GOD WE'RE *NOT* GOD!

We humans are not God, any of us. If *I* (Rick) were God, I wouldn't blame people for becoming atheists. Saint Peter saw the truth clearly: "Salvation is found in no one else [than Jesus], for there is no other name under heaven given to men by which we must be saved" (Acts 4:12). That "system," established by God

Almighty before time, doesn't denigrate humankind: rather we should feel grateful to be the special objects of His special love.

C. S. Lewis (as usual) brilliantly summarized these points:

> Pantheism is congenial to our minds not because it is the final stage in a slow process of enlightenment, but because it is almost as old as we are. It may even be the most primitive of all religions.... It is immemorial in India. The Greeks rose above it only at their peak, in the thought of Plato and Aristotle; their successors relapsed into the great Pantheistic system of the Stoics. Modern Europe escaped it only while she remained predominantly Christian; with Giordano Bruno and Spinoza it returned. With Hegel it became almost the agreed philosophy of highly educated people, while the more popular pantheism of Wordsworth, Carlyle and Emerson conveyed the same doctrine to those on a slightly lower cultural level. So, far from being the final religious refinement, pantheism is in fact the permanent natural bent of the human mind; the permanent ordinary level below which man sometimes sinks, but above which his own unaided efforts can never raise him for very long. Platonism and Judaism, and Christianity (which has incorporated both) have proved the only things capable of resisting it. It is the attitude into which the human mind automatically falls when left to itself. No wonder we find it congenial. If "religion" means simply what man says about God, and not what God does about man, then pantheism almost *is* religion. And religion in that sense has, in the long run, only one really formidable opponent—namely, Christianity.
>
> ...The old atomic theory is in physics what pantheism is in religion—the normal, instinctive guess of the

human mind, not utterly wrong, but needing correction. Christian theology and quantum physics are both, by comparison with the first guess, hard, complex, dry and repellant....

People compare an adult knowledge of pantheism with a knowledge of Christianity which they acquired in their childhood. They thus get the impression that Christianity gives the "obvious" account of God, the one that is too easy to be true, while pantheism offers something sublime and mysterious. In reality, it is the other way around.[4]

One in nature...One *is* nature...we are all One...pantheism is one of the foundation stones of all heresies, as old as—and, actually, a variation of—the age-old sin of pride. That too is about "one," and when the One is anybody but God, the wellsprings of our souls are poisoned. Remember the serpent said, "Ye shall be as gods" (Gen. 3:5 KJV). Augustine of Hippo in North Africa wrote sixteen hundred years ago: "This, then, is the original evil: man regards himself as his own light."[5] Have you noticed, in reading these words, that—roughly in proportion to dangerous ideas and disintegrating cultures—how little, these days, we hear the words "sin" and "evil"? Have New Agers wished them out of existence, or have the rest of us been persuaded to ignore the concepts?

Earlier we identified the worst elements in *The Secret*'s worldview (according to the morality plays in anecdotes and skits on its DVD) not as sin or evil, but inconvenience, embarrassment, and annoyance. In this chapter we can see that New Agers and Law of Attraction advocates would add *ignorance* to that list of nasties. They carry an assumption that humankind—or at least they—

can think its way to truth; wish, with enlightened thoughts, reality to flip; and probably that, if there is a God, someone will come along who is smarter than God and straighten out all the ills of humanity.

The obsession with the One, whether discussed in Athenian amphitheaters three thousand years ago or systematized in DVDs portraying Secretive thought police, is not so much a journey toward the One, the Universal, is it? Most of it would call it egomania. Philosophers would call it solipsism (belief in self as the only reality). Psychiatrists would call it narcissism, after the Greek god who could not take his eyes off his own reflection in the pond. The Bible calls it the sin of pride. And we have (in these pages) called it Selfism. It's a real word, alive and well in *The Oxford English Dictionary*, and maybe it should be used more to call out a cancer in our culture, in our collective selves.

THE SECRET: SOMETHING OLD, SOMETHING NEW, SOMETHING BORROWED...

Contrary to the tsunami of promotion, the message of *The Secret* is not new but as old as the demonic false promises to mankind in the Garden of Eden.

Although I am not quite *that* old, I had the opportunity for the first quarter of my life to grow up in the arcane world of Broadway and Hollywood stars whom I loved dearly, but who had bought into the solipsistic metaphysics that you only had to deny mortal mind and think good thoughts to live in utopian bounty. My wonderful father, Bob "Tex" Allen, was a cowboy star who won the Box Office Award in

1936 and then went to star on Broadway, and my beautiful mother, Evelyn Peirce, was an MGM star. In the world's terms, they were good people, but they had not heard the truth of the Bible and were seeking after "the secrets of the universe" expounded by the false prophets of their age.

Once upon a time when I was on *The Oprah Winfrey Show*, she brought onto the program the man she called her guru, Eric Butterworth, senior minister of the occultist Unity Center of New York City, who explained to the audience that each person is God. I had attended Unity Center with my father and grew up in this "We are all God" community. My parents had immersed themselves in studying the musings of Edgar Cayce, Mary Baker Eddy, Madame Blavatsky, Georges Ivanovich Gurdjieff, and all the others who espouse that we could think and be rich. My father's bookshelves were crowded with "the secret of all ages" books, many of which I read before going off to studies at Dartmouth, Cambridge, and the NYU School of Law.

As the years passed, I noted how much work it was to play God, especially after my mother, who had grown up in Christian Science, died of a massive heart attack when I was fourteen. I later produced a series of television programs on psychic phenomena, hosted by Patrick O'Neill. This gave me many hours to talk with people like J. Krishnamurti, Andrija Puharich, and Sri Chinmoy. They all tried hard to build their reputations as humble, kind, Christ-like deities who could levitate, heal the sick, and read minds, and oh, not to mention, bend spoons. Behind the scenes, however, they disliked each other immensely and exhibited the fallen character of the lost.

Finally, in 1974, the sweet mother of a friend asked me to read the Bible and tell her what was wrong with it. When I read the New Testament in its entirety, I was confronted with the Good News—that we don't have to play God (a heartbreaking and delusional task), that

Jesus is God, and that, by accepting His free gift of salvation, we can live in His kingdom, which offers much better benefits than the occult kingdom of "the secret of all ages."

The first day after accepting Jesus as my Lord and Savior, I saw that the world was more coherent and fulfilled many of the promises that the "name it and claim it" prophets falsely proclaim. Letting go and letting God be God by accepting Jesus as your Lord and Savior is the most wonderful secret of all time.

The people I met in the occult community never loved anyone except themselves, and they seldom engaged in forgiveness. The churches I started to attend after accepting the free gift of salvation in Jesus Christ were marked by extraordinary people who showed compassion, love, forgiveness…as well as the flaws of those who are being remade and perfected by the power of the Holy Spirit.

Today the occultists seem to have gotten the upper hand in the media, but they are not any happier than they were forty years ago. Ruled by and infatuated by self, they suffer the ultimate impoverishment. Their philosophy and metaphysics are deeply flawed. It is easy to poke holes in their logic, but they are not about logic. They are about offering people the vainglorious and damning opportunity to be demigods and get everything that their eyes and heart lust for.

Most people will quickly realize that these promises are empty. Some will continue a lifetime trapped in the blindness of their sad solipsism. Those of us who have crossed over in the kingdom only by the grace of Jesus Christ have great compassion for those trapped in the dark corridors of *The Secret*.

If we love our children, we tell them to brush their teeth, do their homework, and go to bed, etc. If we do not love them, we let them eat all the candy they want, stay up late, carouse, and stew in the juices of their own self-will. Love is proactive. Loving our neighbors means exposing the lies of *The Secret* and telling them the truth of Jesus Christ and His gospel.

—Dr. Ted Baehr

Dr. Baehr is the founder and publisher of Movieguide and chairman of the Christian Film and Television Commission, as well as a noted critic, educator, lecturer, and media pundit. His organization hosts the annual Faith and Value Awards in Media, including the Templeton Foundation Kairos and Epiphany awards. *Movieguide* is a superb reference about current productions, providing synopses, critical summaries, and content information. Here, as an example, is *Movieguide*'s short summary of *The Secret* DVD:

Summary: THE SECRET is a tag team lecture on how to get everything you want by focusing your mind on gratitude, good emotions and visualization. The program directly opposes belief in God while preaching some principles that God ordained. It is a dangerous counterfeit to the truth that sets men free.

In Brief: THE SECRET is a video lecture about "the Law of Attraction." The "Law of Attraction" is a godless, pagan idea that you attract from the universe what you think about in your mind. Thus, if you think positively about getting a nice home, you will get a nice home. Conversely, if you worry about getting cancer you'll get cancer. Your thoughts align the universe in your favor or to your detriment. The program includes wealth and healing testimonies, quotes from famous people in history and short sketches acted out about how to think positively and what happens if you don't.

THE SECRET directly opposes belief in God. The lecturers make a case that will look very attractive to a lot of people. Many will see it as enlightening and life-changing. The danger is that dabbling in metaphysics while denying the existence of God is like playing with fire. If you find someone who loves the program, you should guide them to the real truth that sets men free. Eternal peace, joy and love come from a right relationship to God through Jesus Christ, not happy thought techniques or a mindless personal genie.

(Taken from MovieGuide Web site May 1, 2007 http://www.movieguide.org/index.php?s=reviews&id=7403.)   ∞

THE RISE OF SELFISM

New Agers use science as a prop in their shows, and pseudoscientific terms become sticks with which to beat the uninitiated about their heads. Under this system, groups of "experts" (like *The Secret*'s team, whose expert credentials consist mainly of "speaking," "consulting," "conducting seminars," and of course feng shui management) are dazzled by a set of curious ideas; from these ideas are extrapolated theories of life, existence, creation, divinity, eternity; and a cosmology, or religion, or marketing empire, is established...until the next set of curiosities comes along. It might be a logical (or illogical) extension, or a radical detour, but it *will* come along.

These detours have been given a name: *paradigm shifts*. The man who coined the phrase has observed that new scientific theories, even momentous ones, often are less the result of logic and empirical tests, and more the influence of the proponents' social and psychological biases and other agendas. Fritjof Capra, an eloquent and passionate salesman of New Age science, admitted in chapter 3 of his book *The Turning Point*: "My presentation of modern physics in this chapter has been influenced by my personal beliefs and allegiances. I have emphasized certain concepts and theories that are not yet accepted by the majority of physicists, but that I consider significant philosophically, of great importance for the other sciences and for our culture as a whole."[6]

New Age Science as science ultimately has a contextual problem. It is not oversimplification (any more than the intentional oversimplification of the Lawyers of Attraction) to note that quantum physics is basically still physics; and, for all the revolutionary vistas they imagine, they are forever mirages. Physics deals with the physical world. Writing "Physical = Spiritual" on blackboards does not validate the equation. They look to each other for someone to nod yes about mystical properties of matter; meanwhile there is spiritual truth—including the role of God as master of matter *and* truth, for He is the Creator. In their efforts to recast Einstein's work as a precursor to *The Secret*, New Age thinkers seem to have confused relativity with relativism.

It is not an *ad hominem* attack to observe this tendency in apologists for *The Secret*. They willingly surrender valuable tools themselves in their alleged search for truth. By denying the existence, evidence, and revelation of God, the New Age scientist dooms any satisfactory arrival at truth. For proof we have only to return to one of the original bases of criticism of *The Secret*'s worldview, pragmatism. The team whose photos adorn *The Secret*, and other Law of Attraction advocates, have fashioned a distinctively American materialistic, I-can-have-it-all mentality. Theologian Harvey Cox has referred to "Enlightenment by

Ticketron." The larger point is the American component of quasi-Eastern mystical "enlightenment" practices sends the vaunted asceticism—poverty, humility, self-denial—into the Dumpster. Hedonism is its replacement.

One of the problems in confronting the flesh-and-blood spokesmen for *The Secret*'s ideas is that those ideas often are amorphous and, well, squishy. Countering some of their arguments is like trying to nail jelly to the wall. We have, in this book, approached *The Secret* on its own terms. The appeals it makes often seem to be characterized by cynicism and cruelty to its readers, appealing to fears, greed, and self. We have analyzed the antecedents of the Law of Attraction and have realized that one thing that invites extra scrutiny of our arguments is the glib repackaging Rhonda Byrne has achieved. For instance, except for avatars and several mentions of Buddha, all the trappings and terminology of Eastern mysticism have been scrubbed clean. Concepts of the Universal One, God in Us, etc., have been trotted out as American as Norman Rockwell paintings.

Once again, the idea that "marketing is king" to these movements is not an attack but an observation, something frankly admitted with pride by many New Agers. Mark Anthony Lord, of the Center for Spiritual Living in Chicago, was quoted in *USA Today*: "America was built on having a wonderful life, on being all that you can be," he says. "If you generate a feeling of self that's capable and worthy, you'll attract what you want. I don't care if you use it to get a car." The article continued:

> Attendance is up at his center since *The Secret* caught
> fire, which pleases Michelle Schrag, who attends each

Sunday with her stockbroker husband and three children. Though raised Catholic, Schrag says the center's "emphasis on meditation, which I now do each day, has helped me find happiness in my daily life."

Schrag is typical of a growing breed of American who declares, "I'm spiritual, but not religious," says Catherine Albanese, who heads religious studies at the University of California-Santa Barbara and is author of *A Republic of Mind and Spirit: A Cultural History of American Metaphysical Religion.* "I have to laugh at all the hype around *The Secret*, because for some folks, it's really just religion as usual since the 19th century. Passing on a message of how to get what you wanted from life was a business then, and it's a business now," Albanese says.[7]

BUSINESS AS USUAL

The business angle—the pragmatic, materialistic, want-versus-need aspect of *The Secret*—should be seen as using thoughts as a means to "will" something, whereas in traditional Christianity, prayer is viewed as a way to open oneself to *God's will*. It is here where Christians bump heads, traditionalists versus some in the "name it and claim it," "prosperity gospel," and the "Word of Faith" camps. Those on the extremes of these movements, if divorced from fundamentals like God's sovereignty, can easily become Sunday-morning cousins of the Law of Attraction. "Thou shalt . . ." without ritualistic visualization and such.

Whether Christian presumption or taking God at His Word, leaders of those movements within the church cite biblical sources, however, and not Eastern mystics, rural eccentrics, or infomercial marketers. Once again—for those tempted to grant *The Secret* program a pass because of, say, "good intentions"—people need to remember Christianity points to God, and the New Age points to self. A nice boost to self-esteem, perhaps, but to paraphrase an old saying, "There are no New Agers in a fox-hole when the bombs are going off," you can be sure.

Do boosts to self-esteem work? Of course! Avoid stress? How can that be bad? The motivational-seminar industry attests to the desires but also the occasional efficacy of pep talks. Every year, before our eyes, we see a Vince Lombardi or Marty Schottenheimer fire up a team. Politicians from Ronald Reagan to Bill Clinton have inspired true believers to go the extra mile.

But the lines are being blurred. *The Secret* is already being used in motivational seminars—in otherwise respectable fields like real estate and insurance. I (Rick) was telling an acquaintance about my task for this book, assuming she would share my disdain...and learned that she is a sales rep for a health-and-beauty aids catalog that preaches similar "visualization," even urging workers to pose in front of a Mercedes that could be theirs someday.

So there is a fine line between motivation and greed, faith and presumption, needing and wanting. Fortunately, Rhonda Byrne makes the task a little easier by aggressively ignoring Christianity, denying God. Addressing human nature but pretending evil and sin don't exist require not just a leap of faith but a self-destructive streak that somehow cannot fit on her list of selfist requirements.

Chapter 15

BEYOND *THE SECRET*

Mystery: Visit Mars Hill

The year is AD 51. The city of Athens was not what it once had been. Its glory was beginning to pass. Much of Greek culture was thoroughly plundered by the Romans. In fact, Athens itself had been successfully attacked by Sulla in 86 BC.

A brilliant thinker, communicator, and debater by the name of Paul arrived. He went to a limestone hill located between the Acropolis and the Agora. The small outcropping is known as the *Areopagus*, which means "the hill of Ares," named for the Greek god of war. In Roman mythology Mars was the god of war. Thus the hill was also referred to as Areopagus, or Mars Hill.

Upon arriving, Paul observed that "the city was given over to idols" (Acts 17:16). In fact, it was said there were more gods than men in Athens. Paul saw it as a perfect opportunity to open a dialogue with those who worshiped multiple gods. In the marketplace he daily engaged people in discussion (Acts 17:17).

If you embraced Rhonda Byrne's *The Secret*, we congratulate you for reading this book *The Secret Revealed*. Authors and readers "journey" together, and at this point in our journey, we are now at our own Mars Hill.

It was at this famous location Paul observed an unusual phenomenon. In addition to the many monuments erected to honor various gods, a rather peculiar monument bore the inscription, "TO THE UNKNOWN GOD" (Acts 17:23). The people of Athens apparently did not want to ignore any gods in their worship. Paul seized the moment and began to share that this "unknown god" could actually, in fact, be known.

That is why we would like to meet you here and now at this figurative place in this book, which we are calling Mars Hill.

TO THE UNKNOWN GOD

Ms. Byrne's "unknown god" is known in *The Secret* as "One Universal Mind." In fact, *The Secret* claims, "The One Mind is all intelligence, all wisdom, and all perfection, and is everything, in everywhere at the same time. If everything is the One Universal Mind and the whole of it exists everywhere, then it is all in you!" (pp. 160–161). The concept that everything is God and God is everything is pantheism. (Remember, *pan* equals all; *theo* represents God.) God, in other words, is merely the accumulative total of everything that is.

A less-personal understanding of deity is expressed in Byrne's claim that "the Universe is a mirror," which "is mirroring back to you your dominant thoughts" (p. 49). As if being simply "One Mind" had not sufficiently depersonalized any concept of a divine being, now we have reduced it to a mere reflection of a piece of glass—a mirror. God has become, by this definition, nothing more than a robotic thought-bounce machine.

Rather than portraying humanity as responding and reacting to a personalized God, all ideas are somehow tucked away in "the Universal Mind," which is "waiting for the human mind to draw them forth" (p. 161). Now the Universal Mind has become a bank of ideas from which withdrawals are to be mechanistically made.

Inspiring

The "Universe" not only has a collection of ideas for you to draw out but it is "inspiring" (p. 56). *Inspire* (from the Latin) means "to breathe into." Ms. Byrne is saying the universe breathes into us.

As you know, an impersonal universe does not breathe. Entities that breathe have life. In fact, the existence of breath indicates life. A very ancient and historically trustworthy document states God breathed into humankind life (Gen. 2:7). Humankind—Adam and Eve—were in a two-part creation and initially formed from the dust of the earth. Dust is the source of our material being. To dust we will return after we die.

Although humanity was "formed" by dust, we were not "created" from dust. Humankind was formed from dust but created when God breathed into us. When God breathed into us He created eternal beings. This is much more than merely "forming" us from dirt.

He did not merely blow air into nostrils. God doesn't need air nor does He have nostrils. God is a spirit. He breathed us with a living, eternal type of breath. In other words, He inspired us. When people *expire,* they die. When people are *inspired* they are breathed into. God breathed His eternal nature into us. This impersonal "Universal" about which Ms. Byrne speaks has a name and that name is God, or we could also refer to Him as Father. Welcome to Mars Hill. The Byrnian "unknown god" *can* be known.

Provider

In a previous chapter we discussed *The Secret*'s perception of a "Universe" that provided things for you. *The Secret* claims that the "Universe" brings things to you (p. 51) if you will get "in harmony with the Universal Supply" (p. 163). *The Secret* states an "invisible field" will "supply" things to you, "whether you call it the Universe, the Supreme Mind, *God*, Infinite Intelligence, or whatever else" (p. 163, italics added).

For a split second *The Secret* gets it right. The great supplier of all that is needed in life is God and, for a fleeting moment, it appears Rhonda Byrne could acknowledge that. This is as close as she can come to an admission that there is a *personal* understanding of such impersonal terms as the "Universe." That name is God and this God is personal. He has a personality. In addition, God has intelligence.

In debates between evolutionists and those advocating Intelligent Design, the issue is whether or not there is a Knowing One behind creation, or if it came into being randomly. Byrne uses the term "Universal Intelligence" (p. 163). Could she be suggesting a deist approach to the cosmos? Deism states that God created all that is, but is not involved in it. Theism believes God created all that is and is providentially involved in it, in an ongoing manner. Based on the whole of Bryne's book, it is doubtful she is referring to an entity with personality and intelligence. Surely even those who embrace *The Secret* most vigorously understand there is no lamp of Aladdin and there is no genie, despite Rhonda Byrne's repeated references to them.

However, you do not have to embrace the same emptiness. There is good news for *The Secret* admirers: you do not have to be left with an aloft, distant, cold "force." There is a warm, caring God. The "unknown god" has become known.

Traditions

"Traditions have called *it* so many things," says Byrne. "But every tradition has told us there is something bigger than us" (p. 46). Traditions might have called "it" many things, but one tradition, with its feet in antiquity, prefers to call "it" Him, who is God.

A PERSONAL NOTE

If I (Jim) could talk with Rhonda Byrne herself (and we *did* attempt to contact her as we prepared this book), I would want to help her understand the powerful statement she made when she declared "I *knew* with every fiber of my being that the Universe would provide, and it did" (p. 100). Rhonda, my friend, the universe is not an "it." It is a personal God. And you are correct, He does provide and I'm glad He provided for you—even if you chose to call Him "it." I have good news, Rhonda! The "unknown god" can now finally be known. Welcome, Rhonda, to Mars Hill.

FROM SECRET TO MYSTERY: ANOTHER VERY PERSONAL MESSAGE

One of the many reasons we distrusted *The Secret*'s approach from the start is that it seems to say that we are all gods, or all God; that we can have everything and know everything. This is a microcosm of the American culture today—we are nurtured in the belief that we can experience and own everything. We can have fame for fifteen minutes and riches next week. If test scores are low, we adjust the definition of "passing grades." We acquire, we throw away. If we can't know everything, we declare it not worth knowing.

The Law of Attraction resonates now because it feeds off and feeds into that worldview. If a book says it, maybe it's true; if Oprah endorses it, it has to be true!

But it does not mean that we are any less self-confident to simply admit we are a confused, hurting, vulnerable, needy people. *Secret*-types would say, "This is the time in history when you should break loose from your idea of God!" And we would reply, "This is a time in history when we need God more than ever."

We promised you Mystery. We could have brought out real names, giving real anecdotes about God, in the style of *The Secret*, but our interest was less to show off other people's hearts than to help change yours.

In recent years, I (Rick) have visited a few old monasteries and one old abbey, churches that open themselves up to visitors. These retreats have refreshed me and reacquainted my soul with something that has been deep-down for a long time. These environments are not at all familiar to my background, and I am wary of "meditation" because of the occult connections with some meditation. But the Bible tells us in many places to meditate upon the Word.

Such spiritual oases are rare in this busy, contemporary, world! No church services with forced smiles and loud rock bands. No loud auditoriums. No TVs and cell phones. No street noise.

At the abbey I spent a week where I agreed to keep silent. I read, prayed, thought, sketched, and sometimes, crashed. But mostly I prayed and thought. Can this be bad for any of us? If you're expecting me to say that I came away any of the times knowing God better, I'll let you in on a secret: I didn't. Honest. But here are a couple of secrets I'm happy to tell: that fact bothered me less each time! Also, if I didn't *know* Him better, I *understood* Him more! And certainly, I *loved* Him more and more and more! How is that possible? It's a mystery.

Alone with Him and honest about my thoughts, I have been overwhelmed by the mystery of God who created the universe…and still loves me with an indescribable passion.

- It is a mystery to think that such an imperfect, ungrateful, goof-prone sinner like me could break God's heart, yet He devised a plan that bypassed my inability to approach His holiness: His perfect Son took all my sins upon Himself. Mystery.
- It is a mystery that I can "see" Christ in others when they forgive me of something; that I can experience Christ in myself when I squeeze selfishness out of myself for a little while and serve someone who hurts. A miracle and a mystery.
- It is a mystery that my tears are splashing on the keypad as I write these words. Why? My heart cries out for those people who lust after cash and comfort alone and insult the ideals of service and sacrifice. For those people who think the greatest journey to peace and eternity is through ourselves. *Us?*

I plead with you to put aside the temptation (as old as the human heartbeat) to think yourself on a level with God, or, in fact, some oneness of the universe. It's self-swindling foolishness, doomed to bitter ends. We can't be everything, can't know everything.

The *mystery* I found—feeling closer to God the less I could fathom Him—can bathe you in a peace that passes understanding. "Just accept Me," He says. The beautiful mystery, not a secret, of a life in Christ is that we draw closer to God, yes, but we also *come to realize* that the Creator of the universe wants to know each and every one of us just as deeply as we try to know Him.   ∞∞∞

Protector

This providing God also protects us. *The Secret* claims you should "set the Universal forces ahead of you in everything you do and everywhere you go, by thinking the way you want it to go *in advance*" (p. 57). Once again I have great news for those who have embraced *The Secret*. Rather than try to think your protection into existence, invoking some impersonal force, you can rely on a tender, protective Father to care for you. An ancient writer said it straightforwardly: "The LORD himself goes before you and will be with you; he will never leave you nor forsake you. Do not be afraid; do not be discouraged" (Deut. 31:8).

Think of the best father you have ever met on Earth, whether it be your dad or somebody else's dad. Think of that nearly perfect father. Even that father—no matter how good he was or is—is not as good as your heavenly Father. He not only provides for you but He is your protector and He goes before you. Wonderful news for embracers of *The Secret*!

Creative Force or Creator

And what about Rhonda Byrne's "creative force which is working through you" (p. 50)? Once again that which is unknown can become known. Another ancient writer admonished even teenagers to "remember your Creator in the days of your youth" (Eccl. 12:1). And why should you remember your Creator when you are a youth? The sage stated there are "days of trouble" coming and time will come when you will say, "I find no pleasure in them"—in living (Eccl. 12:1). If you have a firm understanding of your Creator even when you are young, it will aid you in giving meaning and purpose in later years when you are more physically, mentally, and emotionally challenged. He is not merely a creative force. He is a Creator and you are part of His loving creation—that which He cares so much about.

Relationship

How encouraging it must be to one who desperately tries to make *The Secret* work long-term. At some point you will become weary with attempting experience "alignment with the Universe" (p. 62). We have written about moving from "alignment with the Universe" to conformity with God. The next step is from conformity with God to an authentic relationship with God. A Creator who made you a part of His creation did not create you so you would emit thoughts that would return to you in material form. He designed you to have a relationship with Him. That is why He made you. In the ancient writings it states that God made you in His image (Gen. 1:26–27). He gave you the capacity for relationships, specifically a relationship with Him.

Male and Female

But God recognized that this enriched relationship between Him and the human was still lacking something. After each day of the creation process, God responded, "It is good." However, on one occasion He gave a different report. One day He said, "It is not good" (Gen. 2:18). What was not good? It was not good for a human to be alone. Thus, He made another human.

He formed male and female. He formed the greatest bond the earth has ever known, that of marriage—between a male and a female. Exactly how the creation process occurred is not known to us, but what appears to have occurred is that God created the human form "in the image of God," meaning a reflection of God's nature and personality. From that human form (called *Adam*, which means "humankind"), God extracted feminine qualities and formed a female. What remained was distinctly male.

Thus male and female fit together—emotionally, spiritually, physically, and psychologically. In fact, one of the major reasons for the strength of sexual attraction is that male and female were created from one, thus designed to come back together *as a full expression of who God is—that is, the image of God.* A male by himself is not a full expression of God. A female by herself is not a full expression of God.

El Shaddai

In Exodus 6:3, God is referred to by the Hebrew name *El-Shaddai*. *El* means "strong" or "mighty." The root of *shaddai* is not as clear but it appears to mean "breast" or "that which nourishes one," as a newborn is nourished at the breast of his or her mother. In other words, God is *El-Shaddai*, reflecting both the strength that is traditionally associated with masculinity, along with the tenderness that is traditionally associated with femininity. God is neither male nor female. God represents the best of both.

It bears repetition: the reason sexual attraction is so strong between male and female is not merely lust, but a God-designed desire for completeness or oneness for man and woman to come together, thus reflect the image of God—His characteristics.

When man and woman come together in the act of sex they are, in that moment, the fullest expression of God—the full spectrum of God's nature, which include both masculinity and femininity. However, that fullest expression is true only if they are within the monogamous covenant relationship of marriage itself. That is why surveys indicate that martial sexual expression is so much more satisfying and fulfilling than extramarital sexual expression. This is so because God designed the creation to be close to Him as Creator. Within the creation He made male and female with the most unusual capacity for relationship; physical, mental, sexual, psychological.

Why, in response to *The Secret,* are we discussing sexuality? Simply as a way of expressing that God designed us with the desire for holy, pure relationships with each other and with Him. Marriage is a physical picture of the spiritual potential for oneness that God desires to enjoy with us. It must be very encouraging for Rhonda Byrne's readers to discover that the "unknown god" can be known through a relationship—a relationship with Him.

USE OF THE BIBLE

As a reminder of what was noted in a previous chapter, one reason we feel comfortable in using biblical illustrations is because Rhonda Byrne uses them. *The Secret* originally invoked the use of Scripture to speak about the creative process (p. 47). She used—or rather misused—the Bible.

Let it not be lost on the reader that she comes painstakingly close to equating her book to the way the Bible frequently is used. Repeatedly through the centuries Christians have regarded the Bible as so powerful they would open it randomly and begin reading somewhere to find help and guidance. Invoking that same imagery, Byrne claims, "If you are seeking an answer or guidance on something in your life, ask the question, believe you will receive it, and then open this book randomly. At the exact place where the pages fall open will be the guidance and answer you are seeking" (p. 172). Whether intentional or not, *The Secret* is being compared to the Bible for its universal utility.

As a historian, I (Jim) will cautiously venture into the prophetic realm. Ten years from now, Rhonda Byrne's book will be forgotten. The Bible will still be as popular as ever. One hundred years from now, *The Secret* will be a mere footnote in some history book. The Bible, as it has for the last seventeen hundred years, will be flourishing. The Bible, not *The Secret*, is the book to which you can go—even if opened randomly—and it can supply guidance and the answers you seek.

Motive

I (Jim) have never met Rhonda Byrne. I cannot possibly know her motives, but I believe her when she says she really desires to "share the knowledge with the world" in hopes it would "bring joy to the world" (p. 80). The motives may be, as stated earlier, honorable. I applaud her attempt. She clearly is bright and highly creative. I respect her ability. But the best she offers is a disappointing "force," some impersonal, mechanistic worldview.

Great news, reader! The man writing almost two thousand years ago, who was one of the closest friends of Jesus, stated it this way: "These things are written that you may...have life" (John 20:31). How are we supposed to have life? Or as Rhonda Byrne would say, "abundance"? Jesus stated, "I am come that they may have life, and that they might have it more abundantly" (John 10:10 KJV).

Joy

Rhonda Byrne has stated: ask, believe, and receive whatever you want and this will surely bring joy to the world. The most profound figure of human history, Jesus, stated it this way: "Until now you have not asked for anything in my name. Ask and you will receive, and your joy will be complete" (John 16:24). In other words, your joy can be complete, if you ask in His name. Ask according to *His* will rather than your want.

"The Secret" or "The Mystery"?

In AD 60, only nine years after Paul visited Mars Hill, he wrote a letter to a group of people living in the city of Colossae, located in Asia Minor, about one hundred miles east of the better known, seaport city of Ephesus. As he wrote Colossians 2:4, Paul was concerned they were being scammed. Note how his concern reads from different translations:

- I tell you this so that no one may deceive you by fine-sounding arguments. (NIV)
- Now this I say lest anyone should deceive you with persuasive words. (NKJV)
- I say this so that no one will delude you with persuasive argument. (NASB)
- And this I say, lest any man should beguile you with enticing words. (KJV)
- I say this in order that no one may delude you with beguiling speech. (RSV)

- This I say, that no one may delude you with persuasiveness of speech. (ASV)
- I am saying this because I am afraid that someone may fool you with smooth talk. (TLB)

And that is exactly why we wrote *The Secret Revealed*. Defensively, we do not want you to be conned by "enticing words." ("You can have whatever you want." "You are God.")

Positively, we want you to know the Mystery. What mystery? The mystery that Jesus, through God, gave up his "Godlikeness," became a man, and:

- Came to Earth, born as a baby in Bethlehem.
- Had a ministry for three years consisting of teaching and healing broken people.
- Lived a perfect life, a sinless life.
- Was crucified on a cross—not for his own wrongdoing, as He never did wrong.
- Was crucified for the sin of the world, thus restoring fellowship between God and humanity.
- Died.
- Resurrected.
- Will come to Earth someday as King.

And the Mystery includes the exhilarating fact that if I

- affirm these truths
- honestly acknowledge my own brokenness and sin
- confess my need for Him
- thus realizing He is God and I am not,

then I can truly experience what I most want: purpose, meaning, significance, intimacy, and love.

In 1993 (long before *The Secret* was written), Eugene Peterson, a professor at Regent College in Vancouver, British Columbia, paraphrased Paul's concerned letter to his friends in Colossae, originally more than nineteen hundred years earlier. Citing Colossian 2:2–4, Peterson prophetically wrote in *The Message* version of the Bible:

> I want you woven into a tapestry of love, in touch with everything there is to know of God. Then you will have minds confident and at rest, focused on Christ, God's great mystery. All the richest treasures of wisdom and knowledge are embedded in that mystery and nowhere else. And we've been shown the mystery! I'm telling you this because I don't want anyone leading you off on some wild-goose chase, after other so-called mysteries, or "the Secret."

So be it.

AFTERWORD

Do you remember in the opening pages of this book we expressed our statement of purpose? We desire to live up to that promise.

You may recall the name Zapenath-Paneah, appeared on that page. Translated, it means "revealer of secrets."

The Old Testament figure Joseph, regarded as a foreshadow of Jesus, was called Zapenath-Paneah (Gen. 41:45), which means "revealer of secrets,"(Hebrew and Coptic languages). Jesus is not a "hider" of some secret, but a revealer of it. In fact, the final book of the Bible is called Revelation. The Bible is not about hiding secrets, but about revealing truth.

Note that it is not Revelations, plural—but Revelation, singular. There is only one "revelation"—and that is that God was fully revealed in the person of Jesus Christ.

Admittedly, it is a mystery. But it is not a secret.

Here is the heart of our concern for you: behind the appearance of so many "get rich" and "find happiness" promises, *The Secret*'s real intention—certainly its effect—behind every idea and example it offers, is to convince this generation that there is no God. Or that we can have equality with whatever the Law of Attraction's definition of God is, which is worse.

It has been our intention to show you how subversive the so-called Law of Attraction is when hiding behind appeals to greed and selfism, and the danger and futility of those ideas to your life.

We have tried to say to you, reader, "there is a better way." One short story, perhaps, says it best. And with that we bring our time with you to a close.

In 1950, an unknown preacher went to Los Angeles. Thousands flocked to the corner of Washington and Hill Streets, making Billy Graham a household name across the nation.

Graham's preaching led a well-known movie star, radio personality, and singer-composer to embrace Jesus Christ as the truth. The famous entertainer had searched many places to fill his personal emptiness. Later, the celebrity was fired from the radio station due to his new Christian convictions. After his termination, Stuart Hamblen wrote these words:

It is no secret, what God can do. What He's done for others, He'll do for you. With arms wide open, He'll pardon you. It is no secret, what God can do.

To the reader, we close with these important words:

What God can do is no secret.
What He's done for others,
He'll do for you.

Appendix

AN INDEX TO RHONDA BYRNE'S *THE SECRET*

NOTES

Chapter 1

1. Stan Lee was not the inventor of the phrase, nor the concept, of "Suspending Disbelief," as it is found in literature two centuries old. But he is this generation's torch-bearer of the fictional device.

2. The general media has covered *The Secret* extensively and, except for perhaps predictably fawning treatment, has been harsh-to-tough in its coverage and treatment. ABC News *Nightline* (Cynthia McFadden, reporter) did a superb half-hour on the book, seeking out experts in the fields Rhonda Byrne covered. They were uniformly critical, if not astonished, that such a book could gain traction. The she interviewed Bob Proctor, challenging him with the experts' remarks. A transcript is available at <http://www.abcnews.go.com/images/Nightline/Microsoft%20Word%20%20Proctor%20Transcript.pdf> and a transcript of the entire report can be obtained from <http://www.transcripts.tv/nightline.cfm>

Chapter 2

1. Speech by Theodore Roosevelt: March 12, 1912, Carnegie Hall, New York, NY. *The Collected Works of Theodore Roosevelt*, Vol. XVII. New York, Charles Scribner's Sons, 1926, 170.

2. "The Paranoid Style in American Politics," Prof Richard Hofstadter, *Harpers Magazine*, November 1964. *Conspiracy: How the Paranoid Style Flourishes and Where It Comes From* by Daniel Pipes, Touchstone, 1999.

3. Fred DeCordova was the longtime producer of *The Tonight Show Starring Johnny Carson*. Rhonda Byrne was a segment producer on *The Don Lane Show*, the roughly equivalent Australian version of *Carson*. Her own company also produced *Australia Behaving Badly; The World's Greatest Commercials*; and *Oz Encounters—UFOs in Australia*. <http:ezinearticles.com/index.php?The-Powerful-Intentions-of-Rhonda-Byrne&id=521415>

4. The Emerson hunt (who's got the quotations?) is from Blair Warren's provocative site, Twisted Wisdom. <www.Blairwarren.com>

5. The information on Einstein is from "Review of *The Secret*" by Magda Healey in BookBag.uk. <http://www.thebookbag.co.uk/byrnesecret.htm>

Chapter 3

1. Background about the origins of Pragmatism from Louis Menand, *The Metaphysical Club: A Story of Ideas in America*, Farrar, Straus and Giroux, 2002. Menand's book, which shares scarcely any of our disapproval of Pragmatism, is nevertheless recommended as a lively, evocative account of a lunch group of academics who occasionally met for only nine months in 1872, and hatched a momentous movement.

2. The quotation from William James, which should be engraved on every decaying library and outcome-based "school" in America, is from William James, *Pragmatism: A New Name for Some Old Ways of Thinking* Longmans, Green, and Co., 1908.

3. In 1975, New York Mets fan Rick Marschall was Comics Editor at the New York News-Chicago Tribune Syndicate, and a new comic strip was signed: *Scroogie*, about a flaky baseball relief pitcher. Modeled after Tug McGraw, it was written by Tug McGraw (and drawn by Mike Witte). It was in the course of our relationship—a dream-come-true for me at the time—that Tug told me this clubhouse story, the origin of the "Ya Gotta Believe!" chant.

Chapter 4

1. Esther and Jerry Hicks are real, and their website is <www.abraham-hicks.com> The letter from the two Hicks can be found at <www.drewpictures.com/kb.asp?ID=8&Click=4690>

2. James Ray, interviewed by Frank Pastore, KKLA (Los Angeles), March 16, 2007.

3. Quotations from Bob Proctor, Pete Peterson, and Dr. Richard Wender in this chapter are from Cynthia McFadden's report on *The Secret*, ABC News *Nightline*, March 23, 2007.

4. Quotations from Wolf and Hagelin: <http://philaletheia.thetruthtree.com/2007/03/19/selling-the-secret>

5. Beckwith's home page for his Agape center is <http://agapelive.com>

6. The "Secret of Getting Rich" (SGR) scheme was originally announced at <http://losangeles.craigslist.org/sfv/emd/302350838.html> The new version, with Beckwith eliminated and minus the prominent logos of *The Secret*, can be found on many sites, including: <www.quantummanifest.thesgrprogram.com>; <banyangroup.thesgrprogram.com>; <www.healthwealthandhappiness.thesgrprogram.com>; <www.senseiron.thesgrprogram.com>; <http://www.powerwealth.co.uk> Proctor and Canfield's program can be accessed through <www.TheSGRProgram.com>; <www.TheOfficialSecretSeminar.com>; <www.TheLaw.TheSGRprogram.com>

7. Lincoln's statement about the relationship between labor and capital

is from his First Annual Message as president, Dec 3, 1861. *The Collected Works of Abraham Lincoln*, ed. Roy P. Basler; Marion Delores Pratt and Lloyd A. Dunlap, asst. eds., vol. V, *1861–1862*. New Brunswick: Rutgers University Press, 1953, 52.

Chapter 5

1. For more information regarding the wonders of the human brain, see the numerous resources by Dr. Daniel Amen, http://www.amenclinic.com/ This site offers exceptional books and related material on the intricacies of the human brain.

2. For a discussion on the "Law of Magnetism," see James L. Garlow, 2002, *The 21 Irrefutable Laws of Leadership Test by Time*, Nashville: Thomas Nelson, pages 113–128. There is a difference between the pseudo "Law of Attraction" and the time tested leadership principle known as the "Law of Magnetism," which states that "who you are is who you will attract." The former is based on wishful thinking—allegedly emitted to the Universe. The latter is evidenced by the fact that strong leaders—by virtue of the causes in which they are involved—attract persons with like dreams, goals, thinking processes and passions.

3. Garlow, James L., 2000, *How God Saved Civilization*, Ventura, CA: Regal Books, pp. 255–6.

4. The phrase is borrowed from Hurston, Joe, 2006, *Run to the Roar*, Orlando, FL: Charisma House.

5. For a superb treatment of how the

church spoke out regarding women suffrage and abolition of the slaves, see Dr. Donald Dayton, 1976, *Discovering an Evangelical Heritage*, New York: Harper & Row. Also see James L. Garlow, 2004, *God and His People*, Colorado Springs: Victor Books, pages 321–9. In addition, visit www.jimgarlow.com then click on "books," then "How God Saved Civilization," go to Chapter 14 time line regarding abolition and social change. In addition, see Garlow, James L. and Peter Jones, 2004, *Cracking Da Vinci's Code*, Colorado Springs: Victor Books, p. 76.

Chapter 6

1. In the Old Testament portion of the Bible, it states (Proverbs 20:29), "The glory of young men is their strength, gray hair the splendor of the old." In contrast to contemporary culture's unrealistic with eternal youthfulness, aging is normal, and should be embraced. Aging is not something to be dreaded. To see an honest, frank and forthright understanding of the aging process, see Francis Grubbs, 2006, *The Glory of Aging*, Seminole, FL: Christian Law Association, www.christianlaw.org, 2006.

2. I (Jim) am concerned that there are some who will believe *The Secret*'s bizarre weight loss strategy of thinking that "food does not cause weight gain," but rather that "fat thinking" does. This type of casuistry could result in a pattern of eating that could be physically catastrophic. For those who desire to experience proper weight

management, may I direct you to www.hmrprogram.com I (Jim) used these products as part of a medically supervised—seeing a doctor and nurse weekly—weight loss program, operated through a local hospital. Weight loss is not just about "thinking thin thoughts." Any weight management product should be used with the same components that are part of every balanced and healthy weight loss plan: 1. exercise, 2. increase of fruits and vegetables, and 3. monitoring caloric intake.

3. Here are the concepts I followed to encourage proper weight management:

How to Think Like a Loser—by Dr. Jim Garlow © 2005 James L. Garlow

- Thinking—If you are overweight, the fat is in your head.
- Desperation—Capacity to change is in direct proportion to the amount of felt desperation.
- Passion—Passion is what coal is to a locomotive: it empowers to action.
- Strategy—Having a strategy is what tracks are to a locomotive: it gives the capacity to reach the destination.
- Acknowledge—Three words will change your life: "I need help."
- Humility—It's not about you.
- Vision—I am able to see what I can become.
- Ownership—I didn't create my body, and it doesn't belong to me. I am a steward of it. Therefore I will treat it accordingly.
- Excuses—I can have excuses or

I can have results, but I cannot have both.

- Results—I choose to make decisions that yield results.
- Decisions—I will pay attention to even the small, seemingly inconsequential decisions due to the fact that I am simply the cumulative impact of many "small decisions."
- Change—I can change; I do not have to stay the same.
- Skill—Due to my lack of will-power, I will need to develop "skill power."
- Records—Keeping accurate daily records is a way of saying I value life.
- Parameters—Since I did not build adequate fences around my eating habits, well established parameters are my friend.
- Exercise—I do not like exercise. But I love having exercised. I refuse to let the word "exercise" intimidate me any longer. I am an active person.
- Pleasure—I can either have "pleasure now, and pain later," or I can have "discipline now, and pleasure later." But I cannot have pleasure both now and then.
- Discipline—Discipline gives me the dreams of my heart. Lack of discipline is a "dream-destroyer."
- Consequences—Bad actions have bad consequences. Good actions have good consequences. I choose good consequences. Thus I choose good actions.
- Momentum—Momentum is a friend that should be cherished and protected.

- Learning—I choose to learn—daily.
- Silence—In weight loss, I am not the teacher. I am the student. I will remain silent.
- Opinion—This year, my goal is to have 20% fewer opinions.
- Favorites—I will limit myself to those favorites that are not harmful to my goals.
- Routine—In order to break from a destructive "rut," I am willing to accept the routine needed to establish new and healthy habits.
- Variety—I will be sufficiently creative to discover variety within the parameters set around me.
- Success—I will not allow my successes to set me up to fail.
- Failure—I will not allow my failures to cause me to think I cannot succeed.
- Affirmation—I accept the affirmations of others to encourage healthy habits.
- Compliments—While I appreciate compliments from others, I choose to live my life by principles rather than by what others think of me.
- Fear—Although I choose to avoid unhealthy fears, I embrace healthy fears that restrain me from doing those things that will ultimately harm me.
- Criticism—When I am doing what is truly right and assuredly healthy for me, I will not react to, or be deterred by, the criticism of others.
- Endurance—I can outlast the problem I am overcoming.

- Preferences—Preferences can be my friend, but I will not allow it to be my master.
- Convictions—Preferences are something I live by; convictions are what I will die for.
- Principles—Principles are to me what tracks are to a train.
- Hope—Hope does for me what the flange on the train wheel does when the tracks curve: it holds me steady.
- Hunger—I refuse to allow bodily hunger to rule my life.
- Mind—My mind rules over my body.
- Spirit—My spirit rules over my mind, which rules over my body.
- Focus—I choose to fill my mind with wholesome thoughts that take me to healthy results.
- Meditation—My spirit was created for thinking higher thoughts.
- Ongoing—I accept the fact that I must always keep on "keeping on."
- Priorities—Not everything is of equal importance.
- Resignation—I give up. My desire to eat doesn't have to "win."

Chapter 7

1. It strengthens rather than weakens our warnings to readers about some of the bizarre get-rich-quick schemes from the Internet, since they seem so close to *The Secret*, some even using the word "secret" in their breathless headlines and pitches. They merely make our

point about their true nature, so readers won't have to take our word about the polluted ethics. They all silently condemn themselves: if money were so easy to attract, why do they have to charge high prices for their programs—couldn't they share the information and merely attract new incomes by the anointed way they claim to know? See examples like: <http://www.free-money-magnet-course.com>; <http://www.perfect wealthformula.com.; <http://www.livinglifewithoutlimits.com>; and a site with identical testimonials, but where the hostess has morphed from Jan to Kimberly: <http://www.wealthbeyondmeasure.com>

2. Mackay, Charles. *Extraordinary Popular Delusions And The Madness Of Crowds*, London: Richard Bentley, New Burlington Street, 1841. Reprint: Boston: L.C. Page, 1932. This book is still readable and instructive.

3. Special treatments of the Mississippi Bubble and the South Sea Island Bubble, though more specifically related to national economies—a macro-lesson, where ours is a micro-lesson—can be found at "Review of South Sea Bubble: Lessons of History" by Marc Faber, *The Daily Reckoning* e-newsletter, London, England; October 15, 2004 <www.dailyreckoning.com/Issues/2004/101504.html#LESSONS_OF_HISTORY>_

4. See a similar contextualization of Ponzi schemes in "On the Possibility of Ponzi Schemes in Transition Economies" by Utpal Bhattacharya in *Beyond Transition* newsletter, the quarterly publication of the World Bank's Europe and Central Asia (ECA) Department <http://www.worldbank.org/transitionnewsletter/janfeb00/pgs24-26.htm>

5. James, William. *The Varieties of Religious Experience.* Edited and with an introduction by Martin E. Marty. London and New York: Penguin, 1984, xxiv.

6. Roosevelt, Theodore. "An Art Exhibition." In *The Collected Works of Theodore Roosevelt.* Vol. XII, *Literary Essays.* New York: Charles Scribner's Sons, 1926, p. 148. First published in *The Outlook,* March 29, 1913.

7. "Tonight, unhappy with your love, your job, your life, not enough money? Use your head. You can think yourself into a lot better you. Positive thoughts can transform and can attract the good things you know you want. Sound far-fetched? Think again. It's supported by science.

   "Ahead, an hour that can change the way you think about the world and alter your life forever. It's next on *Larry King Live.*"

   Larry King, *Larry King Live,* "The Power of Positive Thoughts," CNN, aired November 2, 2006, 21:00 ET http://transcripts.cnn.com/TRANSCRIPTS/0611/02/lkl.01.html

8. Greg Beato's article in *Reason Magazine,* "The Secret of *The Secret*: A Cult of Self-Help DVD Fleeces the Credulous," can be found at

<http://www.reason.com/news/
show/119132.html>

Chapter 8

1. Review of *The Secret* by Magda
   Healey in *The Bookbag. uk* <http://
   www.thebookbag.co.uk/
   byrnesecret.htm>

2. "I've never regarded being bald as a
   problem. If I did, I could attract all
   sorts of solutions to it, from toupees
   to plugs to hair transplants to
   whathaveyou."
       Vitale, Joe. On *Beyond Marketing
   by Dr Joe Vitale* weblog, Wednesday
   March 14, 2007. http://mrfire.
   blogspot.com/2007/03/on-
   being-bald.html

3. Baldwin, Neil. *Henry Ford and the
   Jews: The Mass Production of Hate.*
   New York: Public Affairs Books,
   2001, *passim.* <http://www.
   neilbaldwinbooks.com/hfj_ch1.
   html>

4. Oliver James in *Times* Online
   (London) Mar 6, 2007 http://
   entertainment.timesonline.co.uk/
   tol/arts_and_entertainment/books/
   article1473581.ece

5. ABCNews *Nightline* (Cynthia
   McFadden , reporter) A transcript is
   available at <http://www.abcnews.
   go.com/images/Nightline/
   Microsoft%20Word%20
   %20Proctor%20Transcript.pdf>
   and a transcript of the entire report
   can be obtained from <http://www.
   transcripts.tv/nightline.cfm>

6. From Dr. Brian Greene's
   biographical statement on his
   homepage: <http://www.columbia.
   edu/cu/physics/fac-bios/Greene/
   faculty.html>. Dr. Brian Greene's

full profile can be found at <http://
www.columbia.edu/cu/physics/
fac-bios/Greene/faculty.html>

7. Ingrid Hansen Smythe holds a
   Bachelor of Music degree, a BA in
   religious studies, and a Masters
   degree in the nature of religion.
   <http://www.skeptic.com/eskeptic/
   07-03-07.html>

8. Prof Norcross's quotation and the
   following conclusion in the text are
   from the *Philaletheia* site, March 19,
   2007 http://philaletheia.
   thetruthtree.com/2007/03/19/
   selling-the-secret>

9. Robert Todd Carroll's reviews
   appear in his generally excellent
   and readable—and certainly
   iconoclastic—site (which is
   festooned with sidebar reminders
   like "It is possible that the most
   important decision in the history of
   therapy was the idea that it should
   be paid for by the hour") *Skeptic's
   Dictionary,* <www.skeptic.com>,
   op. cit. Carroll is the author of the
   print-book *The Skeptic's Dictionary:
   A Collection of Strange Beliefs, Amusing
   Deceptions, and Dangerous Delusions,*
   Wiley, 2003. His review, quoted here
   for its relevance, is of *Crazy Therapies:
   What Are They? Do They Work?* by
   Margaret Thaler Singer and Janja
   Lalich. Jossey-Bass, 1996.

10. Hagelin and Schumm quotations
    from "Quantum Physicists
    Disagree" in *Christian Science
    Monitor,* of all things, March 28,
    2007.

11. Joe Vitale on *Larry King Live,*
    March 8, 2007.

12. For more on the *Titanic* disaster—
    and a truer picture than the

Cameron movie—few books are better than Jay Henry Mowbray's *Sinking of the Titanic* (1912) and Walter Lord's *A Night to Remember* (1955).

Chapter 9

1. Garlow, James L. 1981, *Partners in Ministry,* Kansas City, MO: Beacon Hill Press, see pages 46–49, regarding a discussion of "occupation" versus "vocation."

2. The phrase used for God's name, "I Am who I Am" (Exodus 3:14) is used in part as a way of declaring God's eternality. He is not One Who simply was, once upon a time. He is not Who someday will be. He is in the eternal present tense. God is, by definition, the "I Am (always, eternally present tense) One."

3. Garlow, James L., 2004, *God and His People,* Colorado Springs: Victor Books, outlines the development of numerous denominations.

4. Garlow, James L. and Peter Jones, 2004, *Cracking Da Vinci's Code,* Colorado Springs: Victor Books, p. 224–225.

5. See http://courses.wcupa.edu/fletcher/henley/bio.htm.

6. Garlow, James L., 2005, *God Still Heals,* Indianapolis: Wesleyan Publishing House, outlines how to experience God's healing touch. Especially note pages 251–2, entitled "Blockages to Divine Healing."

Chapter 10

1. Garlow, James L., 2002, *The 21 Irrefutable Laws of Leadership Test by Time,* Nashville: Thomas Nelson. For a discussion of heroic examples

of sacrifice, see "The Law of Sacrifice: A Leader Must Give Up to Go Up" pages 233–250. Contrast Byrne's self-centeredness with the following axioms: "The present generation always stands on the sacrifices of those who have gone before it" (p. 237), "Most of life's real values are learned in the crucible of pain" (p. 244), "Give your life away to a cause bigger than yourself" (p. 247) and "Sacrifice reveals quality of character" (p. 249).

2. Regarding the definition of prosperity, see Garlow, James L., *The Covenant,* Beacon Hill Press, 1999, page 25, "Prosperity is a biblical concept. Although some have distorted this doctrine to mean nothing more than big cars and fancy houses, prosperity is a powerful theme in Scripture. Biblical prosperity is God's desire to meet our needs without our experiencing undue stress. He desires to bless us in the same way any good earthly father wants to take care of his children: 'The Lord will make you abound in prosperity'(Deuteronomy 28:11a)"

Chapter 11

1. Garlow, James L. and Peter Jones, *Cracking Da Vinci's Code,* Colorado Springs: Victor Books, 2004, 200–202, for discussion of the reality of sin, evil, and the devil.

Chapter 12

1. Watkins, James N. *Writers on Writing,* Indianapolis: Wesleyan Publishing House, 2005, two

articles by James L. Garlow, entitled "The Impact of Christian Writing," 17–21, and "Paul and Apollos," 22. Apollos and Paul were contemporaries, both skilled speakers, thinkers, and debaters. There is one difference, however. Paul wrote; Apollos didn't. We have no idea what Apollos said. In contrast, Paul's words—because he wrote—are still being read two thousand years later. The bottom line: writers write, primarily, to influence.

2. For a superb treatment on "making life work," see Colson, Charles, *The Good Life*, Wheaton, IL: Tyndale House Publishers, 2005, and Guiness, Os, *Time for Truth: Living Free in a World of Lies, Hype & Sin*, Grand Rapids: Baker Books, 2000.

3. Billheimer, Paul, *Destined for the Throne*, Christian Literature Crusade, 1975.

4. Garlow, James L. *God Still Heals*, Indianapolis: Wesleyan Publishing House, 2005, 65–80, discussing the "Two Kingdoms."

Chapter 13

1. Garlow, James L. and Peter Jones, *Cracking Da Vinci's Code*, 82–97, discussion entitled "Jesus—Who Was He, Really?"

2. James L. Garlow with Timothy Paul Jones and April Williams, *The Da Vinci CodeBreaker*, Minneapolis: Bethany House, 2006, 50–51, "Chart of Christological Errors." One of the consistent marks or indicators of errant thinking is its Christological position—i.e., its understanding of the person, work, and nature of Jesus.

3. Wattles, Wallace, *The Science of Getting Rich*, Tarcher, 2007.

4. See Garlow and Jones, *Cracking Da Vinci's Code*, 224, for further discussion of Pagan Monism vs. Biblical Theism.

5. Albanese, Catherine, *A Republic of the Mind and Spirit, A Cultural History of American Metaphysical Religion*, New Haven: Yale University Press, 2007.

6. *Emerald Tablet of Mermes* at Sacred Texts.com.

7. James L. Garlow with Timothy Paul Jones and April Williams, *The Da Vinci CodeBreaker*, 141–146. Note the extensive chart outlining the books of the Nag Hammadi discovery.

8. See Garlow, James L. and Peter Jones, *Cracking Da Vinci's Code*, 229–231, for discussion that one cannot follow practices of paganism *and* be a follower of Christ—a Christian—at the same time.

Chapter 14

1. I (Rick) am indebted in this chapter specifically, and in my work on this book generally, and in fact for a large portion of my worldview, to the work published by Walter Martin and Douglas Groothuis. They are scholars of excellent discernment and gifted persuasiveness. So it is at this point I would like to acknowledge them and recommend their work to our readers. I can say that I have incorporated their ideas (as well as those of Saint Augustine and Martin Luther, both still relevant today, and Whitaker Chambers) into my worldview, but any

conclusions I have reached, after this separated-at-birth paean, are wholly my own. Here is a (highly) recommended list of Martin's and Groothuis's prominent books: Walter Martin, *The Kingdom of the Cults*, rev. ed., Ravi Zacharias, ed. (Minneapolis: Bethany House Publishers, 2003); Walter Martin with Jill Martin Rische, *Through the Windows of Heaven* (Nashville: Broadman & Holman, 1999); Douglas Groothius, *Confronting the New Age* (Downer's Grove, IL: InterVarsity Press), 1988; Douglas Groothius, *Truth Decay: Defending Christianity Against the Challenges of Postmodernism* (Downer's Grove, IL: InterVarsity Press, 2000); Douglas Groothius, *On Pascal and Jesus*, Wadsworth, 2003.

2. Mumford, Lewis. *The Transformations of Man* (New York: Harper & Row, 1972), 179.

3. Adams, Henry. *Mont-St-Michel and Chartres*. Boston: Houghton Mifflin, 1918. See also *The Education of Henry Adams*. Boston: Houghton Mifflin, 1918.

4. Lewis, C. S., *Miracles*, New York, HarperCollins Publishers, 1998.

5. St. Augustine of Hippo (Henry Bettenson, translator), *The City of God*, Book XIV, New York, Penguin Classics, 2003.

6. Capra, Fritjof. *The Turning Point*. New York: Simon and Schuster, 1982.

7. "Secret History of The Secret," by Marco R. della Cava. *USA Today*, March 28, 2007.

INDEX

ABOUT THE AUTHORS

DR. JIM GARLOW graduated from Drew University (PhD), Princeton Theological Seminary, and Asbury Theological Seminary. Garlow is the senior pastor of Skyline Wesleyan Church in San Diego, California, and is heard daily on 550 radio outlets nationwide in his one-minute historical commentary called *The Garlow Perspective*.

He is the author of ten books, including the coauthored *New York Times* Bestseller *Cracking Da Vinci's Code,* and has appeared on NBC, CNN, Fox, MSNBC, and CNBC. Other books include *God and His People, A Christian's Response to Islam, The Covenant, The 21 Irrefutable Laws of Leadership Tested by Time,* and *God Still Heals.*

Jim and his wife, Carol, have four children and four grandchildren. You can visit his Web site at www.JimGarlow.com.

RICK MARSCHALL, the author/editor of sixty books and many magazine articles, has been called by *Bostonia* magazine "perhaps America's foremost expert on popular culture." His books have been on music, TV history, political cartoons, biography, and devotions. He has been editor at Marvel Comics and Disney and currently is editor of *Rare Jewel Magazine*, a Christian journal of culture and politics.

Rick assisted his wife, Nancy, in a hospital ministry in Philadelphia after her heart transplant. Their three children are Heather, a youth pastor; Ted, a TV news producer; and Emily, who is doing church work overseas. Rick and Nancy live in Alpine, New Jersey. You can visit his Web site at www. RickMarschall.com.

For more information visit www.TheSecretRevealedBook.com.